DEMOCRATIC
ECONOMIC POLICY

Bruno S. Frey

DEMOCRATIC ECONOMIC POLICY

A THEORETICAL INTRODUCTION

St. Martin's Press   New York

ISBN 0-312-19368-8

Library of Congress Cataloging in Publication Data

Frey, Bruno S.
  Democratic economic policy.

  Bibliography: p.
  Includes indexes.
  1. Economic policy. 2. Economic policy – Citizen
  participation. I. Title.
HD87.F72   1983   338.9   83-9483
ISBN 0-312-19368-8

Contents

Contents

Acknowledgements

This book is based on my *Theorie demokratischer Wirtschaftspolitik* (Vahlen, Munich, 1981). It has been completely revised, with some parts deleted and others added. Many colleagues and friends have read earlier versions of the German manuscript and have made most useful suggestions for improvements. I thank in particular my present co-workers at the University of Zurich, Werner W. Pommerehne, Gebhard Kirchgässner, Friedrich Schneider, Hannelore Weck, Mico Loretan and Jörg Naumann, as well as my former associate at the University of Konstanz, Charles Beat Blankart. Special thanks are also due to my colleagues Dieter Bös (University of Bonn), Klaus Mackscheidt (University of Cologne) and, as always, to my brother and co-economist, René L. Frey (University of Basel). The English has been corrected and improved upon by Roger Bowles (University of Bath) and by Susan Hughes. The final touches to the manuscript have been applied during a delightful stay as Visiting Fellow at All Souls College, Oxford.

Bruno S. Frey
Zurich

Introduction

Many people in the Western World are discouraged and disappointed by economic policy as it is practised today. They expect the government to help solve the problems of present-day life, but the results of governmental action often seem, at best, inadequate. Sometimes economic policies even have an effect contrary to what was intended: the problems become more acute, and at the same time the burden imposed by the state on the people increases because of higher taxes and growing bureaucracy. In this situation many give up; they turn to utopian ideals of a perfect state or – increasingly today – towards the ideal of a market economy with as little government intervention as possible. Others try to find solutions within the confines of their private lives.

This resignation about the limited possibilities of economic policy is in marked contrast to the optimism that prevailed among theoreticians and practical politicians until the mid-1970s. After the Second World War the Keynesian gospel suggested that business fluctuations and economic growth could be steered at will. Samuelson's 'neoclassical synthesis' maintained that both unemployment and inflation could be prevented if fiscal and monetary policy were properly applied. Even greater optimism was spread by the theory of quantitative economic policy in the style of Tinbergen, according to which mathematical techniques of optimization would allow us to maximize social welfare. Econometric models of ever increasing size were developed for this purpose.

There have indeed been great successes in practical economic policy, as is evidenced by the successful creation of upswings during the small recessions of the 1960s. In the 1970s, however, the limits of economic policy became increasingly clear: inflation and unemployment occurred simultaneously, and on the macroeconomic level it became increasingly clear that economic policy intervention can be ineffective or even harmful.

Why is economic policy often ineffective? My book endeavours to answer this question. I shall describe the points at which a successful economic policy can be applied. Both too great optimism and too great pessimism are wrong. There is scope for influencing the course of economic events through political measures, but the economic policy intervention must be well thought out if it is to be effective.

To think about how, where and when to implement economic policy measures is a fascinating task which goes far beyond economic theory. Economic policy is not simply the application of economic theory. Rather, it requires that one moves beyond the borders of the narrow economic area to encompass the political sphere as well. Successful economic policy results only when economic and political actions are combined.

This book is based on the experiences of democratic societies of the Western type, in which (at least in principle) the preferences of the population are respected. For this reason social decisions via referenda, votes and other mechanisms will receive special attention, resulting in a *theory of democratic economic policy*.

This textbook differs from existing works on the theory of economic policy in three ways.

1   Government is taken to be an *endogenous* part of the politico-economic system: it does not act autonomously but is influenced by many different forces. In this process economic and political institutions – in particular, parties, government administration and private interest groups – play an important role. Their behaviour must be analysed with the help of the economic theory of politics; it is not sufficient simply to describe them.

2   The analysis is illustrated with quantitative magnitudes and econometric evidence (although no knowledge of formal econometric techniques is required). The theoretical analysis is in this way related to the real world.

3   The results of modern research are included as far as possible, and an effort has been made to present the content of the theory of economic policy in simple terms. Incentives are given a central role as a determinant of behaviour in the economic policy-making process. The traditional, more narrowly defined, field of economic policy is rejected in favour of an analysis covering the whole society, but many of the techniques developed therein are adopted here. Refer-

ence is also made to the results of interdisciplinary research in political science, systems theory, sociology and psychology.

I have tried to present things in as simple a form as possible without sacrificing their scientific basis. No mathematical knowledge is required of the reader; the emphasis is rather on exercising the typically economic way of thinking, with the reader being taught to understand the results of econometric analysis and to evaluate their importance. This knowledge is a must for the economic (and social) scientist of today.

Each chapter begins with an introductory section, outlining what is to follow and ends with some conclusions. The literature cited at the end of each chapter is very briefly commented on to let the reader know in what way it is relevant.

The book is divided into four parts. In the first, introductory, part economic policy is put into a politico-economic framework, and the way in which the economy can be influenced by economic policy is discussed. It is suggested that discussion of decision-making can usefully distinguish between that which takes place at the level of the social consensus and that which takes place in the current politico-economic process. Part II deals with institutions at the level of the social consensus. These take the form of social contracts concerning the rules governing the political area, the choice between various social decision-making mechanisms, and the ground rules operating in the economic area. Part III deals with the possibilities for economic policy intervention by providing information in the current politico-economic process. The final part discusses economic policy advising. The status, role and incentives of the economic policy advisers are discussed.

PART I

Economic Policy in the Politico-economic System

Economic policy-making takes place within a social framework. The mutual interaction of the economy and the polity is of major importance and has far-reaching consequences for economic policy: When the actors, in particular the government, are endogenous parts of a politico-economic system, the possibilities for influencing its course are limited. The economic advisers can only offer advice that is in the interest of the respective actors. Decisively greater influence can be exerted on the course of economic affairs when the rules of the system are changed; this requires a voluntary and unanimous contract, or 'social consensus'. In Chapter 1 economic policy is put into this general framework and its scope and limits are outlined. My premise is that economic policy in a democracy should conform to the will of the people.

CHAPTER 1

Economics, Politics and Economic Policy

INTRODUCTION

The economy and the polity interact in many ways with respect to allocation, income distribution and stabilization. Neither the economy nor the polity should be looked at in isolation. The decision-makers, or 'actors', all depend on each other; they are endogenous parts of the politico-economic system. The decisions taken by the actors, and therefore the development and outcome of the whole system, depends on the rules and institutions that form the basic framework. The economy's behaviour can be influenced, therefore, by changing the rules and institutions. As will be shown, such changes are possible only by means of voluntary and unanimous contracts, or 'social consensus', in a situation in which the actors' interests in a particular outcome are not yet defined. Such a situation is reached when the actors are uncertain about the position in which they themselves (or their descendants) will find themselves when the framework of rules and institutions yields particular outcomes; in other words, they are living behind a 'veil of ignorance'.

Economic policy at the level of the social consensus differs fundamentally from economic policy in a situation in which the rules and institutions are given, and the decision-makers know their particular interests. At this level of the 'current politico-economy process' the economic advisers can only offer advice that helps the various actors to best realize their interests.

1.1 ECONOMY AND POLITY: THE TWO LINKS OF INTERACTION

The influence of the economy on the polity and of the polity on the economy can be illustrated by way of examples that show the importance of politico-economic interdependence in a modern society.

The Economy Depends on the Polity

Allocation, that is, the use to which available resources will be assigned, is in many areas influenced by government intervention. Agriculture, for example, is more or less isolated from market forces in all the developed industrialized nations: prices of agrarian products are artificially increased, production is helped by subsidies, and imports are kept out of the domestic market by quantitative restrictions. Government intervention is so strong that it is very difficult to analyse the extent to which allocation and income distribution is affected by it. The medical sector is another area that is strongly influenced by government policy, even though a market solution would be perfectly possible. Many hospitals are government-run or heavily subsidized by the state; health insurance is either public or at least strongly regulated by government; and the supply of doctors and other health personnel is also influenced by the government to a large extent.

Other spheres of government influence are income distribution, where social security leads to a huge redistribution between the generations and regional policy tries to reduce the income disparities between geographical regions; and stabilization, where business cycle fluctuations, inflation and unemployment clearly are influenced by fiscal and monetary policy. Until recently it was assumed that these interventions would act to reduce business cycle fluctuations, inflation and unemployment. Recent research results as well as everyday experience suggest, however, that government activities can, wittingly or unwittingly, intensify cyclical swings in the economy and may lead to an increase in the rate of inflation without a reduction in unemployment.

Politics Depends on the Economy

Putting government policy into effect requires economic resources. Equally important is the influence of economic conditions on the government's popularity and chances of re-election. Voters tend to hold the government accountable for the state of the economy; they are thus more likely to support (and vote for) the government when the economy is doing well, and more likely (compared with the usual trend) to vote for the opposition when it is doing poorly.

This mutual interdependence between the economy and the polity, reduced to its simplest and most basic form, is illustrated in Figure 1.1. The economy and polity form a closed system with the two parts linked by feedbacks: the upper link shows political intervention working on the economy; and the lower link shows the influence of economic conditions on the political sector.

This representation is of course highly simplified. Its purpose is to demonstrate how the economy and polity *mutually* interact, and to show that this is not a one-way process in which the government sector only influences the economy.

FIGURE 1.1   *Basic outline of the interdependence of the economy and the polity.*

1.2   VARIOUS REPRESENTATIONS OF POLITICO-ECONOMIC INTERACTIONS

The interdependence schematically presented in Figure 1.1 can be expanded and described either verbally or through the use of models.

Verbal Analysis

John Kenneth Galbraith's conception of politico-economic interdependence in terms of a 'military industrial complex' is a typical example of a verbal analysis and one that has had a strong impact. Government is conceived as being an agent of big business, in which (at least in the United States) the defence sector plays the most important role. Government is used by the large producers to guarantee that their products will be bought. The government and the economic sector are strongly linked through institutions and people active in both areas. In this relationship the interests of business clearly dominate.

The 'New Left' – who in the United States are often called 'radicals' – hold a similar view. In their theory of 'state monopoly capitalism', the state is seen as an agent of monopolies and acts as an ideal capitalist. It is given the task of assuring the loyalty of the masses to the capitalist system, and achieves this with the help of policies aimed at sustaining the economy and social harmonization. The economy is dependent on continuous intervention on the part of the state; and conversely, the state is completely dependent on big business and big finance.

What is characteristic of both Galbraith and the New Left is the conjunction of government and private interests arising from the unlimited dominance of large enterprises. It need not be discussed here whether such a view is valid; what matters is that the economy and the polity are looked upon as interdependent units in a closed system.

Analysis by Way of Models

Models of the mutual interdependence between the economy and the polity have been developed, among others, in the framework of *systems theory* and the *economic theory of politics* (also called '*public choice*').

Economic Theory of Politics. This approach applies the thinking and methods of modern economics to political processes. The interaction between the economy and the polity is central. Application of the same technique of analysis to both politics and economics enables us to deal with overlapping areas which had previously been artificially carved up by the traditional boundaries of the sciences. The starting point for this type of analysis is the economic model of human behaviour – which is quite compatible with that of psychology – according to which individuals and institutions (firms, interest groups and the like) will react to utility and costs in a predictable, systematic way. This behavioural hypothesis holds for both the economic and political areas. Many different aspects of the interrelationship between the economy and polity have been analysed in the framework of this economic theory of politics. The way of thinking can be illustrated with an example.

Example

A democratically elected government may for various reasons profit from actively generating business cycles. For one thing, voters easily forget what has happened in the past and tend to re-evaluate the government's performance in terms of most recent and present conditions. It pays therefore for a government to try to carry out policies that are not particularly popular among the electorate a long time in advance of elections, and to concentrate more on measures that will attract support as the election approaches. A restrictive business cycle policy is therefore more likely to be undertaken at the beginning of a legislative period, and the same applies to ideologically motivated policies. An expansionary policy (whose real income gains and falling unemployment bring in votes) will be undertaken towards the end of the legislative period (provided inflation is not rampant). This model of the 'political business cycle' again shows the close connection between the economy and the polity.

Formal *politico-economic* (or *politometric*) *models* of the interaction between the economy and the polity have been constructed and econometrically tested for various countries, including the United Kingdom and the United States.

The general outline of the models estimated is given in Figure 1.2.

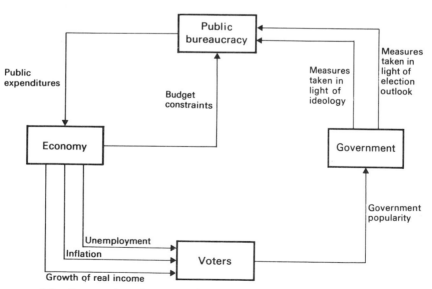

FIGURE 1.2   *Interactions between the economy and the polity in a politico-economic model.*

The lower loop of the figure, running from the economy to the government, describes the influence that the state of the economy (represented by the rates of unemployment, inflation and growth of real income) has on the popularity of the government and its re-election chances. The state of the economy is for the voter an indication of how well the government is doing its job. This relationship between governmental popularity and the economic variables affecting it is called the 'popularity function'.

The figure's upper loop describes how the political sector influences the economic sector of society, which it can try to manipulate in order to ensure its survival. This relationship is called the 'policy function'. The government would of course like to put its ideological ideas into practice. A potentially unpopular ideologically oriented policy will be undertaken only if the government is confident of being re-elected; that is, if its popularity share exceeds a certain minimum level. If its popularity falls below this level, the government will begin to fear that it may not be re-elected and will make an effort to increase its popularity, undertaking an expansionary policy (increasing public expenditures) in order to decrease unemployment and increase the growth of income. The situation will of course be different if the already existing rate of inflation is very high. In this case if may be advantageous for a government to undertake a deflationary policy.

Such politico-economic models have been confronted with competing models relying on purely 'economic' determinants. It turns out that the politico-economic models yield superior *ex ante* and *ex post* forecasts of the real developments.

1.3   CHARACTERISTICS OF POLITICO-ECONOMIC SYSTEMS

In the last two sections an important conclusion was drawn: that the economic and political spheres of society are closely linked, and that government is a part of the system. The government cannot pursue any policy without taking into account the other decision-makers – not even that of maximizing the welfare of the population, because even then it could run into conflict with powerful interest groups.

How is it possible to undertake economic policy in such a system? Is there any possibility at all for the economic policy adviser (the economist) to bring forward proposals, and can it be hoped that they will be followed?

To answer these questions it is necessary to know the composition of the politico-economic system and how 'open' a system it is.

— In a completely closed system there is no relationship between the elements of the system and the outside world; developments are completely endogenous. The historical course is predetermined through the relationships within the system: an intervention from the outside is impossible.
— A partially open system has some exogenous links. Not all inter-actions are completely closed, and it is thus possible to influence the system from the outside. The problem here consists of deter-mining the manner in which such interventions are possible.

Politico-economic systems are partially open because the actors involved are not fully informed. In reality, economic policy-makers are often rather badly informed.

— The voters cannot, and do not want to have to, sort out how far the government is responsible for the existing state of the economy and whether another party would have done better. They are only partially informed as to how far they can make their preferences felt in the political process and whether or not they are well represented by specific interest groups.
— The government does not know with certainty how it must act in order to survive. It knows only roughly the wishes of the voters, and it does not know exactly how many voters can be mobilized by any given interest group. The government and the public bureaucracy are also not fully informed about the possible uses and consequences of their economic policy instruments.
— Interest groups are quite well informed about their own sphere, but they do not necessarily know much about how the different economic policy measures will influence their sector and which instruments will best further their goals.

Politico-economic systems are thus partially open to information inputs from the outside. The economist as economic policy adviser has an opportunity to influence the course of the system by provi-ding information to the decision-makers. The economic policy deci-sions of the various actors wil be affected by this newly gained information. The benefits and costs of actions will be evaluated anew, new possibilities for taking action will open up, and it will be easier to predict the reactions and future activities of the other actors. Information can often affect the behaviour of decision-makers to such an extent that the politico-economic system as a whole will develop in a different direction.

1.4 INFORMATION AND ECONOMIC POLICY

Information relevant for economic policy formation can be provided on two different levels. On the first level, rules and institutions are formed by way of a *social consensus*, which determines the nature of the politico-economic system. The second level consists of the *current social process*, in which the decision-makers act according to their short-range interests *within* the rules and institutions established. At both levels, the information available will have an influence over both the process by which decisions are made and the content of decisions.

Social Consensus

A social consensus has three major characteristics:

1   It regulates basic aspects of society, going beyond the questions of the day-to-day and short-range interests.

2   It arises in a situation of uncertainty. The individuals (and groups) involved do not know in which position they – and above all their descendants – will find themselves in the future, with regard to their position in society, their state of health, and the physical, cultural and environmental circumstances of their progeny.

3   The social consensus is a *voluntary contract*, and the rules must be agreed to unanimously. This consensus applies to social groups as well as to individuals. A social consensus cannot be forced on the people through governmental power. If one or more decision-makers acting in a certain problem area do not participate in the social contract, the increases in productivity and welfare made possible by its rule cannot be exploited. Owing to unanimity of the social consensus, no problems concerning the aggregation of individual preferences arise.

Fundamental aspects of society can be regulated by a voluntary and unanimously agreed contract on the level of the social consensus because such contracts promise to be advantageous for all the groups and individuals in the state of uncertainty. The social consensus makes it possible to find an 'objectivized' regulation of social problems that is divorced from short-range and particular interests without having to sacrifice the basically individualistic foundation of democracy.

The aspects of uncertainty and unanimity may be illustrated with two examples.

Examples

Individuals can agree, on the level of the social consensus, that the poor and the sick are to be supported by a system of social insurance to which every taxpayer must contribute. Such a rule can come about unanimously because none of the participants knows whether he or she (or one of their descendants) will be among the net beneficiaries or net losers from it.

Passenger air traffic has been disturbed by terrorism, which affects all airlines, airports and nations and not only those who are directly hit. It could be advantageous for all countries to draw up a contract on how to deal with the terrorists. Such a rule might be advantageous for both Western and Eastern nations even if in a particular case they would prefer not to extradite. (For example, if a non-criminal fugitive from Eastern Europe forces an airplane to land in the West, the Western country might find extradition to be politically sensitive.) The contract will break down if important members of the decision-making group do not follow the rules of the game; unanimity among the major participants is a precondition for a productive contract.

A social contract may often be informal. Sometimes the individuals and groups are not even aware that such a contract exists; they realize it only if the consensus is called into question. Some of the rules are taken into the formal constitutional law; in this case one can speak of a 'constitutional contract'. As the example of Britain shows, even in this case such a contract need not be formally decided upon and written down. For all social consensuses there is the problem of maintaining them in the event of sharp conflict.

The social consensus lays down rules about the current politico-economic process and sets the framework in which social activities are to take place. In the second part of this book the practical economic policy measures opened up by this approach will be discussed.

Current Social Process

A different approach to economic policy consists of providing information to the decision-makers in the day-to-day politico-economic process. This information will serve different purposes depending on the persons or groups to whom it is addressed. It is useful to differentiate between three main audiences.

Voters and Groups. The information provided by the economic policy adviser serves the purpose of giving the population a better chance to make its own preferences known and to realize them to a greater degree. This also entails providing improved information on the decisions of, and possibilities open to, public decision-makers. Economic policy making, by providing information, serves to make the democratic process more effective, leading to individual preferences being better fulfilled.

Government and Political Parties. The information provided by economic advisers serves to make it possible for decision-makers to reach their *own* goals better. The parties are helped to design a programme that will suit the voters, particularly in the economic sphere, and that leads to gains in votes, so that their chances of getting and staying in power are improved. In a truly democratic system the pursuit of the parties' own interests and those of the government will ensure that the preferences of the population are fulfilled. This is analogous to the theory of the 'invisible hand' in the market.

Public Bureaucracy and other Public Decision-makers. The information provided here by the economic advisers is similar to that offered to the government and political parties. There is however an important difference, in that these institutions (in particular the central bank) are only indirectly dependent on the voters' preferences.

1.5 PROVISION OF INFORMATION BY THE ECONOMIC ADVISERS

Economic policy advisers are, like all other decision-makers, part of the politico-economic system: they are not 'benevolent dictators' who form economic policy according to their own will. The adviser can only advance suggestions to the various economic policy-makers as to how they can bring about a social contract. Whether such a contract comes about, and how far it will extend, will depend on the individuals and groups involved. The same applies to the current politico-economic process, where again economic advisers can only give information: whether the decision-makers then take account of this information is up to them.

Propositions for social contracts may come about as a result of the economic policy advisers' own private interests, if they can gain income (from books, talks and reports) and recognition (scientific reputation, prestige with the population) as a result. Intrinsic motivation may also play a role: many people feel that it is their duty to increase the common good by bringing forward suggestions that will help to develop a social consensus.

In the contemporary politico-economic process the public decision-makers, and the government in particular, continually demand information on how to put their ideological views into practice and how to secure re-election. Among the voters also there is a demand for such information, but it will only partially show up on a market because it is a public good whose supply benefits all voters. However, the private return on consuming such information may be large enough to give rise to a market demand, which will be met by the private mass media (newspapers, books, etc.) as well as the publicly regulated sector (radio, television).

CONCLUSION

Considering the economy and the polity – and the decision-makers acting therein – as endogenous parts of a total system suggests that the possibilities for influencing the course of the economy are limited. The most effective approach for economic advisers is to provide information about how the rules and institutions can be changed by a social consensus. In day-to-day politics the influence of policy advisers is more restricted, because each decision-maker is interested only in knowing how to pursue his or her own goals within the framework given. A further limit is imposed by the fact that the economic advisers are themselves endogenous actors in the system. However, once the limits of economic policy-making are understood, information on the level of both the social consensus and the current politico-economic process can be offered in such a way that the goals of a democratic economic policy – namely, the satisfaction of individual preferences – are better met.

FURTHER READING

The theory of democratic economic policy is built upon political economy. A survey of its present state is given in

Dennis Mueller, *Public Choice*. Cambridge: University Press, 1979;

Hans van den Doel, *Democracy and Welfare Economics*. Cambridge: University Press, 1979.

These two authors concentrate on public choice, which applies the methodology of the prevailing neoclassical theory of economics to politics. The 'new political economy' is broader; it also considers contributions by non-orthodox economists. A discussion of both approaches may be found in

Bruno S. Frey, *Modern Political Economy*. Oxford: Martin Robertson, 1978.

The 'traditional theory of economic policy' assumes that the government can act autonomously to a large extent and (at least implicitly) that it aims at maximizing social welfare subject to the constraints imposed by the economic system. Well-known representatives of this approach are Jan Tinbergen and Henry Theil, whose works are quoted in Chapter 11. A more recent example of this approach is

M. H. Preston, *Theory of Macroeconomic Policy*. London: Philip Allan, 1974.

Sometimes the traditional theory of economic policy is simply understood as the application of economic theory to practical problems. See for example

P. J. Curwen and A. H. Fowler, *Economic Policy*. London: Macmillan, 1976.

Galbraith outlined his views of politico-economic interdependence in

John K. Galbraith, *The Affluent Society.* Boston: Houghton Mifflin, 1952;

John K. Galbraith, *The New Industrial State.* Boston: Houghton Mifflin, 1967.

Econometric estimates of the politico-economic models of the United Kingdom and the United States are presented in

Bruno S. Frey, *Modern Political Economy.*

A re-estimate of the UK model with data from 1958–79, and a comparison with a competing model, is contained in

Bruno S. Frey and Friedrich Schneider, A Politico-Economic Model of the UK: New Estimates and Predictions, *Economic Journal,* 91 (1981), 737–40.

A verbal account of politico-economic interdependence that concentrates on the United States can be found in

Edward T. Tufte, *Political Control of the Economy.* Princeton: University Press, 1978.

PART II

Policy-making by Social Consensus

Economic policy can be formulated through various types of basic agreement. A social contract arrived at in a state of uncertainty can be maintained only under certain conditions. For this reason the consensus approach to economic policy-making is restricted to fundamental questions and long-run aspects. A society that progresses beyond the stage of 'every man for himself' will see the need for establishing political ground rules and institutions, including the delimiting of the private and public spheres and the determination of the degree of federal decentralization of the nation (Chapter 3). On a somewhat lower level, it will need to decide which decision-making procedures are to be used in what area and for what purposes, and how their functioning can be improved. Basic decision-making mechanisms include the price mechanism (Chapter 4), democratic elections and referenda (Chapter 5), the use of public bureaucracy (Chapter 6), and bargaining among interest groups (Chapter 7). The social consensus can also refer to agreements taken in the various economic areas, such as allocation, income distribution and stabilization (Chapters 8, 9 and 10). The concluding chapter of this part evaluates the possibilities and problems of economic policy-making by social consensus.

CHAPTER 2

Basic Aspects

INTRODUCTION

Rules and institutions are established because individuals are aware that they can thereby increase their welfare. This chapter considers how a social consensus about such rules and institutions can be achieved, what role the uncertainty about one's future position (the 'veil of ignorance') plays, how it can be created, and how the requirement that the agreements have to be arrived at by unanimous consent must be interpreted.

2.1 AGREEMENT ON RULES AND INSTITUTIONS

The Increase in Productivity

A group of individuals whose lives are not regulated in any way would necessarily live in poverty and chaos. A large part of their activity and innovative potential would have to be directed towards defending themselves against the attacks of others, and there would be little time and energy left for more constructive forms of activity. In such a situation it would be advantageous for each person to give up part of his freedom and to abide by some rules, on the understanding that all of the others will do the same. Human societies very early became aware of the advantages of such rules for facilitating life and increasing productivity and welfare.

Individuals and groups can form such social contracts in many different areas, ranging from the informal regulation of life in a small (family) group to treaties between nations.

Examples

A group of people sharing a flat (or in a commune) may find it advantageous to have a telephone, but they will also agree that its costs must be
kept within certain limits. The members of the group thus must come to an
agreement on how to use the telephone; they must find a rule acceptable to
everyone. A rule cannot be imposed by force, because the individuals are
free to leave the group at any time. In a small group an informal, verbal
consensus is usually sufficient, but in a larger group a written agreement is
often necessary. The group thus implicitly or explicitly lays down rules
concerning the use of the telephone.

International conflicts, or even wars, are – with few exceptions – unproductive for all nations concerned. It is thus to everyone's advantage to find
rules for governing international life. These cover diplomatic practice (such
as the immunity of diplomatic staff) as well as how to resolve conflicts (for
example, by means of an international high court or intervention by the
UN). Even in war it can be advantageous to all of the participants if some
rules are observed (such as allowing the Red Cross to function undisturbed).

These two examples make it clear that a social consensus is voluntary and unanimous, in the sense that there is no institution on this
level that can force the participants to comply. Each person and
group has an incentive for participating because a situation without
rules would in general be considered to be less favourable. Those
agreeing do not know with certainty the conflicts that will arise in
the future, but they do know that in the absence of rules they will
have to expend a lot more of their energy and resources protecting
themselves against the activities of the others. In specific cases, some
people and groups would be better off without rules (in the second
example given, for example, a nation could gain an advantage by
attacking a Red Cross station); but over a whole series of cases –
that is, over the future as a whole – everyone will gain if the rules are
observed.

Example

In the French army the so-called 'triage' system is used. The wounded are
divided into three groups:

1   people who will die even if they receive medical care: these are not
treated but are visited by a priest;

2   wounded who can be helped and need care: these are attended by a
doctor;

3   wounded who will survive even without a doctor's services: these are left to the nurses.

In a state of uncertainty this system may well turn out to be the best for all of the participants because the scarce medical resources are put to their most effective use. But a wounded individual allocated to the first or third category would of course be better off if he could receive a doctor's aid and intensive care at the expense of the other wounded. Once it becomes known who is wounded and how seriously, triage comes to seem disadvantageous to *some* of those who are wounded.

For economic activity, rules are of the utmost importance. Only if agreements are observed is a division of labour possible. Such agreements need not be written down; custom and practice are often sufficient.

The Importance of General Rules

The social consensus serves to increase productivity by creating institutions (in the broader sense) through agreement. This lays down the best procedures for reaching decisions – but not for deciding particular cases. What matters is that the appropriate process be fixed and followed; the decisions resulting from it will then be accepted regardless of their specific content. Thus a contract on the level of social consensus differs basically from an approach that focuses on the utility that results from individual, isolated decisions.

The difference between an approach oriented towards results and one oriented towards procedures may be illustrated with an example concerning taxes.

Example

Under the result-oriented approach, for example, the consequences of taxes for resource allocation and income distribution are analysed and evaluated; one asks questions such as whether or how the incentive to work is affected by a tax on income. In the context of the procedural approach, however, it is the way in which the decision to impose the tax was reached that is studied. Have special interest groups had too much influence? Has the public bureaucracy manipulated the result in its own favour? Were the political decision-makers, and in particular the voters, informed sufficiently and in an unbiased fashion?

The properties of a tax system (such as whether it is to be regressive or progressive) that has been decided upon by a democratically correct procedure will be accepted. Knowledge of the consequences of certain properties of a tax system – for example the effect of progression on work incentives – is of course a prerequisite of an informed decision arrived by consensus.

Spontaneous and Arranged Social Consensus

Under certain conditions, a social consensus can come about by spontaneous action. This will occur if the advantages of an agreement and the contents of the rules are obvious. Normally, however, this cannot be assumed, since individuals and groups are often short-sighted and do not make contracts because they do not see the long-range consequences. In this case the economic adviser can actively create the preconditions for reaching such a consensus. He must inform the individuals and groups that could benefit from such rules about the possibilities open to them and suggest new kinds of contracts. He must have a nose for innovative solutions, in order to see what preconditions would be necessary for a social consensus, and then to create those conditions.

This problem is quite difficult, because it is often not easy to spot arrangements that can be expected to prove beneficial for all the participants. Usually the strict conditions for a social consensus will not be fully met. It may however be possible to arrive at solutions that will be regarded as improving everyone's position through compromises. If for instance a group feels disadvantaged by a proposal, perhaps its position can be improved by shifting some of the burden on to those who clearly benefit from it – but not so much that the latter no longer have a net advantage. One can try to reach such a 'redistribution' by means of explicit transfers or other types of government activity.

Social consensus comes about when contracts are suggested from which all the individuals in the state of uncertainty assume that their position will be improved. The task of the economic policy adviser thus consists of developing and propagating ideas that will lead to Parento-superior situations (in the *ex ante* sense). The economist becomes a specialist in devising Pareto-optimal agreements, looking for new institutions and procedures that will be acceptable to people and groups because they see themselves as benefiting from them.

Three different social states or levels can be distinguished in the context of a social consensus:

1 a situation without general rules, where the advantages of contracts for achieving Pareto-superior improvements are not yet being exploited;
2 the level of the social consensus, where agreements are made behind the veil of ignorance;
3 the current social process, where the basic social rules already exist and people know what their own position is in the society. Decisions and actions here are to a large extent taken in a state of certainty, in a world of existing institutions and rules.

As already mentioned, the individuals and groups in any specific instance are restricted in their behaviour by the contents of an already existing social consensus. They will try to renegotiate this when they think that they can thereby improve their own position. They must, however, take into account the fact that this may lead to the other participants' no longer abiding by the rules of the game and everyone trying to push through their own short-term interests. Sometimes it will be difficult to find a new agreement that will be unanimously accepted. Those who try to break out may well lose in a situation in which some of the rules no longer hold. Each individual and each group must compare the potential advantages of renegotiation of the consensus with the potential disadvantages of a situation without rules.

Maintaining the social consensus on the level of the current political process is a difficult task. If the rules of the game can be changed without difficulty by simple majority rule, the basic idea of agreement on the level of the social consensus is destroyed: each person and each group would act according to its short-range interests, and the advantages of long-range rules that allow Pareto-optimal arrangements would be lost. Social agreements can be guaranteed institutionally by requiring a *qualified majority* for change. Such regulations can be found in some written constitutions.

When a consensus is being formed, the decision-makers will speculate about the contract's chances of survival in the current political conflicts. If, for instance, an agreement is suggested in which a group that is well organized in the current political process will suffer a disadvantage over a longer period of time, it must be expected that the group will cause revision or repeal of the agreement. Those suggesting the agreement will therefore make an effort to avoid introducing such unstable rules.

2.2   THE IMPORTANCE OF UNCERTAINTY

Individuals and groups will come to a general agreement only if they are uncertain about their own future position in the politico-economic process, for otherwise the wishes of the stronger party would be decisive in each particular instance.

Example

Everyone would like to have his or her preferences determine events. In this sense, everyone would prefer a situation in which he or she would be dictator. However, the individuals would reject the institution of dictator if they were uncertain as to *who* would actually be given the role. In the first case there is certainty; in the second case the decision (to *not* have a dictator) is taken behind the veil of ignorance.

The people and groups involved may not know with certainty how they will be affected by the consequences of a specific consensual rule. Uncertainty makes it possible to accept that individuals are basically rational and selfish and at the same time to reach an 'objectivized' view of social problems.

The uncertainty required for consensus will not always be present, or consistent. There are however some procedures that allow us at least to simulate uncertainty.

Constitutional Assembly.   The idea of social consensus formed in a constitutional assembly comes naturally to American social scientists. They have been strongly influenced by the formation of the United States, in which the constitutional assembly discussed basic questions of the future framework of society (for instance, whether to form a federal state or a confederacy). However, the delegates to that assembly were also quite aware that some of the rules suggested would be to their advantage (or to the advantage of the groups or regions represented by them) in the *current* political process. The state of uncertainty thus only partially exists in a constitutional assembly.

Equal Possibility of Being in the Other Person's Position. In order positively to acknowledge the state of uncertainty, each individual must be capable of imagining how every other person in the society will evaluate benefits and costs. This requires an idea not only of the others' income (budget) and other constraints, but also of their preferences. Such knowledge is traditionally gained through personal contact, either intensive contact with a few people, or extensive knowledge of many (as gained for instance by travelling). Information provided today often comes from the mass media, in particular television, and partly also through the educational process. The procedure here is not directly to increase uncertainty about one's future position but to make clear to individuals how their preferences and constraints would differ if they were in the position of another individual. (If they were not, uncertainty would not matter.)

Ability to Predict Circumstances of Descendants. One may reach a certain degree of objectivity on the level of the social consensus by assuming that the participants are unclear as to which position their children and grandchildren will find themselves in. In so far as there is *some* knowledge about the degree of social mobility possible in the society, however, people may have an idea as to how probable it is, for instance, that the descendants of a rich person will also be rich. The degree of uncertainty is therefore imperfect.

Time Between a General Agreement Being Decided On and its Coming into Force. If an agreement becomes binding only after a certain period of time (say, after two years), uncertainty is introduced because the economic and political conditions may change in the meantime. What might have been advantageous to a particular group at the time that the rule was formulated can be to its disadvantage when it finally comes into force. If this is considered to be a realistic possibility, individuals and groups will have an incentive to form rules that take account of such possible changes. This incentive for an objectivized view will lead to propositions for social contracts that will have a good chance of being generally accepted.

The various possibilities discussed for approaching a state of uncertainty are each suited to different situations. It is clear that complete uncertainty at the level of social consensus is difficult to reach, and will be possible only with regard to particular aspects.

If economic policy advisers want to bring about agreements by social consensus, they must normally be satisfied with an only approximate state of uncertainty. Under this condition, various decision rules may be used. The two decision rules most often employed are as follows.

Maximin Principle

According to this, that alternative should be chosen whose worst consequence is better than the worst consequences of all the other alternatives. The maximin principle is extremely risk-averse: average and even best results are not considered; one concentrates exclusively on the worst results.

Example

Consider the situation in which it is uncertain which of four states (A, B, C, D) will materialize. There are three alternatives (I, II, III) at one's disposal. The decision situation is illustrated in Table 2.1. The numbers designate utility units (utiles). It may be seen that alternative I leads, in the worst possible case (state B), to a utility level of 20, alternative II to at least 30 (state D), and alternative III to at least 50 (state A). The relatively best of the worst results yields a utility level of 50. According to the maximin criterion, alternative III should be chosen.

TABLE 2.1 *Decisions Made according to Maximin Criterion*
(*Arabic numbers indicate utility units*)

| Alternative | State | | | | |
	A	B	C	D	Minimum
I	80	20	40	90	20
II	110	50	70	30	30
III	50	100	90	80	50

This principle is used by John Rawls in his *Theory of Justice* as a decision-making mechanism on the level of the social consensus. He derives from it a principle of income distribution which holds that, among all the social states possible, that one should be preferred in which the poorest group of society is relatively best off (the so-called 'difference principle').

Principle of Insufficient Reason

If there are mutually exclusive alternatives, their occurrence can be considered equally likely if there is no reason for assigning a higher probability to one or other event. If nothing is known, it seems reasonable to expect all outcomes with equal probability. If, moreover, one assumes that the results can be measured in terms of cardinal utility, the decision-making rule of maximizing the unweighted utility of the results follows.

It is not possible to say *a priori* which decision-making rule people will choose in the state of uncertainty. The economic policy adviser making proposals should be aware of this area for leeway and should advance proposals that are felt to be advantageous by the participants on the basis of as many decision-making rules as possible.

2.3 THE INTERPRETATION OF UNANIMITY

A social consensus can be arrived at and maintained only if all (or at least all the important) decision-makers, be they individuals or groups, participate. Otherwise, either the productivity-increasing effect resulting from introduction of the rules will not be fully realized, or the agreement will break down because some of the participants will see that keeping to the rules is not worth-while.

The conflict between agreeing to a rule (which is welfare-increasing for everyone) and the possible advantage to an individual deriving from breaking the contract is a fundamental social problem. The situation may be illustrated by the so-called 'prisoner's dilemma' of game theory. The model has the following characteristics:

1 if there is consensus concerning the rules, the greatest possible utility of all of the participants taken together is reached;
2 if one of the participants does not keep to the rules while all the others do, the one who breaks them can achieve a greater utility as compared with the situation above;
3 a situation of no rules is the worst for everyone.

According to the prisoner's dilemma model, there is an incentive for each person acting in isolation to disregard the rules. As this behaviour is advantageous for the individual, the situation without rules and with the lowest welfare level for all will be an equilibrium. This model may be illustrated with the help of a simple example.

Example

Consider two actors A and B. For simplicity's sake they are considered to be completely identical. In Figure 2.1 the numbers relate to utility units. The number at the top left of each cell shows the utility of actor A; the number at the bottom right of the cell represents the utility of actor B. The number in the middle of the cell shows the total utility (the sum of the individual utilities). Actors A and B each receive 10 utility units (20 units taken together) if they both keep to the rules. Actor A can increase his utility from 10 to 13 units by not keeping to the rules, however, *if and only if* actor B does keep to the rules. B's utility then falls to a very low level (2 units) because only one person is abiding by the agreement. Actor B will make the analogous calculations, so that neither A nor B will keep to the rules. The outcome is that both end up in the worst possible situation.

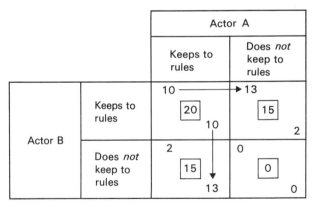

FIGURE 2.1   *The instability of rules as the 'prisoner's dilemma'.*

It may be concluded from the prisoner's dilemma model that measures must be taken on the level of the social consensus to remove the incentives for not keeping to the rules. Such voluntary agreements, for instance that force may be used in order to make people adhere to the agreement, could gain a consensus if they are made in a state of uncertainty and if they are *ex ante* advantageous. The incentive for breaking the rules can above all be obviated through *punishment*. Punishment may take many forms, ranging from ostracism to monetary punishment or even imprisonment and death. A prerequisite is that they be imposed by those who keep to the rules, or by an institution (such as the state) created for this purpose.

The change in the gaming situation that is introduced with punishment may be illustrated using the previous example.

Example

Figure 2.2 shows the consequences of imposing a punishment of 10 utility units on norm trespassers, as compared with the situation shown in Figure 2.1. Breaking the rules is now not profitable for either A or B. The punishment of 10 units diminishes the utility from 13 to 3 units, so that a worse state is reached than if the rules were kept.

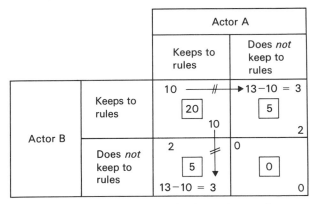

FIGURE 2.2   *The stability of rules with punishment.*

CONCLUSION

Productive economic activity presupposes a consensus about the fundamental rules and institutions of a society. This entails fixing the individual's political rights (in particular, property rights) and the limits of the private and collectively managed spheres of the society. The state, as the most important collective institution, is given the right to use force, but the rights of the individual are protected by the institution of the division of power and regional decentralization. The fundamental democratic right consists of the population's direct participation in the political and economic sectors (economic democracy). These fundamental rules in the forms of rights and institutions in the society will be discussed in Chapter 3.

Somewhat less fundamental is the agreement on the decision-making procedures to be followed in the current social process. A consensus as to where and how far a certain decision-making mechanism is to be used and what political measures are to be taken to improve its functioning will lead to productivity increases. The price system, democratic voting mechanisms, hierarchical decisions by the public bureaucracy and bargaining among private interest groups are all possible social decision-making systems. These procedures will be discussed in Chapters 4–7.

The agreements reached on the level of the social consensus may also be analysed with respect to the economic areas concerned. Chapters 8, 9 and 10 will examine the contributions a social consensus may make in the areas of allocation, income distribution and stabilization. In this context, contracts covering redistribution, intergenerational contracts (for example, old age pensions) and attempts to stabilize prices with the help of general rules (incomes policy, concerted action, constant expansion of the stock of money) will be discussed. Chapter 11 will deal with the possibilities for, and the limits of reaching agreements at the level of the social consensus.

FURTHER READING

Basic contributions to the social consensus as an approach to economic policy have been made by James Buchanan. The following works are central to the topic:

James M. Buchanan, *Freedom in Constitutional Contract. Perspectives of a Political Economist.* College Station and London: Texas A & M University Press, 1977;

James M. Buchanan, *The Limits of Liberty. Between Anarchy and Leviathan.* Chicago and London: University of Chicago Press, 1975.

Buchanan limits his constitutional consensus to the rules contained in a written constitution; he therefore speaks of constitutional contracts and compares the contracts reached in a constitutional assembly with pre-constitutional anarchy. Both states, however, are special cases only from the point of view of modern economic policy. Moreover, Buchanan only considers constitutional contracts among individuals, thus excluding the possibility of consensus among groups. Social consensus in the sense discussed in the present book also covers informal agreements among groups.

Important philosophically oriented contributions are

Friedrich A. Hayek, *Legislation and Liberty. A New Statement of the Liberal Principles of Justice and Political Economy*. London: Routledge & Kegan Paul, 1973–79.

John Rawls, *A Theory of Justice*. Cambridge, Mass.: Harvard University Press, 1971.

A worthwhile interpretation of the constitutional contract is

Dennis C. Mueller, Constitutional Democracy and Social Welfare, *Quarterly Journal of Economics*, 87 (1973), 60–80.

A critical evaluation is given by

Scott Gordon, The New Contractarians, *Journal of Political Economy*, 84 (1976), 573–90.

The various decision-making rules in the case of complete uncertainty as well as the prisoner's dilemma are discussed in

Duncan Luce and Howard Raiffa, *Games and Decisions*. New York: John Wiley, 1967.

The need to agree voluntarily to the use of force is stressed in

William J. Baumol, *Welfare Economics and the Theory of the State*, 2nd edn. London: Bell & Sons, 1975.

CHAPTER 3

Fundamental Political Rights and Institutions

INTRODUCTION

A consensus about fundamental political rights and institutions is advantageous for all individuals in a state of uncertainty. Once the rights and collective (governmental) institutions are set, the course of the political and economic processes is largely determined. They thus constitute the heart of the social consensus.

Individuals and groups can make their preferences known in the future politico-economic process only if their basic political rights are guaranteed, including the fundamental separation between the privately and collectively organized sectors of society. People can live together productively only if they permit the state to enforce the rules of law; but at the same time they must make sure that the state does not become dictatorial, unnecessarily violating their preferences. The separation of powers and regional decentralization serve as important constitutional limits to the monopoly of the state.

This chapter discusses the various forms that the basic political rights and institutions may take. It emphasizes federalism as an institution restricting the government's power over individuals, and the rights for participation in the political and economic spheres. Various possible forms of industrial democracy are treated.

3.1 BASIC INDIVIDUAL RIGHTS

A democratic society is possible only if the individuals have basic rights, including:

— the right to speak and to assemble;

— the right to choose among different forms and media of information;

— property rights.

The advantage of having a social consensus about such rights is obvious.

Property rights play a particularly important role for economic welfare. If there are no such rights, those who work and produce goods must devote a large part of their efforts and income to defending the fruits of their activity against those who would like to possess them. This anarchical state is unproductive; everyone is better off if property is protected by collective rules.

Property rights are productive only if they are well defined and effectively protect the (legitimate) owner. These rights need not necessarily be private but may well belong to a collectivity, say a commune. In many cases, however, private property rights are the best institutional arrangement because it is in the owner's own interest to safeguard and to maintain the property rights collectively transferred to him.

3.2   THE SEPARATION BETWEEN THE PRIVATE AND COLLECTIVE DOMAIN

It is quite unlikely that a social consensus can be reached with respect to which matters should belong to the private, and which to the collective, sphere. Over time there is a constant change in this respect, owing to technological developments, shifts of preferences and influences from the outside world. In the state of uncertainty, however, there is the possibility of reaching a consensus on *how* to take the decisions about what is to be in the private and what in the collective domain. This presupposes that the individuals and groups know the consequences of the choice of a particular decision-making rule.

Consensus about a Decision-making Rule

The most important aspect of a decision-making rule is the size of the majority required for a decision. On the level of the social consensus, the individuals and groups are faced with two kinds of cost.

1   *External costs* arise when the collectivity takes a decision against one's personal interest. The larger the majority required, the smaller is the danger of belonging to the minority. In the extreme – with the unanimity requirement – these external costs are zero because any individual can prevent a decision that he does not like. In Figure 3.1 the external cost curve falls from left to right with an increasing share of individuals required for a collective decision.

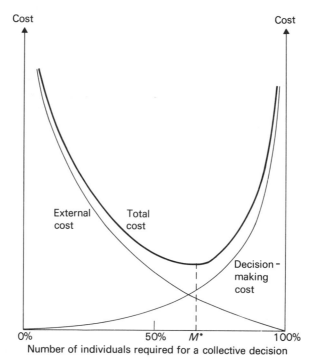

FIGURE 3.1   *Determination of optimal majority.*

2   *Decision-making costs* consist of the costs that arise when the collectivity (society) is to decide a question. The smaller the majority, the easier it is to reach a decision. When the decision-making rule comes near to unanimity, it becomes more and more difficult to reach a decision. The danger of so-called strategic behaviour in-creases: if someone knows that his consent is needed for a collective decision, he has the possibility of 'exploiting' those expecting to gain most. In the case of the rule of unanimity, everybody is in this strategically favourable position, so the decision costs are extremely

high. In Figure 3.1 the curve of decision costs is shown to rise from left to right with an increasing share of individuals required for a collective decision.

Individuals (and groups) will take into account both types of costs when they determine an *optimal majority*. The external cost curve and the decision-making cost curve can be added, for they are both denominated in terms of subjectively expected utility losses. The optimum is given where total costs are lowest. In Figure 3.1 this optimal majority is indicated by M^*.

The optimal majority M^* has three properties:

1 the higher (*ceteris paribus*) the external costs are, the larger is M^*; the higher (*ceteris paribus*) the decision-making costs are, the lower is M^*;

2 the shapes of the external and decision-making cost curves differ according to the matter considered. For each problem there may be a different majority that is optimal when it comes to making decisions about allocating activities as between the private and collective domains. For example, in the narrowly personal area (such as the kind of music one listens to) the external costs are likely to be higher because individuals probably experience a large utility loss if a collective decision is imposed. On the level of social consensus, individuals will therefore allow collective decisions in this area only provided a large majority is required;

3 the optimal majority is 50 per cent by chance only. Simple majority thus has no special significance as a decision-making rule with regard to the determination of the private and collective domains.

3.3 THE STRUCTURE OF THE STATE: SEPARATION OF POWERS

The basic elements of the construction of government institutions is one of the most important topics to be settled by social consensus. The separation of powers and the regional decentralization of public activity (discussed in the next section) are important facilities for checking the power of the state and forcing politicians to take the preferences of individuals and groups into account.

The classical separation into executive, legislative and judiciary powers is designed to prevent a monopoly of power by the state and to safeguard individual liberty. The three powers should control each other; this idea of 'checks and balances' is particularly well developed in the American system. The relationship between the three powers is not stable over time; in some periods the executive gains in weight, in other periods the parliament dominates, and in still other periods the judiciary may take over areas formerly in the hands of the executive or legislative branch.

The economic adviser can advance suggestions that serve to prevent a monopoly of power and strengthen the balancing capacity of the separation of powers. Two such propositions are:

1 no members of the executive may sit in the legislative assembly. (this principle applies in the United States but not in the Federal Republic of Germany, where, for example, in 1977 46 per cent of the members of the federal parliament (Bundestag) were public employees);
2 the membership and presidency of public committees must rotate automatically after fixed time intervals.

Such proposals have a chance of being implemented only in something approaching a state of uncertainty, that is, before particular persons and groups know their positions of interest. The public officials already sitting in parliament would, of course, try everything to keep their position, and the members (and presidents) of committees would strongly oppose automatic rotation.

3.4   THE STRUCTURE OF THE STATE: REGIONAL DECENTRALIZATION

Voting with their Feet

The preferences of individuals and groups have a better chance of being fulfilled when the state is organized in a decentralized way. The competition between the various regional suppliers of public goods and services provides incentives to take the wishes of the population into account in the political process. Federalism is built on the same idea as that of the market, where the firms compete for the consumers' outlays, and of democracy, where the parties compete for votes.

In a federal constitution the citizens may move to another region if they are dissatisfied with the combination of public output and taxes existing in the region in which they live. The population thus makes its wishes felt by 'voting with their feet'. The elected representatives of federal subunits must make an effort to provide that level and distribution of public goods and services which induces the population to stay and attracts additional people from the outside. This competition brought about by individual migration decisions leads to an efficient (Pareto-optimal) supply of public output. However, as the demand for publicly supplied goods and services depends strongly on personal income levels, it is likely that a regional differentiation of the population according to income groups will result, which may be considered unfavourable from the point of view of income distribution and social justice.

The model just sketched disregards various costs that reduce mobility between regions. The decision to move to another region is strongly dependent on whether there are adequate opportunities for work. Mobility is also small because there are restrictions imposed from other areas of public activity (in particular, one may lose subsidized public housing and would have to wait a long time in the new region before reaching the same privileged position again). Finally – at least in Europe – people resist moving because they do not like to leave their friends. The model discussed is therefore applicable primarily to the choice of residence within the limits of a metropolitan area.

Advantages and Disadvantages of Federalism

The goal of the *economic theory of federalism* is to analyse the determinants of the optimal degree of centralization (or decentralization); in other words, the regional breakdown of a country that best suits the wishes of the population. Knowledge of the advantages and disadvantages of decentralization allows the individuals to take an informed decision on the level of the basic social consensus.

Generally speaking, decentralization is well suited for allocation while centralization helps to solve problems of distribution and stabilization.

The following arguments support decentralization.

1 There is a greater scope for taking into account all those preferences that differ between regions. It has been shown that the popu-

lation is more likely to participate politically, and thus to make its wishes clear, in small than in large, anonymous communities. The governments of the federal subunits find it possible to supply those public goods that cater for the special preferences of the local population. The higher and more intensive political participation of the population puts pressure on the politicians to supply the goods efficiently.

2   It can be expected that planning and administrative costs will be smaller in the case of decentralized supply. This is mainly due to the savings in information costs made possible by the closer contact between suppliers and demanders of public goods. The proposition that centralization decreases administrative costs has been proved wrong empirically in many instances (in particular in Germany, where a great number of formerly independent communes have been united into larger units in the seventies).

3   Regional decentralization gives a better chance of innovation in the political process. In Switzerland, for example, the right to vote for women was introduced in some cantons many years before it was admitted by the (male) electorate at the federal level. The same applies to various forms of social policy.

The following arguments support centralization.

1   Benefits and costs crossing the boundaries of a region (known as 'spill-overs'), and the resulting biases, are smaller the more centralized a country is. If a region is able to consume the goods supplied by another region (termed 'benefit spill-ins'), it has little incentive to provide the goods itself because the population can benefit from the supply without participating in the cost of providing it. The regions from which benefits spill out into adjacent regions do not take into account these 'external' benefits in their supply decision; the public goods supply will therefore generally be too low. Spill-overs between autonomous federal subunits thus lead (as in the case of external effects in the price system) to a Pareto-inferior allocation of resources. This inefficiency may be an argument for centralized decision-making in the face of public goods with strong regional external effects.

2   In some parts of public activity there are *indivisibilities*, as for example in the case of a nuclear power plant. A centralized decision

and supply may be warranted if the regional units are not able to provide these goods co-operatively.

3   In some cases public production is subject to *increasing returns to scale*, which may make it worthwhile for goods to be supplied from a higher level of the federal system.

4   The mobility of the population as well as the exchange of goods may lead to such a close connection between parts of a country that it may be sensible to co-ordinate public supply (for example, the school system). This may under some circumstances require centralized decision-making.

5   From the point of view of an individual deciding on the level of the social consensus, it may be advantageous for a *minimal provision of certain public goods* to be guaranteed in all regions of the country. There may, in particular, be two reasons:

— the public goods concerned may be of interest in the future (they may be 'option values'), though no (political) demand is presently exerted because one does not know in which region one will live;
— a minimal supply of certain (basic) public goods (for example social security) may reduce the tensions between regions of different per capita income, and may thereby be an important element in securing the existence of the country as a whole.

In both cases, a centralized decision is required to bring about the minimum supply, because the individual subunits have no incentive for providing the goods.

6   A *redistributional policy* has to be undertaken at the central level. An individual federal unit has no capacity for raising the necessary taxes from upper-income recipients, because they will move out of the jurisdiction to evade the higher taxation. If on the other hand the redistribution is undertaken by a region via the provision of goods and services mainly benefiting low-income recipients (for example via high social welfare payments), there will be an immigration of low-income people into that region from other areas. The region is thus unable to finance the redistributional policy in the long run. An example is provided by New York City, which almost went bankrupt because of such a policy.

7   An effective *stabilization policy* can be undertaken only at the central level. If a single federal unit embarks on an expansionary

policy, a large part of the multiplier effect gets lost in the form of spill-overs into other areas. Neither will a federal unit have any interest in undertaking a restrictive policy to combat inflation, because a large part of the effect would benefit other regions. In both cases we have the same problem: the public good 'stabilization' will not be supplied at all or will be under-supplied by a federal subunit; each one takes the position of a 'free rider'. The units below central government, moreover, lack adequate instruments for an effective stabilization policy. In particular, they cannot influence the monetary base. On the contrary, they have a budget to balance: in a boom there are high tax receipts, which will be spent; in a recession the expenditures must be reduced because tax income falls. The federal units are thus forced to undertake a destabilizing fiscal policy.

Possibilities for a Social Consensus

Economic advisers may try to bring about a social consensus in the following respects:

1 by determining the degree of centralization (or decentralization) that individuals and groups find desirable, taking into account the advantages and disadvantages of each solution;
2 by choosing the appropriate area of each jurisdiction. Spill-overs bias the allocation of resources; the limits to which the benefits and costs of public goods extend should therefore relate to the competence of the government of the subunit. This *fiscal equivalence* is fulfilled if those who benefit from the public goods also pay the cost. The principle of fiscal equivalence requires a very large number of federal units; for each public good a different size is required because the area of benefit and cost diffusion differs as between goods. A large number of jurisdictions, on the other hand, would create high costs of co-ordination and administration. Individuals behind their veil of ignorance must strike a balance between the costs imposed by a deviation from fiscal equivalence and costs accruing from the multiplicity of jurisdictions.

3.5 DEMOCRATIC RIGHTS: POLITICAL PARTICIPATION

Individual members of society must arrive at a consensus about the possibility of *direct* participation in political decisions in the current social process. Only a few aspects of elections, referenda and citizens' initiatives will be discussed here.

Elections

Choosing between competing parties and politicians is an essential form of political participation in a democracy. A consensus must be found on which election rules to choose (see Chapter 5) and on how often elections should take place. The length of the legislative period is an important determinant of the government's time horizon. If it is short, the government has continually to consider its chances of re-election. It concentrates then on short-run measures and creates marked 'political business cycles'. If the legislative period is long, there is the danger that government disregards voters' preferences over extended periods and follows a policy that suits its own preferences. Lengthening the election period thus has both advantages and disadvantages. Recently, proposals have been advanced to introduce legislative periods of variable length. They go beyond those constitutional provisions that simply limit the maximum length (as for example in the United Kingdom and Canada).

— The length of the election period may be determined by a random mechanism, stipulating, for instance, that the probability of the election period lasting longer than three years is 30 per cent, more than four years, 40 per cent, more than five years, 25 per cent and over six years, 15 per cent. The government then has to take into account that it may be in power a short or a long time.
— The more successful the government's policy is, the longer it can stay in office. If the party in power is able to achieve low unemployment, low inflation and rapid growth, it may stay on; otherwise, the voters have the constitutional option of calling for an election.
— The longer a party has been in office, the more time the following government may be allowed to undertake a new policy before it has to meet the test of an election. Changing a policy requires the introduction of new laws, and public bureaucrats need to be induced to support the new line (or if not to be reshuffled accordingly). All this is the more difficult the longer the previous government has been in office; it is therefore reasonable that the succeeding government should have more time available to undertake the reforms it finds necessary.

These propositions have to be discussed and their advantages and disadvantages evaluated when a social consensus is to be reached.

Popular Referenda

The classical *assembly of the people* has been preserved in some Swiss cantons (Landsgemeinden), in some communes in Switzerland and in parts of the north-eastern United States. This most direct form of democracy is of limited importance today. More important are the institutions of the obligatory and optional *referendum* and of the *initiative* as it is mainly practised in Switzerland.

Example

Since the Swiss Confederacy was established (in 1848), there have been 223 referenda about changes of the constitution and of laws at the federal level. Of these, 135 (61 per cent) have been accepted and 88 rejected by the voters. In the same period 74 'initiatives' have been undertaken, of which only 7 have been accepted. The Swiss electorate has to decide about ten times per year on federal matters, and in addition there are referenda and initiatives on the level of cantons and communes. The issues cover a wide range, including economic policy decisions (for example, whether to change a turnover tax into a value added tax, and whether to increase that tax).

The institution of the referendum has been applied in various representative democracies to obtain the opinion of the electorate on issues that government and parliament have been unwilling or unable to decide. Denmark, France, Ireland and Switzerland have mandatory referendum provisions in their constitution. Referenda are often used in American states, particularly in California, as well as in Australia. There have been over 500 referenda in the world up to 1979, a large proportion of which, however, have taken the character of a plebiscite in favour of the ruling government (or dictator). Examples of serious referenda are the votes taken in the United Kingdom, Norway, Denmark and Ireland on whether to join the European Community, and in Sweden and Austria on nuclear power policy.

Citizens' Initiatives

Another form of direct participation of the population in politics that has gained momentum in the last decade is the 'citizens' initiative'. This is devoted mostly to issues such as the environment or nuclear power plants. The parties and the governments of all levels are forced to deal with these issues, which are taken up by a spontaneously formed group of citizens outside the established political institutions. These 'initiatives' make their demands felt by organizing demonstrations, sit-ins and other propaganda activities. Democratic activity can thereby be exercised, public activity made more transparent, government controlled more strongly, and dubious projects can be prevented. But owing to the spontaneous eruption of such initiatives, the problems that can be tackled are few in number and often emotive. Initiatives are formulated when individuals are directly involved in a controversial area and when the problems are imminent. Research has shown that the composition of citizens' initiatives is mainly of members of the upper middle class. The participants often lack the endurance necessary to bring about long-run effects; as a rule, initiatives need quick success. This disadvantage can be overcome by stronger organization, but this means that the spontaneity and the element of direct democracy is lost.

Citizens' initiatives may be a useful means of revealing strongly held or minority preferences. The economic policy adviser can point out to the individuals the advantages of having rules and institutions that induce the established political decision-makers to be sensitive to the preferences that are revealed. So far, citizens' initiatives have had limited direct success, and sometimes they have been used by extremist groups to push their own cause. The influence of initiatives may, for example, be increased if the written constitution admits the possibility of a *popular initiative*, which forces the government to put a question directly before the people. Experience in Switzerland suggests that the threat of an initiative is often sufficient to induce the parties in power to consider the wishes of the population.

3.6 DEMOCRATIC RIGHTS: ECONOMIC PARTICIPATION

Motives for Introducing Economic Democracy

Economic democracy means that elements of democracy are introduced into the economic area, in particular into firms. It is proposed mainly for two reasons:

1   to overcome the discrepancy between political democracy and
     economic hierarchy: Labour and capital should have equal
     rights;
2   to reduce the alienation of the employees who feel themselves to
     be of no importance and to have no influence in the firm, and
     who therefore do not derive satisfaction from work.

Economic democracy can be advantageous for both workers and
employers (management and capitalists); it may well be the outcome
of a social consensus. The workers expect economic democracy to
give them a stronger say in the firm. The advantages for the employers are less obvious:

— tensions may be reduced, leading to fewer strikes;
— the workers will become more closely attached to the firm they
  are employed in, which raises work incentives;
— part of the responsibility of management can be shared with, or
  relegated to, the employees;
— the firm gains more weight in the political struggle for subsidies,
  tax exemptions and protection against outside competition, as it
  can now speak more convincingly in the name of employers and
  employees alike. In modern economies such sectoral interests are
  often more important than the classical conflict between labour
  and capital.

Economic democracy also has disadvantages for both sides of the
labour market. The management fears that it is further reduced in its
capacity to take decisions. For the workers, economic democracy
may mean that the pursuit of more far-reaching goals, such as the
nationalization of all private enterprises, is postponed or given up
completely.

Levels of Economic Democracy

Three stages of workers' participation in the firm can be distinguished.

Participation at the Plant Level.   This kind of participation is restricted to practical questions at the place of work and the plant. It
involves the right to be informed and to be heard, for consultations
to take place between employers and elected representatives of the
workers, and for the veto to be exercised in certain circumstances.

Co-determination. This form of economic democracy entails workers having an influence in all matters relating to the enterprise, including investment decisions. Workers' representatives sit on the board of directors and the board of managers.

Workers' Self-management. This variant of economic democracy introduces various elements of direct democracy. The enterprise belongs to those employed in it. The most important characteristics are:

— all employees have the same vote in the firm's decisions and participate democratically;
— the employees share the profits of the firm but cannot individually sell any part of the property;
— outside intervention in the firm's affairs is prohibited; workers' self-management thus presupposes a decentralized market economy. The bureaucratic tendencies of planned economics are resisted;
— the workers can choose the firm in which they want to work, and the firms can decide autonomously whom to hire. The members of the firm decide according to democratic rules (which they set for themselves in the firm's constitution) who (if anyone) is to be dismissed.

Analysis of Economic Democracy

Worker participation is much debated today. The discussion is mostly confined to an *ad hoc* exchange of the presumed advantages and disadvantages of this kind of democracy. An analysis from the point of view of economic theory is rarely undertaken. In order to highlight the issues involved, two approaches will be sketched here; the *theory of property rights* and the *theory of the co-operative firm*. As we shall see, they stress different aspects and therefore come to different conclusions.

The View of the Theory of Property Rights. This approach starts from a model of the economy with effective competition between resource owners. Competition relates to goods as well as to the workforce of various levels of qualification, and also to the means of financing. The owner of a firm unites the factors of production (he forms a *team*) in a way that leads to the most efficient production of the good. He offers the other input owners a contract according to which he organizes production and pays them their (marginal) output. As compensation for his activity, he receives the positive difference between turnover and cost (the profit), but he has also to bear a possible negative difference (a loss). The firm is an institution formed of voluntary members in which the entrepreneur is given the task of finding the most efficient form of production. He has an interest in providing the other input owners with the right incentives to produce, such that the firm as a whole functions best. The hierarchical structure of the firm is the result of a series of voluntary contracts between resource owners.

This view of the firm leads to two conclusions with respect to economic democracy.

1   It is unnecessary to introduce co-determination by law. In a competitive economy, nobody can be exploited because everyone is free to supply his labour to whom he chooses. Individual liberty is guaranteed not by the democratic rights within the firm, but rather by the effects of competition.

2   Co-determination will be offered by the entrepreneur in his own interest *if* there is a demand for it. Given the same qualification, a worker will receive a higher wage for a given job without participatory rights than he would if he had the privilege of participating democratically; the lower wage is the result of the worker implicitly buying the good 'democratic participation'. If economic democracy increases the firm's productivity, the entrepreneur will introduce it in his own interest, without asking for a compensation.

The view of the firm, as seen by the theory of property rights, and the consequences for the introduction of economic democracy depend largely on the assumption that there is effective competition in all the markets and that the substitution between alternative job conditions (with and without co-determination) is possible. These possibilities must further be perceived by the individuals and be used fully.

In reality, these conditions are not even approximately met. In a modern economy there are many restrictions and rigidities that prevent the price system from functioning in the way the theory of property rights postulates. The workers often feel burdened by the job conditions; in many cases there are no adequate alternative job

offers available, or they will not be known because of high information and transaction costs. For the workers it is therefore often
advantageous to accomplish their desire for better job conditions
and more participation by resorting to *collective* action; that is, by
employing the political process to specify the rights for economic
democracy.

The View of the Theory of the Co-operative Firm. This approach
stresses the positive effects of workers' co-determination and co-
ownership. Economic democracy improves the relationships among
employees (horizontal level) and between management and workers
(vertical level). Both serve to raise productivity and allow a more
rapid introduction of technical innovations; at the same time, the
workers are more satisfied with their jobs. There is thus no conflict
between economic efficiency and economic democracy.

The main reason why economic democracy should have these
positive effects is to be found in the fact that there is greater cohesion
among employees. As the workers receive a part of the profits and
can influence job conditions, they will see to it among themselves
that everyone works well and that shirking is ostracized. A good
work performance will be favourably looked upon by colleagues.
The hierarchical system of controlling work will be replaced by a
horizontal, informal control among equals.

In a traditional hierarchical firm where payment is used to set the
work incentives and in which there are no participatory rights, concerted action by the subordinates against management and owners is
advantageous. If one particular employee is working harder, the
managers will assume that the productivity of all workers can be
raised. So workers will agree not to work too hard and fast. This
effect is well known when the piece-wage is fixed, but it holds in
principle for all levels of hierarchy, possibly not least among lower
and middle management. Another incentive for collusion among the
employees against the firm's top executives and owners is that there
are only a limited number of higher jobs available in a firm. Harder
work by all who are competing for the higher posts increases only
the utility of those who finally get the job; the increased efforts of all
the others often leads to increased profits, in which the employees do
not share.

The positive relationship betwen economic democracy, productivity and job satisfaction proposed by the theory of the co-

operative firm does *not* presuppose altruistic behaviour on the part
of the workers. On the contrary, it is assumed that they act according to their own interest. It differs mainly from the theory of property rights in that the *social interdependence* within the firm
assumes a central role. Co-operative behaviour among employees is
assumed to be strengthened when there is co-determination and
profit-sharing.

Empirical research

The theory of property rights and the theory of the co-operative firm
stress quite different aspects and effects of economic democracy.
They reach almost opposite conclusions.

— The theory of property rights suggests that co-determination
  would be introduced if there were a demand for it and if it raised
  productivity. The fact that we do not observe co-determination in
  the absence of legislative coercion is taken to indicate that it is
  neither demanded nor efficient.
— The theory of the co-operative firm argues that industrial democracy increases both job satisfaction and productivity, and that it
  improves general labour relations. It is not widely practised because people are insufficiently or incorrectly informed about its
  merits, and because there are public goods effects involved.

The propositions advanced by the two theories require testing at
an empirical level. So far there are only a few preliminary studies
enquiring into whether co-determination increases productivity. Two
pieces of empirical work will be discussed here, one relating to a case
study in Sweden, the other to a cross-section analysis in Germany.

A Swedish Case Study.   In 1971/72 the Swedish employers' association analysed the effects of co-determination in a chemical firm with
a diversified production programme. The study concludes that it
leads to improved co-ordination and better problem-solving capacity. More efficient production methods were being introduced at a
more rapid pace and with lower transaction costs; the workers were
more ready to learn so that their opposition to technical progress
was low. Increasing the quality of job conditions did not result in
lower productivity.

A German Cross-section Analysis. A sample of 42 firms with between 20 and 600 employees and different degrees of co-determination was selected. Economic democracy extends from limited rights of participation in decision-making in specific areas to the right to co-determine fully all matters relevant to the firm as a whole. The empirical analysis concludes that the productivity of labour and the productivity of capital as well as the growth of labour productivity, are higher in the set of firms that had extended co-determination. As these differences may be due to factors unrelated to economic democracy, a multivariate regression analysis was used in order to control for these influences. The results indicate that those resources directly related to the extent of co-determination are indeed more productive in firms that had extended industrial democracy. This positive effect is attributed to improved trust and co-ordination within the firm.

The two studies sketched above may be interpreted as indicating that economic efficiency increases, or at least does not decrease, with co-determination. This result is only preliminary; further empirical analyses may come to different conclusions. In particular, it is necessary to inquire more thoroughly into the question of what forms of economic democracy are likely to increase, and what forms are likely to decrease, economic efficiency.

Existing Institutions of Economic Democracy

In various countries there is a basic consensus that economic democracy is a productive social institution without which a modern industrial society cannot exist. Prominent examples are Germany and Yugoslavia.

Co-determination in the Federal Republic of Germany. Economic democracy in the form of legally prescribed co-determination of employees is well developed in Germany. Since 1951, the seats in the board of directors in selected heavy industries (mining, steel) have been divided equally between owners and employees, with a 'neutral' member having one additional seat. The employees have the right to name one of the members of the board of managers. A law passed in 1976 expands this co-determination to *all* corporations having more than 2000 employees. Still, there is not full parity between 'capital' and 'labour'; the board of directors constitutes a 'third' party, which represents upper management.

Worker Self-determination in Yugoslavia.   The Yugoslav experiment with economic democracy may be considered as an alternative mode of social organization alongside capitalism and bureaucratic planning. Self-determination was introduced after 1950 as a response to the huge bureaucratization and mismanagement brought about by planning of the Soviet type. By 1965 the economic reform was complete, but subsequent development has been full of experimentation and learning.

The employees of a Yugoslav plant are its 'owners'. The workers do not, however, manage the firm. This task is given to a workers' council, which is elected by all employees. It determines the production programme and the use of resources. For day-to-day operations, this board elects a manager for a period of four years; he may be re-elected.

The practical experience of self-managed firms does not fully live up to expectations. The highly qualified employees and upper management take part much more often and more decisively in the firm's decisions. University graduates account for most of the discussion taking place in the councils, while the blue-collar workers speak rarely, and the unskilled workers hardly ever. The envisaged job rotation does not take place, either. The managers are in fact almost always re-elected, even if they are of doubtful efficiency.

The functioning and the consequences of the Yugoslav self-managed firm can be analyzed with the help of economic theory. The goal of the firm can be assumed to consist in maximizing the income per employee. The employees of a firm will be willing to hire an additional worker only if he produces at least the average share of distributed profits on top of his own wage. (A capitalistic, profit-maximizing firm hires additional workers as long as their marginal product is higher than the wage rate they have to be paid.) For this reason, the Yugoslav firms are reluctant to admit new workers. The existing jobs are 'monopolized': family members are privileged, the worker must pay an 'entrance fee', or be satisfied initially with a lower wage rate. Maximizing average income leads to more capital-intensive production than is the case in a capitalistic firm. This may be one of the reasons for the high rate of unemployment in Yugoslavia.

CONCLUSION

No economic policy undertaken by a government and its administration will closely follow the wishes of the population if the individuals do not possess basic political rights and if the fundamental institutions of the state do not allow the people's preferences to be expressed. In that sense, a democratic economic policy presupposes that the basic framework within which day-to-day policy-making takes place is adequately set. It has been stressed in this chapter that the separation of powers – including their regional separation, in the form of federalism – and the participative rights in the political and economic spheres are two prerequisites for the fulfilment of individual preferences. A social consensus about such rules is thus of central importance.

FURTHER READING

The discussion on the separation between the private and public domains is based on

James M. Buchanan and Gordon Tullock, *The Calculus of Consent. Logical Foundations of Constitutional Democracy.* Ann Arbor, Michigan: University of Michigan Press, 1962.

An attempt to measure empirically the value given by individuals to rights on the basis of referenda is given in

Eli M. Noam, The Valuation of Legal Rights, *Quarterly Journal of Economics*, 96 (1981), 465–76.

The economic theory of federalism is discussed in

William E. Oates, *Fiscal Federalism.* New York: Harcourt, Brace, Jovanovich, 1972.

A good collection of articles is

Wallace E. Oates (ed.), *The Political Economy of Fiscal Federalism.* Lexington, Mass.: Lexington Books, 1977.

The institution of the referendum as it exists in various countries is treated, for example, in

David Butler and Austin Ranney, *Referendums. A Comparative Study of Practice and Theory.* Washington DC: American Enterprise Institute, 1978.

The impact of referenda and intiatives on the behaviour of governments and public bureaucracy has been empirically analysed for the case of Switzerland by

Werner W. Pommerehne and Bruno S. Frey, Bureaucratic Behaviour in Democracy: A Case Study, *Public Finance*, 33 (1978), 98–112.

The theory of property rights has been strongly influenced by

Armen A. Alchian and Harold Demsetz, Production, Information Costs and Economic Organization, *American Economic Review*, 62 (1972), 777–95.

See also

Eirik G. Furubotn and Svetozar Pejovich, Property Rights and Economic Theory: A Survey of Recent Literature, *Journal of Economic Literature*, 10 (1972), 1137–62.

The theory of the co-operative firm is dealt with in various articles in

Alasdair Clayre (ed.), *The Political Economy of Co-operation and Participation.* Oxford: University Press, 1980.

The case study of Sweden discussed is treated in

Carl-Olof Faxén, Does Employee Participation in Decision-Making Contribute to Change and Growth? *American Economic Review, Papers and Proceedings*, 68 (1978), 131–4.

The econometric cross-section analysis of German participatory firms is taken from

John R. Cable and Felix R. Fitzroy, Productive Efficiency, Incentives and Employee Participation: Some Preliminary Results for West Germany, *Kyklos*, 33 (1980), 100–21.

Co-determination in Germany has recently been discussed in

Alfred L. Thimm, How Far Should German Co-determination Go? *Challenge*, 24 (1981), 13–22.

The Yugoslav system of self-management is discussed and analysed by

Jaroslav Vanek, *The Participatory Economy. An Evolutionary Hypothesis and a Strategy for Development*. Ithaca, NY: Cornell University Press, 1971.

CHAPTER 4

Decision making via the
Price System

INTRODUCTION

Individuals and groups can choose among different methods of making social decisions by social consensus. The economic adviser can provide information as to which procedure is best suited to which decisions. The functioning of the social decision-making mechanisms and their corresponding institutions must be known; the decision-makers seeking a social consensus can thus be informed of the advantages and disadvantages of each mechanism, allowing them to decide upon the most productive rule. Moreover, the economic decision-makers must be informed about ways of improving the functioning of the social decision-making mechanisms.

The decision-makers will not rely on one decision-making procedure alone. Rather, they will choose a combination of the mechanisms at their disposal. The 'best' combination cannot be determined *a priori*; it will result from an evaluation of the properties of the various procedures by the individuals and groups at the level of the social consensus.

Social decision-making procedures can be classified in various ways. This chapter deals with the price mechanism, discussing its strengths and weaknesses and the main approaches designed to improve its functioning:

— *anti-trust policy* (section 4.2), which should serve to restrict monopolistic tendencies and to stimulate competition. *Government regulations* imposed on particular firms and economic sectors are also directed towards this goal;
— *consumer policy* (section 4.3), which aims at strengthening the consumer's position against that of the producers;

— *structural policy* (section 4.4), the goal of which is to promote adjustments in the structure of production. The most extreme form is the direct control of capital formation (known as 'investment steering').

4.1   PROPERTIES OF THE PRICE SYSTEM

In present times the price system seems to lose more and more ground in the decision-making process to administrative and bureaucratic factors. Even in countries whose economies are based on the market mechanism, there is an increasing tendency to plan and to regulate the economy. On the other hand, there have been some fundamental decisions to introduce the market and therewith the price system (as for example in the Federal Republic of Germany in 1948). The increased use of elements of the market in socialist planned economies, in particular in Hungary, is also noteworthy. Finally, in the United States there is presently quite a strong movement for freeing the economy from direct government intervention (for *deregulation*).

Within economic theory, the central role of the price system as a social decision-making mechanism was cast into doubt by the 'Keynesian revolution', at least with respect to macroeconomics. In recent years the champions of the price system, under the leadership of the 'monetarists' and the 'supply-side economists', have once more gained in importance.

In order to be able to make a well-reasoned assessment on the role of the price system and the policies to improve upon it, it is necessary to compare the actual functioning of the price system with the actual functioning of economic policy interventions. There is little use in comparing a non-optimally functioning price system ('market failure') with idealized institutions of economic policy-making, or in comparing badly functioning economic policy institutions ('government failure') with an idealized market. Individuals and groups need to be informed by economic advisers about how the decision-making mechanisms actually function in a real-life politico-economic process. They have to compare *imperfect* decision-making mechanisms and *imperfect* institutions. With this knowledge they will be able to determine the weight they want to give to the price system and the supporting economic policies.

The most important *strengths* of using the price system are as follows.

— Economic resources are allocated efficiently.
— The selfish and competitive behaviour of individuals leads (under specific circumstances) to the best outcome for all. There is no need to set any incentives for the 'right' behaviour by any outside authority.
— The decentralized system of decision-making by consumers and producers reduces information and transactions cost.
— Everyone is free to choose according to his own preferences; behaviour is not directly regulated.
— Changes in relative prices induce people to introduce technical progress, to change the structure of production and to undertake organizational reforms.

There are two kinds of *weaknesses* of the price system: either it does not function well, or it cannot be applied. The major shortcomings of the market mechanism are more numerous.

— Markets may be incomplete, there being only few demanders and/or suppliers. In the case of increasing returns to scale, the competitive principles destroy themselves. The supplier with the largest output can offer goods at the lowest price, and will drive out the other competitors, thereby creating a monopoly.
— In the presence of external effects or the characteristics of a public good, the identity of those benefiting and those carrying the cost no longer holds. This leads to a misallocation of resources in that too much or too little is supplied. This is often referred to as the problem of 'free riding' and the 'tragedy of the commons'.
— The allocation of resources can be biased if there is 'moral hazard'. This arises if a supplier of insurance against a risk is unable to distinguish adequately between true risk (of, say, a house burning down after being struck by lightning) and negligence (when, for example, a house burns because the owner does not take the precaution of extinguishing his fire properly, secure in the knowledge that he is insured). There can also be a misallocation of resources owing to 'adverse selection'. This occurs if the supplier of insurance is unable to ask for a premium that is higher for bad than for good risks. This may result in there being no market for some types of risk, so that the corresponding (socially worth-while) activities will not be undertaken.

— The price system is sometimes slow in bringing about the necessary supply reactions when they are needed – for example, when a war breaks out.

— Some markets do not exist or are considered to be immoral. Some transactions are forbidden in most societies because they conflict with basic human values (selling parts of one's body or even one's blood, for example – and, of course, engaging in slave-trading), or because they are incompatible with democracy (for example, buying parliamentary seats or bribing public officials). It should however be pointed out that human history shows examples of almost everything having been marketed at one time or another; in England and France, at one time, parliamentary seats could be openly bought.

— The distribution of income resulting from the price system is usually not considered to be just. This aspect is of central importance for the practical application of the price system.

— Full employment of resources, especially labour, and stable prices are not guaranteed. The state must intervene with fiscal and monetary policy in order to stabilize the price system. This 'Keynesian' view has recently been challenged by the 'monetarists', who argue that the private market economy is stable, and that instability is produced knowingly or otherwise by the government or the central bank. Even if this is true, it may take a very long time for full employment and price stability to be reached after an exogenous disruption. The costs to individuals arising in this transition period may be intolerably high.

4.2 ANTI-TRUST POLICY AND REGULATIONS

Institutional arrangements that serve to intensify competition can overcome some of the shortcomings of the price mechanism and reinforce some of its advantages. Such arrangements, of course, can only improve those shortcomings that result from hindrances to the price system's allocative qualities. On the other hand, it is not to be expected that an improved functioning of the price system will remove the problems created with respect to income distribution and stabilization; if anything, it is likely that they will be intensified.

The objective of strengthening competition is to break up monopolistic positions – in the widest sense – and to offer consumers an

effective choice between various suppliers, which in turn forces producers to supply efficiently. *Anti-trust policy* (which will be discussed
next) seeks to achieve this goal by creating the conditions of a competitive market as far as possible. *Regulation* (which will be discussed
subsequently) accepts the monopolistic positions as given and attempts to achieve by way of (generalized) instructions a better fulfilment of the consumers' wishes and more efficient production.

Arguments For and Against Anti-trust Policy

In the economic literature, various reasons are given for why competition ought to be strengthened:

— allocative efficiency can be improved;
— technical, or *X-efficiency* as it is often called, is higher, and therefore prices lower, than in the case of a monopolistic market;
— more technical progress is made and introduced than under less
  competitive market conditions.

The following arguments are advanced against anti-trust policy:

— if increasing returns do in fact exist, large firms can produce more
  cheaply than small ones;
— only large enterprises can successfully compete on international
  markets.

Laymen and politicians, however, usually have quite different
quarrels with large and monopolistic firms:

— monopoly prices are unjust from the distributional point of view;
— monopolies are responsible for inflation and unemployment;
— monopolies restrain technical progress by suppressing new goods
  and processes protected by patents;
— monopolies manipulate consumers through advertising;
— large firms are the main culprits of environmental destruction;
— monopolies push small firms out of business and lead to an alienation of the workers;
— monopolies use their power for political goals and thus threaten a
  free society.

In order to find a social consensus on whether, and on how far, to
restrict monopolistic firms, it is necessary to determine whether these
charges are well founded. In this book, only some of them can be

discussed. The next section deals with the allocative inefficiencies created by monopolies. The following sections are concerned with X-efficiency, technical progress, returns to scale and the possibilities and actual working of anti-trust policy.

Monopolistic Supply and Allocative Efficiency

The model of perfect competition cannot be used directly for the purpose of economic policy because it depends on very specific conditions which are rarely, if ever, fulfilled or attainable. The conditions not being fully met, one has to turn to the *theory of the second-best*. This approach, however, does not allow any generally valid assertions as to whether more intensive competition improves allocative efficiency. Only if the sector considered is strongly isolated from the rest of the economy does an anti-trust policy that brings about marginal cost pricing improve economic efficiency. The behavioural rules for the firms deduced for specific cases are extremely complex and hold only for narrowly determined parameter constellations.

Applying the theory of the second-best bears the danger that more and more biases are introduced into the economy, in particular when restrictions assumed to be immutable do in fact change. This may lead to a complete mix-up in economic policy. For these reasons the economic policy adviser will find little help in the theory of the second-best when he makes suggestions for an institutionalization of anti-trust policy at the level of the social consensus.

The concept of *workable competition* opens up another, and more practically oriented, avenue to anti-trust policy. Deviations from the conditions of perfect competition are taken as the rule rather than the exception. Whether competition is effective is judged by the results. Competition fulfils its role if it meets the preferences of the consumers as well as possible. There are various criteria for judging whether competition works – the level of factor productivity, the speed with which new products and new processes are introduced, the spectrum and quality of goods and services, and so on. Workable competition can exist within an oligopolistic or even monopolistic market structure; it may even happen that consumers are less well off where there is a structure of atomistic suppliers.

The concept of workable competition gives a better basis for the institutionalization of an anti-trust policy than does the abstract model of perfect competition. In particular, the dynamic aspects of competition can be better assessed.

Whether to undertake an anti-trust policy, and to what extent, depends crucially on how large the allocative inefficiencies brought about by monopolization actually are. There have been various attempts to measure empirically the welfare losses due to monopolies. These losses can be captured only at the level of the firm; their macroeconomic importance is calculated by aggregating the results over all firms.

The welfare loss due to monopolization can be measured by the decrease of consumer surplus arising when the quantities and prices of a monopoly are compared with the Pareto-optimal supply of a firm under perfect competition. Figure 4.1 shows the corresponding equilibrium quantities and prices, and the loss in consumer surplus.

With perfect competition, profit-maximizing firms offer the quantity X_c, so that the given competitive price p_c is equal to marginal cost MC. In the figure, the marginal costs are taken to be constant for simplicity; they are thus equal to average cost (they include normal interest payments for the capital invested). Profits are zero. A

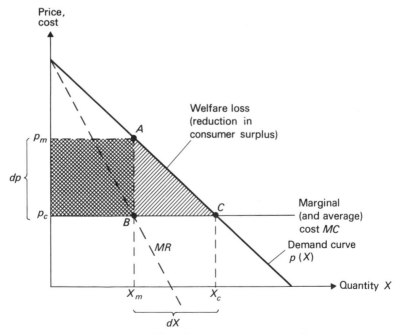

FIGURE 4.1   *Welfare loss owing to monopolization.*

profit-maximizing monopolist, on the other hand, sets the quantity he supplies at X_m and the price he charges at p_m so that marginal revenue MR equals marginal cost MC. The consumers have to pay a higher price and choose to buy a smaller quantity than under perfect competition. The welfare cost amounts to the reduced quantity of output dX, evaluated at the corresponding price $p(X)$ – this is shown by the trapezoid X_mACX_c – minus the value of the reduced resource input. They are evaluated at opportunity cost, that is, the competitive price. The value of saved resources thus is $dX \cdot p_c$, which corresponds to the rectangle X_mBCX_c. The net loss for the consumers – the reduction of the consumer surplus – equals the hatched triangle ABC. This welfare loss is often named 'dead-weight loss'.

Empirical estimations

The first attempt to measure the welfare loss empirically was undertaken by Harberger. He assumes that the price elasticity of demand equals minus one, and concludes that the welfare loss amounted to 0.07 per cent of gross national product in the United States in 1929. This loss is extremely small. Other authors, such as Schwartzman and Kamerschen, reach similar but slightly higher estimates, using somewhat different assumptions.

Newer estimates include additional negative effects of monopoly on welfare. All those expenditures can be considered socially wasteful that are used to keep up the monopoly position and the corresponding profits, for example by maintaining excess capacity, by differentiating products unnecessarily, by forcing protection from foreign competition, by giving funds to parties and by bribing politicians and public officials. The maximum size of these expenditures is given by the size of the monopoly profits. It can therefore be argued that the social loss due to monopolization includes the whole area between the monopoly and competitive price (dp) from zero up to the quantity sold. This area, additional to the loss of consumer surplus, is indicated by the double-hatched quadrangle p_mABp_c in Figure 4.1. According to Posner, this results in a welfare loss of between 1.8 and 3.4 per cent of GNP for the USA.

Some authors, such as Cowling and Mueller, also consider all advertising outlays as social loss. If these are added to the two types of cost already mentioned, there is a welfare loss of 13 per cent for the USA in 1963–66. The corresponding figure for the United Kingdom is 7.2 per cent of GNP for 1968/69.

The results of various empirical estimates of the welfare losses due to allocative inefficiency are given in Table 4.1. This table shows that

TABLE 4.1   *Welfare Loss due to Monopolization*

Study (author)	Country	Year	Size (share of GNP) (%)
Harberger	USA	1929	0.07
Schwartzman	USA	1954	0.1
Kamerschen	USA	1956–61	1.8
Posner	USA	—	1.8–3.4
Cowling and Mueller	USA	1963–66	13
	UK	1968–69	7.2

Sources: author's compilation from original studies:
— Arnold C. Harberger, Monopoly and Resource Allocation, *American Economic Review, Papers and Proceedings*, 44 (1954), pp. 77–92;
— David Schwartzman, The Burden of Monopoly, *Journal of Political Economy*, 68 (1960), pp. 627–30;
— David Kamerschen, Estimation of the Welfare Loss from Monopoly in the American Economy, *Western Economic Journal*, 4 (1966), pp. 221–36;
— Richard A. Posner, The Social Cost of Monopoly and Regulation, *Journal of Political Economy*, 83 (1975), pp. 807–27;
— Keith Cowling and Dennis C. Mueller, The Social Costs of Monopoly Power, *Economic Journal*, 88 (1978), pp. 727–48.

the empirical estimates of the welfare losses due to monopoly yield increasingly higher values. Cowling and Mueller's estimates are roughly one hundred times larger than those of Harberger or Schwartzman (around 10 per cent compared with 0.1 per cent of GNP). This increasing size is due mainly to the broader definition of what constitutes the welfare losses attributable to monopoly.

The empirical results presented here do not on the whole indicate that the social welfare costs of static allocative inefficiency are very high. It seems rather that society experiences only a small loss as a result of suppliers failing to follow the rules of perfect competition (not setting price equal to marginal costs). Moreover, when interpreting Table 4.1, three points should be kept in mind:

1 anti-trust policy can at best reduce the welfare losses *once*; the United Kingdom, for example, could increase its consumer surplus by 7 per cent of GNP. This is not much compared to a steady growth rate of GNP which cumulatively raises output and welfare;

2 expenditure on advertising is not necessarily wasteful, because part of it serves the useful function of informing consumers. Ad-

vertisement also often has an entertainment value. The estimates of loss by Cowling and Mueller given in Table 4.1 are therefore overstated. The same applies to the costs of defending a monopoly position: the size of monopoly profits only indicates a (probably quite irrelevant) upper boundary;

3   the estimates show what a *perfect* anti-trust policy could at best attain if it were completely *costless*; the costs of undertaking the anti-trust policy itself (administration, costs of errors, and so on) are disregarded.

X-efficiency

The maximum output that can be produced with a given set of inputs is called 'technical' efficiency or 'X-efficiency'. In traditional economic theory, it is assumed that firms produce on their production possibility curve, and that the cost functions show the minimal attainable cost of producing a given output. Organization and the incentive structure within the firm are influences that the theory omits.

X-inefficiency can arise for three reasons:

1   the contracts between employers and employees are incomplete and at times vague: the input factor labour cannot, therefore, be used to the optimal extent by the firm;
2   it is either not possible or too costly to monitor the performance of employees precisely: the employees therefore have a chance to behave inefficiently, or even to shirk;
3   the firm's management is not fully informed about the production possibilities: in some areas the most efficient way of producing is unknown.

A monopoly that produces above-average profits is not directly confronted with the need to survive. Therefore it can be assumed that this market structure allows X-inefficiency to arise. When competition is stiff, however, firms not producing at minimum cost will be pushed out of the market by efficient firms. The likely existence of X-inefficiency in a monopolized market is one of the more important arguments in support of anti-trust policy.

So far no compelling empirical evidence on the importance of X-inefficiency for the whole economy has been found. In the literature one finds more or less anecdotal stories about cases of inefficiency with monopolies and large firms. These examples suggest that X-inefficiency is of considerable importance. The connection with the degree of competition in a market is, however, an open question. The possibility may not be excluded that lively competition between a few oligopolistic suppliers is more effective in preventing X-inefficiency than the 'night-cap competition' between a large number of small competitors.

Technical Progress

Monopolistic firms are the main innovators; this is argued by well-known economists such as Schumpeter and Galbraith. This proposition directs our attention to an additional and important aspect going beyond the static allocative efficiency of the model of perfect competition.

The connection between innovation and the extent of competition has been analysed empirically in a great number of studies. Three relationships in particular have been examined:

1 expenditure on research and development per unit of output has been shown to increase up to a threshhold size of firm and then to decrease; this threshhold differs as between sectors of the economy;
2 there is as yet no evidence for the view of Schumpeter and Galbraith that higher concentration leads to more research and development; the empirical studies suggest rather that a 'medium' degree of concentration somewhere between perfect competition and pure monopoly brings about the highest degree of innovative activity;
3 if there is little rivalry between suppliers, small and medium inventions are introduced quickest. Large and important innovations, on the other hand, are more quickly brought in when there is a well developed rivalry between suppliers.

Economies of Scale

Should an anti-trust policy be undertaken if production is subject to decreasing returns to scale resulting in small firms producing at lower cost? Or are large firms more efficient owing to increasing returns to scale? Empirical analyses have reached the following conclusions.

— In cross-section studies it is not possible generally to find any marked scale effects in one direction or the other. The 'utilities' (transport, power plants, gas works) may be an exception. In the public sector, say, the postal service or police, increasing returns to scale have also been found. However, average costs fall only down to a threshhold and rise thereafter. The size of the threshhold (measured for example by the number of employees) differs between economic sectors.

— The time-series analysis of economies of scale is subject to great measurement problems because it is difficult, or even impossible, to differentiate between the effects of scale and the effects of technical progress occurring over time. The existing empirical studies suggest that there are approximately constant returns to scale.

On the whole, the research undertaken indicates that the supposed existence of increasing returns to scale is no convincing argument for tolerating large firms and monopolistic market structures. To justify a large firm on this ground it would be necessary positively to demonstrate that there are increasing returns to scale in this particular sector.

Approaches to Anti-trust Policy

Anti-trust policy can be differentiated according to the point of application and its intensity.

Measures for intensifying competition can be applied by considering the market structure, conduct or performance of firms.

In the first case it is assumed that the number of firms (as measured by the degree of concentration) is a sufficient indicator of the extent of competition. Concentration may take various forms: it can be horizontal or vertical, or it can extend over conglomerates (where completely different products are supplied within one firm). Capturing competition by the degree of concentration has the advantage that it may be measured in a relatively easy and objective way. Moreover, it approaches the problem at its base: the possibility of building up market power is prevented. It is, however, dubious to infer directly from the development of, and sectoral differences in, the degree of concentration how well the price system functions. This measure considers only one aspect among many. It is not at all clear whether consumers' preferences will be better fulfilled when the degree of concentration is reduced by anti-trust policy.

Anti-trust policy can also be applied by considering the behaviour of firms. This implies that within a given market share the firms have considerable leeway to vary their behaviour. The problem is to determine, and to measure empirically, whether a particular firm is behaving in such a way as to restrict competition. This approach also underlies regulation, because the anti-trust institution usually tries to coerce firms to behave in a specific way by subjecting them to instructions (see the next section).

The third way that anti-trust policy can be applied is to direct attention to performance. No intervention is deemed necessary if the firms produce at low cost and if they introduce new goods and processes rapidly. This approach, based on the idea of workable competition, is difficult to operationalize because performance entails many different aspects and because there is no definite point of reference. However, some hints may be gained by comparing the performance of firms across economic sectors, regions and countries.

There are four different intensities of anti-trust policy.

1   Competition can be strengthened or established if the entry of new suppliers into the market is encouraged by reducing legal and financial barriers and giving positive incentives through tax reductions and subsidies. Moreover, the government can establish public enterprises which compete in the market.

2   The behaviour of those firms that restrict competition may be prevented. It is difficult to monitor restrictive practices, because there may be tacit collusion and 'parallel behaviour' between the suppliers. It is easier to control those restrictions that are directed towards a specific supplier (for example by boycotting him) or to discriminate in the form of differentiated prices and terms of delivery. Anti-trust policy can endeavour to prevent competing firms from being thrown out of the market or being subjugated to a dominating firm or a suppliers' interest group.

3   Anti-trust policy is more severe if all explicit or implicit supply restrictions among the market participants are prohibited. Such agreements may for example refer to future prices, to the geographic region awarded to a supplier, or to the division of the supply quantity among the suppliers.

4   The most severe anti-trust policy consists of prohibiting all forms of mergers between firms that may lead to a domination of a market

by one firm. (In the case of merger, formerly independent firms form a new unit which often reduces competition among suppliers.)

Regulation

If the conditions for competition are impossible or very difficult to attain, or if competition is inefficient, a government institution may be established to force firms to behave in a socially useful way. Regulation is particularly applied to natural monopolies, which produce under increasing returns to scale. Under these technical conditions average costs fall with increasing output. The Pareto-optimal equalization of prices with marginal cost then leads to a deficit. These relationships are illustrated in Figure 4.2. At the inter-section of the falling marginal cost curve MC with the demand curve $p(X)$, price is lower than average cost AC, resulting in losses. It would, on the other hand, be socially wasteful if a large number of small firms produced the quantity X_{SF} each at a profit, because the advantages of mass production would not be exploited. It would be preferable if one firm produced, for example, quantity X_T where

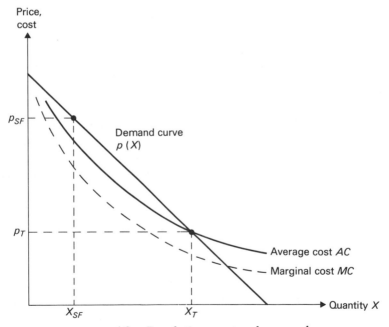

FIGURE 4.2 *Regulating a natural monopoly.*

average cost equals price p_T. No monopoly profits would exist and at least part of the benefits of mass production would be exploited. The main objective of regulation is to bring about the quantity of supply X_T.

Regulation can proceed either by fixing a 'fair rate of return' or by directly setting prices. Fixing a fair rate of return on capital is intended to protect the consumers against exploitation by the single (or few) supplier(s), but still to take advantage of the increasing returns to scale. This procedure is confronted by three major difficulties.

1   The prices that may be charged by a firm are based on cost and on the profit rate set by the regulatory agency (*cost-plus pricing*). This kind of price setting leads to distortions and inefficient production:

— the regulated firms have an incentive to overstate their cost in order for the regulatory agency to grant a higher price. The firms will attempt to label some part of profit (perhaps the perquisites of management) as cost;
— regulated firms have no incentive to reduce cost. Lower costs could not increase (the regulated) profit but would have to be used to reduce the price.

In order to prevent such behaviour, the regulatory agency must control the firms. It must monitor its costs precisely and must be able to recognize and indicate possibilities for reducing costs by technical innovations and organizational reforms.

2   A regulated firm has an incentive to produce more capital-intensively than a non-regulated firm. In the case of a firm subject to a maximum rate of return on capital, increasing the stock of capital not only entails costs but also increases the admissible profit. However, empirical studies have been unable to locate this over-capitalization effect. This may be due to the fact that such firms do not intend to maximize profits, but rather pursue other goals.

3   A fair rate of return may lead to difficulties in the case of firms with low profits or losses. If the regulated firm is confronted with a price-elastic demand curve, raising the price will not help because revenue falls. Such a firm will attempt to get rid of those products not bringing profit or to reduce the quality of the goods and services supplied. The regulatory agency will make an effort to prevent both

reactions. If it succeeds, the unprofitable firm must be supported by the government or be nationalized.

This discussion shows that effective regulation is very difficult. It is not sufficient to fix a fair rate of return. The regulatory agency is forced to establish a whole net of controls: it must monitor costs, see that technical progress is introduced and survey the range and quality of goods and services supplied.

Instead of fixing a rate of return, the regulatory agency can also directly set prices. In order to promote certain products, low prices can be fixed which do not cover average cost and therefore lead to losses. In exchange, prices above average cost will be granted in other areas of production. The profits produced there will compensate for the losses in the areas with low prices. There are many examples of such *cross-subsidization*, for example in profitable/unprofitable air routes or in telecommunications.

The regulated firms react by supplying large amounts of the products with high prices and little of the products with low prices. The regulatory agency is therefore forced to control quantities as well as prices. Non-regulated firms coming from the outside will also attempt to supply in the area with high prices – to engage in 'cream-skimming'. In order to salvage its plan, the regulatory agency must keep out these competing firms by erecting entry barriers. Moreover, it must control the investment policies of the regulated firms in order to prevent the prices falling too much as a result of the enlarged supply. This means that there is another far-reaching intervention into the firms' behaviour and into the market.

The Behaviour of Anti-trust and Regulatory Agencies

The decision-makers seeking a social consensus have to know how the institutions undertaking the anti-trust and regulation policies function in practice, not how they should function ideally. The economic advisers can make it clear that these agencies are not able, nor do they intend, to maximize 'social welfare'. The persons involved in anti-trust policy and regulation are best assumed to pursue their own selfish interests. The actual anti-trust and regulatory policy observed depends on the behaviour of three decision-makers.

1 The *members of an anti-trust and regulatory agency* have an interest in minimizing the conflicts with other decision-makers in order not to be burdened with unnecessary trouble. They will moreover be

interested in establishing a good reputation, as well as in extending their agency to give them greater influence and possibly even higher income. These goals can be reached if the agency takes into account the interests of the other decision-makers, in particular those directly affected by their policy. As a rule, the latter are well organized and can create difficulties for the agency by passively obstructing the orders, by withholding information the agency needs, and by appealing to the courts. The population, on the other hand, will scarcely react to the policies. An individual citizen is rarely confronted directly by the issues and has little incentive to supply a public 'good' in the form of an effective anti-trust or regulatory policy. The agency therefore has little interest in paying special attention to the wishes of the general public. It is much more important for it to get along well with the economic sectors with which it directly deals. It will take into account their wishes, and possibly even will promote them actively. As one of the wishes of these sectors always is to prevent competition, the anti-trust and regulatory agencies cannot be expected to undertake a vigorous policy to foster competition.

2   The *government* must evaluate whether it is advantageous to pursue an active competition policy against the well-defined interests of particular economic sectors. The interests of 'capital' and 'labour' in such sectors are in line with each other and therefore particularly effective in politics. As a rule, the government will conclude that it does not pay to antagonize the special interests of particular economic sectors.

3   The *economic sectors affected by an anti-trust or regulatory policy* will attempt to make the policy fit their own interests. Barriers to entry and investment controls that reduce the competitive pressure are particularly advantageous. The sectors affected will try to persuade the agency to prohibit substitute products and to support complementary products. In order to reach these goals, the sectors will promise to support the agency and the government financially and politically, provided they adopt an 'appropriate' policy.

The interaction of the decision-makers leads us to expect the following type of anti-trust and regulatory policy:

— monopoly power in certain areas will be strengthened and the agency will be closely connected with the sectors to be regulated.

The agencies even identify with the interests of 'their' sector. In most countries, for example, it is a matter of course that the ministry of agriculture represents the interests of the farmers.
— in order to protect suppliers, competition will be restricted; entry barriers will be erected and some form of competition, such as comparative advertising and discounts, will be prohibited.

Serious empirical research on the benefits and costs of anti-trust and regulatory policy seem thus far to be available only for the United States.

Empirical evidence

A study by Breyer and Macaroy of the US Federal Power Commission, which regulates the area of gas pipelines and the production of gas and electricity, concludes that the consumers have gained no, or at best very little, net utility from regulation. The commission is an ineffective institution for the purposes for which it was established.

An analysis by Posner on the social costs of regulation finds that the regulatory costs make up between 10 per cent (for milk) and 30 per cent and more (for medical services, road transport and oil) of the revenue of the sectors affected. The overall regulatory costs are estimated to be around 1.7 per cent of GNP.

Weidenbaum differentiates between the direct administrative cost of the regulatory agencies and the indirect burden imposed on the private sector due to regulation. The total costs are calculated by taking the lowest cost estimates of a number of detailed studies of particular economic sectors. He estimates that in the United States in 1976 the direct administrative cost amounted to $3.2 billion, and the private sector had to carry indirect costs of $62.9 billion. The total cost of federal regulation of over $66 billion amounts to about 3.6 per cent of GNP. Another study, by Downing and Lawson, estimates that total cost including state regulation reaches a figure of 9.4 per cent of GNP for the same year.

One must hasten to add that these studies look only at the *costs* imposed by government regulation; if the benefit side is also considered the overall effect may well be positive.

Conclusions for Economic Advising

Whether or not individuals and groups reach a social consensus to institutionalize an anti-trust and/or a regulatory policy depends on the evaluation of the relevant elements. In addition, the other aspects mentioned at the beginning of this chapter should be considered, though there is so far no sound theoretical and empirical evidence available (for example on the influence of monopolistic firms on individual preferences through advertising).

The economic adviser can make the following suggestions, which may become part of a social consensus.

— Only unequivocal evidence of the effects of an increase or decrease of the existing state of competition is useful. The adviser has to identify those economic sectors and firms in which, for example, increasing returns to scale do exist, and in which technical progress is overwhelmingly promoted by large firms.
— Anti-trust and regulatory policy should be directed towards decreasing the restrictions on competition. In particular, the barriers to entry should be removed. The resulting potential competition is likely to improve allocative and X-efficiency, and to increase technical and organizational change.
— Competition can be actively strengthened by establishing public enterprises to compete with private monopolists, and private firms with public monopolies.
— The institutional design of the anti-trust and regulatory agencies must be paid great attention. If the institutions are badly constructed, competition will be hampered rather than strengthened. To reduce the tendency of the agency to identify too closely with 'its' economic sector, it is useful to establish agencies that are monitored by both producers and consumers of particular goods and services. The opposition of those injured by a particular agency policy will then make itself felt within the agency. To improve the weight of consumers and taxpayers within the agencies, institutions of direct participation may be devised.

4.3   CONSUMER POLICY

The price system is often criticized because it is taken to disregard the preferences of consumers. Three kinds of criticisms may be distinguished:

1   consumption *per se* is criticized by the New Left and some environmentalists because it is believed to make people unhappy;
2   consumers are manipulated by producers: according to Gal-

braith, this results in a disequilibrium between private and public consumption owing to firms' advertising;

3   particular goods are of insufficient quality: the consumers cannot take advantage of the choice possibilities because they are badly informed and not adequately protected against deception. This view is advanced, for example, by the American 'consumerism' movement.

The underlying theme of these criticisms is that the consumers have a much weaker position in the price system than the producers. The market that is designed to meet the wishes of the demanders does not function properly.

Economic advisers can inform the individuals and groups of ways of enabling consumer preferences to be better fulfilled within the price system. They can suggest rules and institutions of consumer policy which may find a consensus. The anti-trust and regulatory policies (discussed in the previous section), which may be considered to be a form of indirect consumer policy, are here supplemented by a *direct* consumer policy.

The consumers' role in the price system can be improved by strengthening the individual consumer's position, by collective action of consumers, and by weakening the relative position of producers.

1   An individual consumer is better able to fulfil his wishes in the market the better informed he is about the properties of the goods supplied. In many cases the producers have an incentive to offer product-specific information, because this improves the utility gained through the product, resulting in a greater demand for it. The consumers are also informed by commercial enterprises, which offer their specialized knowledge in the market at a price and thus operate as the consumers' agents. They will be able to sell their knowledge in the long run only if they are able to offer a useful service to consumers. This will be the case if they make an effort to inform as objectively as possible. Examples are the consumer guide journals or the French *Guide Michelin*, which is bought because consumers believe that it can judge competently the quality of hotels and restaurants.

Information will not be provided on all goods and services by the price system itself. As soon as there is a public good element involved (that is, when the information cannot be transmitted only to those consumers who pay for it) – and this is quite often the case –

the consumers will be informed insufficiently. Also, there is in general very little information supplied on how best to use the goods and services supplied by government.

The individual's position in the market will also be strengthened by a good consumer education. Such education is not devoted to particular goods but is designed to make consumers more critical and more aware of properties of goods generally, thus allowing them to improve their buying decisions.

2   Activities designed to strengthen the consumers' position in rela-
tion to producers have, to a considerable extent, the properties of a public good. A particular consumer has little incentive to participate in the cost of such activities but will tend to behave as a 'free-rider'. There is little chance therefore that consumers will be able to form themselves into an effective interest group.

Self-organized collective action will take place only under the following conditions.

— When the shortcomings in the goods and services supplied are grave and very obvious, a spontaneous reaction in the form of consumers' strikes and boycotts is possible. These will, however, as a rule be effective only in the short run.
— In well-defined goods markets consumer organizations may exist in the long run provided they offer the individual consumers a specific incentive to join, in the form of a private good. An indi-
vidual may then find it advantageous to pay the membership fee because otherwise he would not receive the private good supplied jointly (or would have to buy it at higher cost). Automobile associations function on the basis of this principle: they are able to fight in the political sphere only because they offer their members a great many private services.
— The interests of consumers may be taken up by 'political entre-
preneurs', who hope to win votes and influence by supporting their case.

As self-organized collective action by consumers takes place under restricted conditions only, the decision-makers may seek a social consensus about strengthening the consumers' position by establishing public institutions designed to support consumers. In many countries (in particular in the Federal Republic of Germany) such

consumer organizations are financially supported by the state. Another possibility which has recently received considerable attention is the appointment of a (publicly-financed) ombudsman for the consumers. He surveys advertising and marketing methods, accepts complaints about deficient goods and services, and seeks to remove the nuisances by voluntary bargains with the firm or sectors concerned.

Whenever consumer interests are collectively organized and promoted, there arises the problem of providing incentives to the executives of such organizations to fight for the real interests of consumers. It must be expected that these organizations will become concerned with their own affairs and pursue their own goals. Such a development is the more likely the larger the share of public subsidies received, the latter being independent of how successfully the cause of consumers is advanced.

3   The producers' position in relation to consumers can be weakened by consumer legislation. This may involve regulations concerning price, quality, marketing and the introduction of goods. The producers can also be made liable for the goods supplied. These regulations are of use only if they can be made effective by the consumers at a low cost. Such costs may be lowered by admitting 'class actions', in which anyone can sue in the name of the many persons involved.

Laymen often think that, the better is the protection of consumers by way of regulations, the better off consumers will be. In particular, they often assume that, the stricter the liability rules are, the better will be the position of consumers. It may, however, be shown that this is not necessarily so, and that there may also be disadvantages for the consumers.

Liability rules affect the behaviour of both producers and consumers. When liability rules are introduced by social consensus it is important to know the advantages and disadvantages connected with any such rule. The consequences of introducing four types of liability rules will be discussed here.

1   The buyer carries all the risk associated with a product. The consumer will make an effort to be aware of the product quality (*caveat emptor*) and will have an incentive to choose and use products carefully. The buyer has a comparative advantage in this respect

because he knows best the purpose for which he wants to use the goods. The transaction costs are thus high for consumers only if they use the product rarely and at infrequent intervals.

2   The producers are liable for deficiencies in the product. The consumers then carry only part of the risk; this induces them to choose the product less carefully. Compared to the rule of *caveat emptor*, the producers will supply fewer potentially deficient goods, because they must take into account the possibility that they might be held liable. They will also ask higher prices, because they will be induced to supply more goods at high quality and low risk of deficiency. The area of choice for consumers will thus be restricted. The supply of risky, but cheap products will be smaller.

3   The producers are liable when the consumer is dissatisfied with the product. There need not even be a deficiency in the material or construction of the good. This liability rule will induce consumers to be very negligent in their handling of the product. They know they will not carry the cost if they use it for the wrong purposes and thereby damage or destroy it. Because there will also be more accidents in product use, the social costs of consumption will rise. The producer will supply even fewer products that are susceptible to negligent and mistaken use. They will supply only very carefully checked and foolproof products, which will push up prices. The consumers' choice will be even more limited.

4   The government compensates consumers for all damages that arise in the use of products, irrespective of who is responsible. The social costs of such a liability rule will be very high because neither the producers nor the consumers will have to carry any of the cost of negligence; they do not have to account for the consequences of their actions. The producers may supply badly designed and deficient products, while the consumers have no incentive to be careful when choosing and using the goods.

Economic advisers can inform individuals and groups about the weak position of consumers in the economic process and can make suggestions on how it may be strengthened by information, education, collective action and by liability rules. By pointing out the advantages and disadvantages of the various institutional arrangements, advisers can help to bring about a consensus on the fundamental properties of consumer policy.

4.4 STRUCTURAL POLICY

The price system results in a given structure of production with respect to economic sectors and regions. Individuals deciding at the level of the social consensus need not necessarily agree with this production structure but may consider rules and institutions that bring about a different pattern of goods. In the course of economic development, inefficient branches will disappear and others become important. It is difficult or even impossible to reach a consensus on the desirable structure of production in the current politico-economic process because the interest of individuals and groups are strongly influenced by the sector with which they are connected. Few would be ready, for example, to support a structural policy abolishing the sector to which they are attached. The basic institutions and rules about structural policy have therefore to be agreed upon by social consensus behind the veil of ignorance; that is, individuals will not know with which sector they and their heirs will be connected.

Structural policy has a very important impact on future economic growth. This policy can promote economic development in two ways.

1 It can help to bring about the structural changes necessary for growth by offering help with adjustment. Opposition to structural change on the part of the declining sectors can thereby be overcome. This effort can be directed at enterprises as well as at workers. Improved education and special courses for adapting new skills help to decrease unemployment resulting from structural changes.

2 Structural change can be actively promoted by supporting those sectors in the economy that are assumed to have good prospects. Alternatively, the government may withdraw all support from those sectors that are not considered viable in the future, particularly if they are inefficient.

The instruments of structural policy can affect supply or demand. On the supply side, the input of labour and capital, as well as of technical progress, can be influenced. Demand can be affected by varying the public budget. Often, direct subsidies and (less visible) tax relief measures are used. Protection may be offered by means of direct government regulation in the form of fixed or minimum prices, government guarantees to buy certain goods, barriers to entry and restrictions of capacity, closing markets against potential competitors, quantitative import restrictions, manipulated price increases of foreign goods (through import duties), and technical regulations which make it difficult or impossible for foreigners to compete.

Example

The agrarian market of the European Economic Community provides many examples of a structural policy using the instrument of protecting suppliers. Prices are fixed politically and sales are guaranteed. As the prices are fixed above the world level, there is chronic oversupply of such goods as butter, corn, beef and milk powder. Production is not directed to meet the consumers' wishes, but to maintain a certain structure of production, in particular to keep the agricultural sector alive.

Another instrument of structural policy is *investment guidance*, an approach extensively discussed in Germany (Investitionslenkung). The government directs the sectoral distribution of private investment in order to take into account 'social preferences', which are taken to be disregarded by private investors. According to the proponents of this approach, what constitutes these social preferences may be determined by the democratic mechanism of voting or by the views of an 'enlightened elite' (among which the proponents of investment guidance count themselves). A hierarchy of wants is established, ranging from basic individual needs, to basic social needs, to superior individual needs, to superior social needs, and finally to private luxuries. The government has to see to it that private investments are undertaken in such a way that these needs are fulfilled in sequence.

Structural policy can be formulated by: a council of scientific experts on structural questions; a political assembly in which the main social groupings are represented; or an executive agency for the practical implementation of the policy. The following major problems will arise when a structural policy is to be undertaken.

1　The technical problem consists in finding reliable data on structural changes in the past and in forecasting likely future developments. In order to undertake a reasonable policy, it is important to have an idea about which sectors have good economic prospects and which ones must be expected to shrink. Such forecasts are extremely difficult to make; the forecaster ideally should have at his disposal a model of economic and political developments in the whole world, which of course is impossible. Therefore he must make more or less arbitrary assumptions about future conditions within and outside the country. On this basis the likely structural change will be forecast, presupposing (among other things) knowledge about future technologies. The forecaster will have to know which new production processes will be introduced and which new goods will appeal to consumers.

2   It must be decided which groups should be represented in the councils and assemblies for structural policy, and what their proportions should be. There is a strong danger that well-organized groups will be over-represented or that they will at least bring forward their interests too forcefully. We have to expect that in such institutions coalitions will form with the goal of maintaining existing economic structures, especially when labour and capital in a particular sector act jointly. As structural change mainly benefits future generations by promoting economic growth, it should be considered which group (if any) represents the interests of future generations.

3   The agency given the power to undertake the structural policy does not necessarily contribute to more rapid structural change and thereby to an increase in future welfare. (As mentioned earlier, the formal goals of an institution should not be confused with its actual behaviour.) As prestige and a quiet life may be assumed to be important arguments in the utility function of the top executives of such an agency, the intensive and well organized interests will be privileged, whereas the less visible, broad and badly organized interests will be neglected. The economic sectors whose size and existence are threatened by structural change will be given more weight than the anonymous taxpayers and consumers. Therefore it is likely that the agency will undertake a policy designed to maintain the existing economic structure, with the general public having to pay the cost. Economic advisers can make suggestions about the institutional form of the agency so that incentives are created to promote, and not to hinder, structural change.

CONCLUSION

The price system has advantages and disadvantages (the latter are usually called 'market failures'). Its functioning can be improved by various policies. This chapter has discussed anti-trust and regulatory, consumer and structural policy. It has been shown that all these attempts at improvement also entail social costs. Often, there is a wide gap between the officially declared goal of improving the functioning of the price system and the policy actually undertaken. Often economic policy measures lead to results that are in gross contrast to the official goals. A structural policy, for instance, as a rule does not promote structural change but rather helps outdated economic sectors to survive.

The large gap between official goals and actual policy can be attributed to two causes:

1 *government failure*, entailing a distorted functioning of the democratic decision-making mechanisms;
2 *administrative failure*, entailing an inadequate working of the public administration.

Government and administrative failures will be considered in subsequent chapters. In accordance with this discussion, it should always be kept in mind that the advantages and disadvantages of the price system should be compared with the advantages and disadvantages of those decision-making mechanisms designed to improve upon the price system. The individuals and groups setting the basic rules in society have to choose between alternative ways of ordering the current politico-economic process. What they need, therefore, is a *comparative analysis of institutions*.

FURTHER READING

A good and simple introduction into the properties of the price system is given by

Kenneth J. Arrow, *The Limits of Organization*. New York: Norton, 1974.

A definite and precise presentation of the theory of general economic equilibrium is

Kenneth J. Arrow and Frank H. Hahn, *General Competitive Analysis*. San Francisco: Holden-Day, 1971.

A modern discussion of externalities may be found in

William J. Baumol and Wallace E. Oates, *The Theory of Environmental Policy. Externalities, public outlays and the quality of life*. Englewood Cliffs: Prentice Hall 1975, part I.

Texts on anti-trust or monopoly policy are, for example

Joe S. Bain, *Industrial Organization*. New York: Wiley, 1959,

J. M. Blair, *Economic concentration. Structure, behavior and public policy*. New York: Harcourt, Brace, Jovanovich, 1972.

Strongly empirically-oriented is

Frederic M. Scherer, *Industrial market structure and economic performance*. Rand McNally: Chicago, 1970.

A good British text is

Charles Rowley, *Anti-trust and Economic Efficiency*. London: Macmillan, 1973.

The theory of X-efficiency has been developed by

Harvey Leibenstein, *Beyond Economic Man: A New Foundation for Micro-Economics*. Cambridge, Mass.: Harvard University Press, 1976.

The relationships between the extent of competition and technical change are surveyed by

Morton I. Kamien and Nancy L. Schwartz, Market Structure and Innovation: A Survey, *Journal of Economic Literature*, 13 (1975), 1–37.

Charles Kennedy and A. P. Thirlwall, Surveys in Applied Economics: Technical Progress, *Economic Journal,* 82 (1972), 11–72.

Evidence on the existence and non-existence of economies of scale is given, for example, in

C. Pratten, *Economies of Scale in Manufacturing Industries.* Cambridge: University Press, 1971;

Aubrey Silberston, Economies of Scale in Theory and Practice, *Economic Journal,* 82 (1972) (Supplement), 369–91.

Various approaches to the theory of regulation are discussed by

Richard A. Posner, Theories of Economic Regulation, *Bell Journal of Economics,* 5 (1974), 335–58.

The empirical evidence on the benefits and costs and regulatory policy referred to in this chapter is presented in:

S. G. Breyer and P. W. Macaroy, *Energy Regulation by the Federal Power Commission,* Washington DC: Brookings Institution, 1974, Table 5.1;

Richard A. Posner, The Social Cost of Monopoly and Regulation, *Journal of Political Economy,* 83 (1975), 818, Table 2 (excerpt);

Murray L. Weidenbaum, The High Cost of Government Regulation, *Challenge,* 22 (1979), 37, Table 4 (excerpt).

Consumer policy is discussed in

Peter Smith and Dennis Swann, *Protecting the Consumer: An Economic and Legal Analysis.* Oxford: Martin Robertson, 1979;

OECD, *Consumer Policy in the Member Countries.* Paris: Organization for Economic Co-operation and Development, 1972.

The discussion of liability rules in the text is based on

Roland McKean, Products Liability: Implications of Some Changing Property Rights, *Quarterly Journal of Economics,* 84 (1970), 611–26.

An empirical analysis of structural change is provided, for example, by

Hollis B. Chenery and Lance Taylor, Development Patterns: Among Countries and Over Time, *Review of Economics and Statistics,* 50 (1968), 391–416.

In Anglo-Saxon economics, structural policy is not treated as a whole as in German economics; see, for example,

Hans-Friedrich Eckey, *Grundlagen der regionalen Strukturpolitik.* Cologne: Bund Verlag, 1978.

An exception is

Alan Peacock, *Structural Economic Policies in West Germany and the United Kingdom.* London: Anglo-German Foundation, 1980.

The actual workings of structural policy are analysed within public choice; see, for example,

Anthony Downs, *An Economic Theory of Democracy.* New York: Harper and Row, 1957;

Peter Bernholz, Economic Policies in Democracy, *Kyklos*, 19 (1966), 48–80.

CHAPTER 5

Democratic Decision-making

INTRODUCTION

One of the most important tasks for individuals and groups is to reach agreement on the democratic decision-making procedures to be used. In order to reach a sensible decision in a state of uncertainty, economic advisers will need to inform people and groups about the characteristics of the various decision-making mechanisms.

There are a number of decision-making procedures that can be followed in a democracy. Among the direct mechanisms, the simple majority rule (with its various advantages and disadvantages) is the most important. The indirect mechanisms work via elections. Usually it is the strength gained by the parties in parliament that decides who will form the government, which in turn has the power to undertake policy-making decisions in the current process. In the United States and some other countries, the chief executive is directly elected by the people. Democratically elected governments formulate business cycle, allocation and distribution policies in a characteristic way. This has to be taken into account when it is endeavoured to reach a social consensus.

There are many other democratic decision-making mechanisms, some of which are fairly new. It is worth considering these because they manage to avoid some of the important disadvantages of simple majority rule, making it possible to introduce new social decision-making rules that are advantageous to everyone in the state of uncertainty.

5.1 MAJORITY RULE

The best known and most widely used among democratic decision-making mechanisms is majority rule. In many societies, a *simple majority* is accepted without question: of two alternatives, the one is chosen that receives more than half the votes. A *qualified majority* requires that two-thirds or three-quarters (or some other share above 50 per cent) decides for one of the two alternatives. In the extreme, qualified majority converges to the rule of *unanimity*, wherein every member of the electorate must support an alternative before it becomes the collective decision. This rule, by definition, secures a Pareto-optimal outcome among the alternatives at issue (an outcome that is Pareto-optimal in an overall sense is reached only if the selection of alternatives is chosen unanimously). Often, however, no definite decision is reached with the unanimity rule because there is an incentive to act strategically. In particular, individuals who fight tenaciously against an alternative may be able thereby to gain special advantages.

If there are more than two alternatives, or if voters may abstain, it is necessary to distinguish between *absolute majority* (in which an alternative gets more votes than all other alternatives taken together) and *relative majority* (in which an alternative gets more votes than any other alternative).

Simple majority rule has three important advantages.

1   Each person has one vote. In practice, however, some individuals are excluded from voting (for example by being too young) and some groups consistently participate more than others (for example, upper-income more than low-income individuals).
2   The rule is easy to understand and has a high legitimacy among the population.
3   It is cheap to organize. This holds, however, only in the case of two alternatives. If there are more alternatives, a common rule (attributed to Condorcet) is to set sequentially two alternatives against each other. That alternative is chosen which beats any other alternative.

The simple majority rule has, however, six major shortcomings.

1   Logically inconsistent results are possible. This fact is known as the 'Condorcet paradox'. No definite winner can then be determined, because every alternative can be beaten by some other alternative. One then speaks of *cyclical majorities*. The Condorcet paradox may be generalised to the *impossibility theorem* (or Arrow paradox), which holds for all voting rules in which the decision is reached by pair-wise confrontation.

2 Preference intensities cannot be revealed because the voters can only say 'yes' or 'no' (or abstain).
3 The simple majority rule is not necessarily 'just', because a stable majority may consistently exploit a minority.
4 A voter has little incentive to become informed because the probability that he will cast the decisive (or pivotal) vote is normally very small.
5 Strategic voting can be advantageous. (This behaviour applies, however, to almost all voting and aggregation mechanisms; it corresponds to free-riding in the framework of the price system.)
6 The simple majority rule is subject to manipulation. If there are more than two alternatives, the sequence in which the alternatives are presented to the voters can determine the outcome. In public referenda there are, in general, only two issues between which the voters can decide. The pre-selection, formulation and material interpretation of the issues to be voted on is of great importance. One must therefore expect that pressures develop outside the formal process in efforts to influence the outcome.

This discussion of the advantages and shortcomings merely serves to show that, as is the case with all other decision-making systems, majority rule is imperfect.

5.2 ELECTIONS AND DEMOCRATIC GOVERNMENTS

In a representative democracy the formal participation rights of citizens are restricted to parliamentary elections. There are two (pure) types of election systems:

1 with proportional representation, the number of seats is distributed according to the share of the vote received by a party;
2 with majority representation, that party receives the seat(s) in a precinct that has a (relative) majority of votes.

In most countries, the two systems are mixed in one way or another.

The behaviour of a democratically elected government can be analysed theoretically and empirically by assuming that it maximizes its own utility subject to various constraints. The utility of politicians is increased when they are able to put their wishes into action. The major constraint is imposed by their wish to be re-elected. Their chances for re-election depend (among other things) on the state of the economy: they are lower, the higher are rates of unemployment and inflation, and higher, the higher is the growth of real income. Governments are also restricted by administrative and legal constraints as well as by financial constraints, for example, by budgetary constraints and the state of the balance of payments. This model has been estimated econometrically (or rather: politometrically) for various countries, with good *ex ante* forecasting results.

The model of government in a representative democracy allows us to draw some conclusions about its behaviour in the current politico-economic process.

1 Over time, a government will vary government expenditures and taxes in predictable ways. If government is confident of being re-elected, it will undertake an ideologically motivated policy, most usually immediately after it has come to power. Thus, for example, left-wing governments increase public outlays and nationalize enterprises according to their party programme. Right-wing governments will try to reduce public expenditures, and fight inflation. If politicians are afraid of losing a forthcoming election because of their low popularity ratings, they will undertake an expansionary policy as the election date approaches. (This will occur unless the rate of inflation is extremely high, leading voters to favour a deflationary policy.) This behaviour results in a wilfully produced *political business cycle.*

2 With respect to allocation and distribution, producers will be favoured at the expense of consumers. The 'producers' in this case comprise both capital owners and employees in a particular sector. The government undertakes policies in favour of producers, who will be conscious of the resulting rise in income and accordingly will support the government party. The resulting increases in prices and/or taxes, as well as the quantitative restrictions, are as a rule scarcely perceptible to the consumers, who will react only to increases in the price of basic goods such as milk, bread and housing, and more recently also in public transport and energy. Democratic government will also favour projects whose benefits are highly visible and quickly attainable, because this improves their prospects for re-election. A government will carry the cost of projects without visible short-run benefits, only if it is confident of still being in power in the next (or later) legislative periods, so as to reap the fruits of its investment. Public activities with invisible *costs*, on the other hand, are favoured by democratic governments; and they are very imagin-

ative when it comes to disguising the costs of their actions – the activity is financed from a multitude of sources, and the tax system is made complicated and difficult to understand. Moreover, the government makes an effort to burden the private sector only indirectly, in particular by guaranteeing a sector's income through price-fixing and regulation. This results in even experts finding it difficult or impossible to calculate the amount of direct and indirect subsidies flowing into a sector. Finally, democratically elected governments favour organized groups who undertake activities to maintain and enlarge their income and fight with determination when a public activity threatens their economic position. But the wishes of non-organized groups may be taken into account by government if the groups are large in number and can be decisive in elections. This applies, for example to old-age pensioners, who are not organized as an interest group but are courted by political parties because of their vote potential.

There are various rules and institutions that the economic advisers may suggest for a social consensus which improve the functioning of democratic elections and induce governments better to fulfil the population's wishes.

1   As has already been pointed out, the classical constitutional rights are a precondition for citizens to be able to express their preferences. If they are violated in important respects, elections are of no use.

2   Competition between the parties is the mechanism that makes parties interested in the voters' wishes. Only if this competition is vigorous will the re-election constraint be sufficiently strong to ensure that the government is forced to take account of individual preferences. To secure competition between the parties, economic advisers may suggest facilitating the entry of new parties. Such proposals have a chance of being adopted only behind the veil of ignorance, since the parties established in the current political process would fight strongly against easing the way for new parties. New parties can, for example, be supported financially or by the granting of generous television time. The existing forms of party financing are often in favour of established parties, which is not surprising in view of the fact that the mode of financing has been decided by the established parties themselves in the current political process.

3 Various measures can be undertaken to strengthen the direct relationship between public expenditure and taxes, and to make this relationship clear to the citizens:

— an 'information agency' independent of government could help voters to know the costs and benefits of public programmes. Such an agency would, for example, calculate (under various assumptions) how much a representative taxpayer is burdened by the direct and indirect subsidies going to the agricultural sector. This institution must be devised in such a way that it has an incentive to provide the citizens with such information, and does not become prey to the interests of the government, public administration and interest groups.
— the tax system can be simplified so that the voters may more easily see the costs of public activity.
— expenditure laws can be given a fixed lifetime (via 'sunset laws'), after which they have to be debated and voted upon again by parliament.
— the government may be allowed to make additional expenditures only if the necessary additional taxes or reductions in other expenditure items are explicitly and precisely stated, showing the consequences for the *individual* taxpayers. There may also be a rule that only direct income transfers that show up in the public budget be allowed.

Such information helps citizens to compare the expected utility derived from public activity with the corresponding cost in terms of individual tax prices for the (additional) publicly supplied good. The voters then have more scope for defending themselves if they consider the relationship between benefits and costs unattractive. A government subject to democratic competition is then forced to explain to the voters the *net* benefits of its activities, and to take their preferences into account.

5.3   NEW VOTING MECHANISMS

Innovations are often planned and introduced at the technical level – rockets, for example, or electronic calculators. Social innovations are, however, equally if not more important. Consider procedures for deriving collective decisions: there is a need for a new voting mechanism or mechanisms that would be able to account for individual preferences and would overcome some of the shortcomings of traditional majority rule. Such a mechanism would be a productive social innovation fitting all individuals and groups.

Some voting rules – in particular the rank-order method and point voting – were developed long ago but are not often used for collective decision-making. The *rank-order method* (which is also known as the 'Borda count') allows individuals to state the intensity of their preferences when they vote. They are, however, restricted to a given point schedule. For example, an individual may allocate three points to the most preferred, two points to the next and one point to the least liked alternative. That alternative receiving the highest number of points is the social choice. Under *point voting*, individuals are free to allocate a given number of points (say, 100) among the alternatives in any proportion they wish. An individual might give 80 points to his first choice, 20 points to the next best and no points at all to the third alternative. Again, the alternative receiving the highest number of points is the social choice.

Under both decision rules, but particularly with point voting, individuals have an incentive to vote strategically. It is advantageous, for example, for a voter to allocate *all* the points to his most preferred alternative (even if he considers other alternatives to be acceptable) in order to increase the chance that his preferred alternative becomes the social choice. The advantage of being able to express one's preference intensities thus results in a disadvantage: the increased incentive to misrepresent one's true preferences by strategic voting.

In the following sections of this chapter, five recently developed voting rules will be outlined:

1 approval voting;
2 probabilistic voting on the basis of a referendum;
3 probabilistic voting on the basis of point voting;
4 voting by veto;
5 voting by imposing a tax (a preference-revealing mechanism).

Approval Voting

Under this decision-making mechanism, voters are allowed to vote for – or 'approve of' – as many issues (or candidates) as they wish – but not more than one vote may be cast for each issue. The winner is the issue with the greatest vote total.

Example

In a post-election survey of the 1968 presidential election in the United States, 44 per cent of the voters reported voting for Nixon, 42 per cent for Humphrey, and 14 per cent for Wallace. Under approval voting, a great many supporters of Nixon would also have approved of (that is, cast a vote for) Humphrey, and vice versa. Wallace supporters would have cast many more approval votes for Nixon than for Humphrey. Under certain assumptions, it has been estimated that Nixon would have received 70 per cent, Humphrey 61 per cent and Wallace 21 per cent. Nixon would have turned out to be a much clearer winner than under the relative majority rule. This outcome seems to reflect voters' preferences well: it has been calculated that in a pair-wise contest Nixon would have defeated Humphrey 53 to 47 per cent, and Wallace 82 to 18 per cent.

It has been shown that approval voting gives fewer incentives for strategic voting while allowing voters not just to express the highest preference but to denote the issues (candidates) that they find acceptable and those they do not. This voting rule also has the advantage of being easy to understand and practicable. No ranking of the issues (candidates) as in the Borda count is required.

Probabilistic Voting on the Basis of a Referendum

This voting rule proceeds in two steps. First, the number of votes going to each of the two alternatives is counted as would be the case with majority rule. Second, the social choice is determined by attributing probabilities to the alternatives according to their percentage shares in the vote, the final decision being based on the probabilities.

Example

Assume that, in a referendum about a bridge project, 60 per cent of the voters are for, and 40 per cent against, building the bridge. The social decision is to build the bridge with a probability of 60 per cent, which can be done by putting 60 red 'yes' and 40 white 'no' balls into an urn. If a red ball is randomly chosen the bridge project is the social choice.

This voting rule is especially advantageous when the majority is small, as for example in the case of 55 per cent yes and 45 per cent no. Under simple majority rule, the large minority is suppressed, while under the probabilistic voting rule each vote has the same weight in the outcome.

Many people find this voting rule rather difficult to understand because they are not accustomed to the use of a random mechanism.

Probabilistic Decisions on the Basis of Point Voting

This voting rule proceeds in three stages:

1 first, the individuals allocate points to the various alternatives according to their preference intensities. The respective point shares can be interpreted as individual probability assignments;
2 second, the individual probabilities are aggregated by calculating the weighted mean for each alternative;
3 third, the social decision is determined by using a random mechanism based on the aggregate probabilities.

This voting rule is not subject to the paradox of voting because an overall comparison of all the alternatives is undertaken. It also has the advantage of taking into account the preference intensities of all the individuals, and not just of the majority. This decision-making mechanism is, however, rather difficult for the ordinary voters to understand. The second and third steps in particular may prove to be too unorthodox to be acceptable.

Voting by Veto

In contrast to the new voting rules discussed so far, this mechanism allows a choice to be made about the issues to be decided upon. Each individual may present his own proposal. The social decision is taken by each individual's deleting from the set of alternatives that proposal to which he is most strongly opposed. The order in which the voters are given the opportunity to decide alternatives is assigned randomly. That one which remains is the social decision.

The voting rule is illustrated for the two-person case; it can easily be generalized to many voters.

Example

Consider a situation in which a gift of *B* pounds must either be accepted *and* divided among two persons, or be rejected (in which case the status quo is maintained). Each voter proposes a distribution of the sum of money B. There are thus three alternatives.

Assume that voter I's proposal V_I consists in voter I receiving $B - 1$ pounds and voter II receiving 1 pound; while voter II's proposal V_{II} consists in the reverse distribution $(1, B - 1)$. The third alternative is the status quo S, with nobody receiving anything $(0, 0)$. Assume further that the random mechanism gives voter II the right to delete one alternative from the set (V_I, V_{II}, S). He will delete V_I because this distribution of B is much more unfavourable for him than his own proposition. Voter I will then delete alternative S from the remaining set (V_{II}, S), because proposal V_{II} gives him at least one pound. The social decision thus is V_{II}.

It would be mistaken to conclude from this example that the voter who gets to choose first has a decisive advantage. It may be shown that this advantage becomes smaller and smaller, the larger the number of voters.

Voting by veto has some good properties:

— the social decision is Pareto-optimal because the status quo alternative is always deleted. It should be noted that under alternative decision-making rules it often happens that no equilibrium distribution of a given sum of money is reached, so that nobody receives anything;
— in the case of many individuals participating, there is a tendency for an egalitarian distribution;
— the preference revelation is unbiased. Each voter must make an effort to take other voters' preferences into account because otherwise his proposal will soon be deleted;
— the veto power of each voter prevents exploitation by the majority.

The major disadvantage of this voting rule is that it is rather complicated and difficult to understand. Its implementation is costly, also. As is the case of a great many other decision-making rules, the outcome may be distorted by coalitions, and the incentive to participate declines increasingly the more individuals are involved.

Voting by Imposing a Tax

A voting outcome constitutes a public good for the individuals participating because the outcome *applies to all*. A voter can therefore impose a negative external effect on other voters, as the aggregate outcome can be more unfavourable to them owing to the participation of that particular voter. Under the voting mechanism discussed here the imposition of this marginal external effect is 'punished' by a tax, so that a Pareto-optimal outcome is brought about.

Example

Consider three voters, I, II and III, and two alternatives A and B. The relative individual utilities (utils) attributed to these alternatives are given in Table 5.1. This table shows that alternative A gets 20 (column 1) and B (column 2) 40 utils, so that B should be the social decision. Voters I and II have no effect on this outcome, as is shown by columns (3) and (4). Even if they did *not* participate, alternative B would get more utils than A and would be chosen. (If for example voter I did not participate, the sum of utils for B would be 30 (column 4) as against 20 for A (column 3). If, however, voter III did not participate, the outcome would change: alternative A would get 20 utils (column 3) and B 10 utils (column 4). The fact that voter III participates thus reverses the social outcome, imposing a negative external effect on voters I and II. They suffer a loss of 10 utils because they would attribute to A 20 utils and to B 10 utils. The vote tax imposed on voter III must therefore be equivalent to 10 utils (in monetary terms).

TABLE 5.1   *Voting by imposing a tax: three voters and two alternatives*

Voters	Individual utilities		Sum of utilities assigned by other voters		Voting tax
	A (1)	B (2)	A (3)	B (4)	(5)
I	0	10	20	30	0
II	20	0	0	40	0
III	0	30	20	10	10
Sum	20	40			

This 'preference-revealing process', as this voting rule is often called, has important advantages. The social decisions are Pareto-efficient because the vote tax gives an incentive to vote such that the effect on the other voters is taken into account. The rule does not generate the inconsistent results encountered in the voting paradox, and the voters have an incentive to reveal their true preferences. Each voter can influence the social decision by paying the marginal cost imposed on others in the form of the vote tax. He cannot win by overstating or understating his preferences.

This voting rule has also some major weaknesses, in particular that voting is no longer anonymous since the stated preferences must be attributable to specific voters in order to calculate their vote tax. Moreover, it does not give any incentive to participate. Possibly most important, this voting rule is very complicated (a computer is needed to calculate the voting tax) and is probably incomprehensible to the voting public.

CONCLUSION

The new voting rules sketched have some advantages over simple majority rule, but also some disadvantages. Individuals and groups must evaluate these advantages and disadvantages when they consider which voting rule should be used under which conditions. As none of the new voting rules has the same combination of positive and negative characteristics, the one chosen may have strong consequences for the policies undertaken in the current politico-economic process. Economic advisers will be most successful if they suggest using a voting rule where its comparative advantages are greatest:

— for economic policy questions where marked differences in preference intensity are typical, the preferred voting rule would allow for intensity of preference to be expressed;
— in areas in which the supply of public goods is to be determined and where there is therefore a special incentive for strategic voting, a voting rule immune to the latter is warranted;
— for economic policy problems where the protection of minorities is crucial, a voting rule producing Pareto-optimal outcomes is to be recommended;
— for policy questions of a long-term nature, which can be revised only at high cost, a voting rule that prevents the paradox of voting is best suited.

The economic adviser will probably not reach a consensus if he suggests introducing a new voting rule in areas where simple majority rule has long since been applied and where it has functioned well, or where the advantages of the new rules are small compared with the complications and costs created by their introduction. The citizens are not accustomed to the new decision-making mechanisms, and for that reason will resist them. A consensus about their introduction is most likely to be achieved in areas where thus far there has not been any democratic decision-making apparatus and in newly instituted committees with no tradition of majority voting.

FURTHER READING

The simple majority and several other voting rules are treated, for example, in Dennis Mueller's book on *Public Choice*, cited in the first chapter.

The history of voting rules, in particular the contributions by Condorcet and Borda, are discussed by

Duncan Black, *The Theory of Committees and Elections*. Cambridge: University Press, 1958.

A definitive treatment of the general problems involved in the aggregation of preferences is

Amartya K. Sen, *Collective Choice and Social Welfare*. Edinburgh: Oliver and Boyd, 1970.

The analysis of the behaviour of democratically elected governments is also based on the economic theory of politics, in particular on politico-economic modelling. A survey is given in

Bruno S. Frey, Politico-Economic Models and Cycles, *Journal of Public Economics*, 9 (1978), 203–20

as well as in *Modern Political Economy*, cited in the first chapter.

Approval voting is more fully discussed in

Stephen J. Brams and Peter C. Fishburn, Approval Voting, *American Political Science Review*, 72 (1978), 831–47.

This article also contains the illustration of the US presidential elections of 1968 given in the text.

The two rules of probabilistic voting have been developed by

Bruno S. Frey, Wahrscheinlichkeiten als gesellschaftliche Entscheidungsregel, *Wirtschaft und Recht*, 21 (1969), 14–26;

Michael D. Intriligator, A Probabilistic Model of Social Choice, *Review of Economic Studies*, 41 (1973), 553–60.

The voting by veto rule is due to

Dennis C. Mueller, Voting by Veto, *Journal of Public Economics*, 10 (1978), 57–75.

The preference revealing mechanism is discussed in

Nicholas Tideman and Gordon Tullock, A New and Superior Process for Making Social Choices, *Journal of Political Economy*, 84 (1976), 1145–59.

CHAPTER 6

Bureaucratic Decision-making

INTRODUCTION

In large sectors of society decisions are taken bureaucratically, by using a formalized, hierarchical procedure. The bureaucracy's behaviour to a large extent determines the outcome of the politico-economic process. Only when the behaviour of the public bureaucracy is suitably restrained may it be expected that the population's preferences will be adequately taken into account.

Bureaucratic public institutions behave in a way that is quite different from other decision-makers. Public bureaucracies tend to try to enlarge the budget at their disposal ('budget maximization') and to secure for themselves a terrain in which they can act at their own discretion. Members of the public administration (civil servants) have little incentive to act efficiently; it is more important to them to keep to formal rules. Empirical comparisons between private and public institutions suggest that firms exposed to competition produce at lower cost than do public firms.

In the current political process, the four most important decision-makers (voters, interest groups, parliament and government) have little incentive and few possibilities for efficiently controlling the public bureaucracy. However, it is possible to introduce rules and institutions by social consensus with which the public administration can be controlled, in particular by sharpening the budgetary and political restrictions.

6.1 PUBLIC BUREAUCRACY AND ECONOMIC POLICY

When fixing the ground rules for the current politico-economic process one must consider the *actual*, rather than an idealized, behaviour of the public bureaucracy. Economic policy advisers can inform the decision-makers about how public bureaucracies behave. They will in particular point out the differences between actual behaviour and altruistic behaviour based on the idea of 'public welfare' or the 'common good'. This information will help decision-makers solve two questions with respect to a possible social consensus.

1 What problems is public bureaucracy able to solve well? What are its advantages and weaknesses compared with those of other institutional arrangements?
2 What can be undertaken at the level of the social consensus in order that public bureaucracies do indeed fulfil the individuals' preferences in the current politico-economic process?

These questions can be answered adequately only if something is known about the importance and the behaviour of public administrations.

6.2 THE IMPORTANCE OF PUBLIC ADMINISTRATION

Many people today tend to identify public administration with 'bureaucratization', and some even point to the danger of a new Leviathan. It is difficult to say whether such fears are well founded. It is even quite difficult to grasp the sheer size of public bureaucracy. Furthermore, its size depends very much on the definition of the public sector. The number of public officials changes drastically depending on whether or not employees of the public railways and the post office are included. There is no rule about how to define the extent of the public sector as such; what matters is that an adequate definition is chosen for the problem one wants to study.

One measure of the size of the public administration that is often used is the proportion of public employees in total employment. Table 6.1 shows the development of this share over time in industrialized countries. According to this table, every fifth employee in the United Kingdom, and every fourth employee in Sweden, works in the public sector (whose definition varies, however, between countries). In the United States, Austria and Belgium this applies to every sixth employee, in Germany, France and Italy to about every seventh, and in Switzerland to every tenth. The share of public employees is much lower in Japan (6.4 per cent in 1978), but even there it has strongly increased since 1960, when it was below 3 per cent). In all ten countries included in the table the share of public employees

TABLE 6.1   *Share of Employees in the Public Sector, various Countries, 1960–78*

	1960	1970	1978
	%	%	%
Japan	2.9	5.8	6.4
Switzerland	6.3	7.9	10.1
Italy	8.6	10.9	14.2
France	12.3	12.4	14.3
Germany (F.R.)	8.0	11.2	14.5
United States	15.7	18.0	16.7
Belgium	12.2	13.9	16.9
Austria	10.8	14.1	18.3
United Kingdom	14.9	18.0	21.3
Sweden	12.8	20.6	28.8
(Unweighted) mean	10.4	13.3	16.2

Note: A comparison between countries is limited because the public sector is defined in different ways in the various countries. The definition used here comprises general governmental institutions that supply non-market goods and services, and extends to all federal levels.

Source: John P. Martin, Public Sector Employment Trends in Western Industrialized Economies, mimeo. Paris: OECD, 1980, table 1 and own calculations.

has grown markedly between 1960 and 1978: the unweighted mean of this particular measure of the size of the public sector has in the 18 years increased by six percentage *points*, from 10.4 to 16.2 per cent.

However, the share of public employees in total employment is an inadequate measure for evaluating the importance of public administration in the politico-economic process. This indicator should be complemented by an output measure, showing the consequences of the activities, interventions and regulations of public administration in other decision-making systems. An often used indicator that aims to capture the importance of public administration is the share of public expenditure in the gross national product. Table 6.2 shows the long-term development of this share excluding public enterprises, for three developed industrial countries. In the United Kingdom, the United States and Germany the share of public expenditures in national income increased greatly over the first three-quarters of this century. In the United Kingdom, this share increased from roughly

15 per cent to almost 50 per cent of GNP, in the United States from 8 to 35 per cent, and in the Federal Republic of Germany from 12 to almost 40 per cent.

The share of public expenditures in GNP is, however, at best an *indirect* indicator of the output side of public administration, and thus of its importance in the politico-economic process. On the one hand, part of administrative behaviour has no budgetary consequences (if for example the private sector is affected by public regulations), while on the other hand, a few public officials can undertake huge budgetary activities (huge redistributional transactions can in principle be performed by a few public employees by pushing computer buttons). The indirect consequences of the public administration's activity in the form of regulation has been discussed in Chapter 4, and some quantitative estimates have been advanced.

The statistics available on the level and the development of the public sector suggest the same overall conclusion: public administration is of major (and increasing) importance in the politico-economic process.

TABLE 6.2 *The Share of Public Expenditures in National Income in the United Kingdom, the United States and Germany, 1900–75.*

Year	United Kingdom (share in GNP at factor cost)	United States (share in GNP at market prices)	Germany (share in NNP in market prices)
	%	%	%
Around 1900	14.4	7.9	12.3
Around 1913	12.4	8.5	15.4
Around 1925	24.2	12.2	22.4
1930	26.2	12.3	26.9
1938	30.0	19.8	42.4
1949	40.0	23.0	31.6
1955	36.6	24.5	30.1
1960	37.2	27.0	30.3
1965	41.9	27.3	33.9
1970	42.1	31.7	32.1
1975	46.8	35.0	38.6

Source: Konrad Littmann, Oeffentliche Ausgaben II, *Handwörterbuch der Wirtschaftswissenschaften, Band I.* Stuttgart, Tübingen and Göttingen: Fischer, Mohr and Vandenhoeck and Ruprecht, 1977, Table 1 (excerpt), 353.

6.3   MODELS OF PUBLIC ADMINISTRATION

Public employees can be assumed to maximize their *own* utility subject to the constraints imposed. This behavioural assumption allows the development of a theory of hierarchical institutions.

The top bureaucrats, who to a large extent shape the behaviour of the civil service, derive utility from their own income, the prestige they gain by performing well ('performance excellence'), a quiet life with no major conflicts, and the indirect income derived from perks such as official cars and journeys. For many purposes, these arguments in the bureaucrats' utility function can be reduced to a single factor; the size of the budget of the administrative unit. Direct and indirect income and prestige increase the larger are the expenditures that the bureaucrats may undertake, and the better is the chance of being able to meet the demands of the clientele groups, thus allowing the bureaucrats to lead a quiet life.

The top bureaucrats and the administrative units as a whole have to take into account four different constraints. They are restricted by (1) the size of the budget allocated to them, (2) the large number of rules, regulations and laws that public employees must observe, (3) the rule that major conflicts with government have to be avoided (the public officials know, on the other hand, that the government depends on them and has but limited scope for controlling them owing to its insufficient information; the same applies to the parliament and its commissions which are supposed to control bureaucracy); and (4) constraints imposed by well organized interest groups. Bureaucracy must make an effort to minimize such conflicts.

The typical behaviour of public administrations can be illustrated with the help of two *paradigmatic models* which contain the elements just mentioned.

Budget Maximization

One assumption that can be made concerning public administrations is that of budget maximization, in which the bureaucrats' utility function is taken to be positively and directly related to the size of the budget. Most public bureaux have a monopolistic position in relation to parliament because they are the only suppliers of a particular publicly supplied good or service. This monopolistic position allows an administrative unit to fix the options available to the demanders by supplying only one package: a *particular* quantity of a public good, supplied at a *particular* 'price' in the form of budgetary costs. This package is chosen so that the budget (and therewith the utility of public officials) is maximized. The quantity supplied is larger than would be Pareto-optimal.

The model of budget maximization is illustrated in Figure 6.1. Part (a) shows the total utility produced by the supply of increasing quantities of the publicly supplied good according to the parliament's views and the corresponding total cost. Part (b) indicates the marginal utilities (the parliament's marginal willingness to pay) and the marginal cost. Marginal utility falls, and marginal cost rises, with increasing supply. A Pareto-optimal supply would obtain at quantity P, where the maximum net utility is produced and where marginal utility equals marginal cost. Public employees have, however, an interest in supplying as much as possible of the good: they will offer the parliament *only* the option of 'buying' quantity B. At this quantity, parliament's consumer surplus (net utility, as shown in Figure 6.1b) is completely exploited in order to maximize the budget (that is, the cost) of the administrative unit. Area CDE is equal to area EFG in Figure 6.1(b). Parliament is forced to accept this unfavourable option because of its lack of information for determining quantity P.

Budget maximization can be considered to be a special case of a general model of public bureaucracy: The public employees' utility is determined solely by the budget size, and the only constraint imposed is parliament's willingness to pay.

Exploiting the Discretionary Opportunities

Public administrations are only incompletely controlled by government and voters. One important reason is the difficulty of measuring the output of non-marketed goods and the efficiency with which they are produced. The government has no real incentive to control public bureaucracy effectively: the cost of information is high and the government is afraid of antagonizing the public bureaucracy on which it depends. The voters too lack the incentive and the means of controlling public bureaucracy effectively. An improvement in

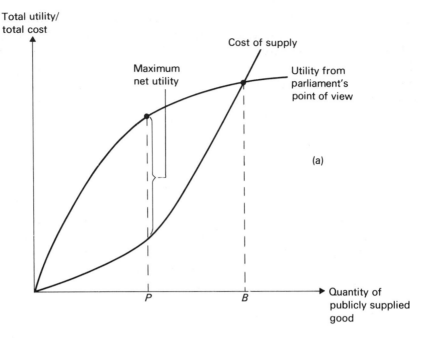

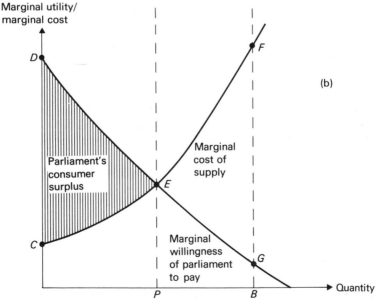

FIGURE 6.1   *The budget maximization model: (a) total curves; (b) marginal curves.*

administrative performance is a public good that will not be supplied by individuals. For a particular person or group it does not pay to get into trouble with the public administration; it is simpler to yield to its wishes in order to make them more favourable to one's own wants. Moreover, individuals do not have the information required to control the public bureaucracy.

Public officials take advantage of these severe limits on the degree to which government and voters can exercise control. They create for themselves a discretionary area within which they can maximize their own utility. Public employees in particular will not make a great effort to supply public goods at the lowest possible cost.

The creation of a discretionary area can again be interpreted as a special case of a more general model. The public administration's utility lies in the discretionary area that enables it to lead a quiet life and to appropriate goods for its own purposes. The political constraints are explicitly considered, but it is shown that they do not seriously restrict public bureaucracy.

Further Properties of Bureaucratic Behaviour

The behavioural elements developed above allow us to draw further inferences about the typical behaviour of public employees and their institutions.

1   Public officials have little incentive to act in a socially optimal way, because a particular member of the public administration is seldom subjected to the consequences (the benefits and costs) of his decisions. While the output of the civil service is a public good that affects all, the costs of decision-making have to be borne by only the public employees involved, and therefore will be kept as small as possible. Bureaucrats do, however, have reason to stick to the formal rules and regulations, because if they make a mistake in this regard they may be punished severely. As has been mentioned, a public official may also have an intrinsic motivation to perform well and thereby to gain the respect of his colleagues.

2   Outdated bureaucracies rarely die, because it is not obvious whether the services of a particular bureau are still in demand. As there is no efficiency test (such as there is in the market-place), an administrative unit is usually not dissolved; instead, new tasks are devised for it. This reorientation is guided not so much by the popu-

lation's preferences as by the benefits that the corresponding administrative unit can gain.

3   Bureaucratic decisions are systematically distorted owing to different risks associated with alternative actions. For a public official who is supposed to make a decision, the consequences of committing a formal mistake may be very high; he may be officially censured or even dismissed. He will therefore make an effort to act in a formally correct way. Wrong decisions with major budgetary consequences may put the bureaucrat into an uncomfortable position because his competence will be put into doubt; whereas wrong decisions without direct budgetary consequences have almost no negative effects on the public official making them. Opportunity costs arising, for example, by not using a plot of land for building or by causing time losses to the population are of little importance; a typical civil servant will therefore not take much trouble to evade such costs. The least risk is associated with not making any decision at all, because it is difficult, and often impossible, to prove the net benefits that would have been created had a decision been made.

4   Public administrations tend to be excessively labour-intensive. The government can win votes by offering people jobs in the public sector at good salaries and with high side benefits.

5   Restrictive rules and regulations to be observed by the public officials cause inefficiencies and reduce their work incentives. Often, it is impossible to act efficiently. As a rule, hiring and promotion procedures and salary structures are rigidly fixed so that there is little or no scope for rewarding individual performance.

6.4   EMPIRICAL COMPARISONS OF PUBLIC AND PRIVATE PRODUCTION

Methodological Approaches

A comparison of the efficiency of public administration with other decision-making mechanisms can be drawn only in those areas in which alternative arrangements are possible. The extent of allocative inefficiency is almost impossible to measure, since most empirical studies restrict themselves to the evaluation of the *cost of production* ('technical' inefficiency) in the public as compared with the private sector.

TABLE 6.3   *The Importance of Public Enterprises, Various European Countries, 1975/76*

	Share in value added	Share in total employment
	%	%
Federal Republic of Germany	10.0	7.5
Great Britain	11.8	7.9
France	12.0	11.9
Austria	19.2	13.8
Italy	25.1	24.2

Note: The shares are not strictly comparable between countries because public
enterprises are defined in different ways.

Source: Charles Beat Blankart, *Oekonomie der öffentlichen Unternehmen.*
Munich: Vahlen, 1980, Table 1.

Table 6.3 shows that public enterprises are of considerable importance in modern industrial economies. According to this table, in
Great Britain, Germany and France more than 10 per cent of value
added is produced in public enterprises, and the corresponding share
in total employment is between 8 and 12 per cent. In Austria these
shares of public production and employment are even higher, and in
Italy one-quarter of all value added and of all employees are in the
public sector. Such a table does not, however, allow any conclusion
to be drawn about whether output is produced more efficiently in
the private or public sectors because different goods and services are
involved. A comparison of efficiency requires that the cost of producing a homogeneous product be considered. Only under this condition does it make sense to think about which institutional
arrangement (private or public production) is less costly.

To compare homogeneous products one may proceed in two different ways.

1   If the goods and services produced in the private and public
sectors are equal in all (relevant) respects, the costs of production
may be directly compared. This condition obtains in rare cases only.

Example

In Australia there are two airlines, the Trans-Australian Airways (TAA),
which is public, and the Australian National Airlines (ANSET), which is
private. Owing to public regulations, the two airlines fly the same routes,

TABLE 6.4   *Productivity Differences Between a Private (ANSET)
and a Public Airline (TAA) in Australia: Average, 1958–74*

	Freight and airmail	Passengers	Revenue
Advantage of private compared to public production	+50%	+13%	+11%

Source: D. G. Davies, Property Rights and Economic Efficiency: The Australian Airlines Revisited, *Journal of Law and Economics*, 20 (1977), 223–6.

use the same types of airplanes and set the same prices. In Table 6.4 the efficiency of the two institutions is compared on the basis of indices. This table indicates that the private company produces at lower cost than the public company. The difference is most striking in the case of freight: the private airway is 50 per cent more efficient.

2   If the public and private enterprises do not produce exactly the same goods, the differences must be accounted for with the help of statistical procedures. One such procedure is to use multiple regression analysis, which controls for the different influences on costs not connected with the question of production being private or public. The cost differences between private and public production are captured with the help of dummy variables. The procedure is best illustrated with an example.

Example

Consider the cost of refuse collection in the case of private and public supply. The average cost per household may depend on the quantity of refuse per household, the quality of collection (such as its frequency), technical conditions (for example the population density in the refuse collection area), the mode of financing (via general taxation or specific charges), and finally on the institutional arrangement of production – whether refuse collection is in the hands of private or public enterprises. The estimation equation used for a cross-section analysis of refuse collection areas thus is:

$$
\begin{aligned}
\text{average cost of refuse collection} = &\ \alpha_1 \cdot \text{(quantity)} \\
&+ \alpha_2 \cdot \text{(quality)} \\
&+ \alpha_3 \cdot \text{(technical conditions)} \\
&+ \alpha_4 \cdot \text{(mode of financing)} \\
&+ \alpha_5 \cdot \text{(institutional arrangement)} \\
&+ \varepsilon.
\end{aligned}
$$

where ε captures all random influences that do not systematically influence refuse collection. The first four groups of variables (with parameters α_1, α_2, α_3, α_4) are introduced to control for the cost differences due to factors *not* connected with the institutional arrangement of production. The question of whether private or public production is cheaper is answered by the dummy variable 'institutional arrangement' (*D*). It is defined so that in the case of private production it takes the value 1 ($D = 1$) and in the case of public production the value zero ($D = 0$). A negative sign on the coefficient α_5 suggests that private production *ceteris paribus* leads to lower cost. If $\alpha_5 > 0$, the analysis suggests a cost advantage of public production. This equation has been used to explain the cost of refuse collection in the 103 largest Swiss cities for the year 1970. The coefficient α_5, referring to the institutional arrangement of production, turns out to have a statistically significant negative sign. This suggests that private refuse collection is more efficient than public.

A Survey of Studies

Table 6.5 collects studies undertaken to test empirically the relative cost efficiency of private and public production for various areas of production and countries. Without precise information on the data and estimation methods used, great care must be taken in the interpretation of this table. The general picture given by the studies so far undertaken indicates that public production is more costly than private production. The study of the Canadian railways listed in the table suggests, however, that what may matter more is whether there is *competition* among producers (which is more often the case when the supply is left to private enterprises).

6.5 CONTROLLING THE PUBLIC ADMINISTRATION

As has been pointed out, the population, the interest groups and the politicians (government and members of parliaments) have little incentive and opportunity to control public administration in the current politico-economic process. For this reason, rules and institutions that induce the civil service to follow the wishes of the population, and that check its power, must be introduced by social consensus. These rules and institutions serve to strengthen the constraints on bureaucratic behaviour mentioned above: competition may be introduced, and budgetary and political restrictions may be directly tightened. These three approaches are now discussed in turn.

TABLE 6.5 *Comparisons of Efficiency (Costs) of Private and Public Production*

Area, author and year of study	Units and organizational forms	Findings
Utilities		
Electricity		
Wallace and Junk (1970)	137 firms by regions in the USA	Public firms have 40–75% higher operating costs and 40% higher investment cost per kWh.
Meyer (1975)	90 firms over time and by regions in the USA	Public firms have lower operating costs but higher transport and distribution costs.
Spann (1977)	Firms in four major US cities	Private firms are as efficient, and probably more efficient, with respect to operating cost
Water utilities		
Mann and Mikesell (1976)	Firms by regions in the USA	Public firms have 20% higher costs.
Morgan (1977)	143 firms in six US states	Public firms have 15% higher costs.
Crain and Zardkoohi (1978)	112 firms in the USA	Public firms are 40% less productive.
Health and insurance		
Hospitals		
Clarkson (1972)	USA	In non-profit-making hospitals 'red tape' is more prevalent
Wilson and Jadlow (1980)	1,200 US hospitals producing nuclear medicine	Proprietary hospitals deviate less than public hospitals from perfect efficiency index.
Insurance claims		
Frech (1979)	Contracting out of Medicare claims by US Social Security administration: 12 profit-making and 66 non-profit-making firms	Mutual insurance firms are 45–80% more costly than proprietary firms.
Refuse collection		
Pier, Vernon and Wicks (1974)	26 cities in Montana	Municipal supplies are more efficient.
Kitchen (1976)	48 Canadian cities	Municipal suppliers are more costly than private ones.
Pommerehne and Frey (1976)	103 largest Swiss towns with a population of between 5,100 and 423,000	Operating costs are significantly lower for private than for municipal firms.
Stevens and Savas (1977)	314 US cities with a population between 2,500 and 720,000	Municipal firms are 10–30% more costly than private firms.
Collins and Downes (1977)	St Louis County, Missouri	No significant cost differences.
Spann (1977)	Various US cities	Public firms are 45% more costly.

TABLE 6.5   (*continued*)

Area, author and year of study	Units and organizational forms	Findings
Transport		
Railroads		
Oelert (1976)	West Falia, Germany	Public firms have on average 160% higher costs compared with the contract price of private firms.
Caves, Christensen and Swanson (1980)	Canadian National (public) v. Canadian Pacific (private) railroads	No significant differences in productivity; CN was less efficient during the highly regulated period before 1965, its productivity has since increased more quickly than that of CP.
Airlines		
Davies (1977)	ANSET (private) and TAA (public) airline in Australia	Private airline is clearly more efficient than the public one.
Banks		
Nichols (1967)	California Savings and Loans co-operatives and mutuals v. stock companies	Mutual firms have 13–30% higher operating costs.
Davies (1982)	Australian banks	In private banks productivity and profitability are higher than in public banks.
Cleaning		
Bundesrechnungshof (1972)	German Federal Mail, Telephone and Telegraph	The cleaning of offices is 42–66% more expensive if undertaken by the public corporation itself than if it is contracted out.
Fischer-Mendershausen (1975)	Hamburg, Germany	Cleaning costs could be reduced by 30% if 80% of the space were contracted out.
Weather forecasting		
Bennett and Johnson (1980)	US Weather Bureau v. government's private contracted for service.	Government service is 50% more costly.

Sources: Thomas E. Borcherding, Werner W. Pommerehne and Friedrich Schneider, Comparing the Efficiency of Private and Public Production: An International Survey. *Zeitschrift für Nationalökonomie*, 89 (1982), 127–56; and Charles Beat Blankart, *Oekonomie der öffentlichen Unternehmen*, Munich: Vahlen, 1980, Table 6. The individual contributions are cited in these works.

Introducing Competition

The power of the public administration to pursue its own goals rather than the population's wishes may be checked by giving consumers the power to choose between various suppliers. A social consensus may be reached that bureaucratic units have to compete with one another for the budget allocated for a specific purpose. Competing bureaucratic units can also be created on purpose.

Example

In the United States the three branches of the services and the Marines often compete for the same budgets, for example for air defence.

Of course, such an arrangement works only if collusion between the administrative units can be prevented.

As a result of a social consensus, public monopolies may be terminated, allowing private competitors to enter the market. The bureaucratic units will be forced to work more efficiently the more they are exposed to private competition.

In many areas of public activity a combination of public and private supply is possible. It is difficult to find any area that has not been supplied by private production in some country or other at one time or another. Public production of publicly supplied goods and services is not necessary; there are many ways of introducing competition between private and public enterprises.

Examples

In the following areas the same (or very similar) products are supplied by private and public enterprises in various West European countries:

— education (schools, universities);
— health (hospitals, cemeteries);
— refuse collection and disposal;
— communications (postal services, telephone and telegraph, radio, television);
— traffic and transportation;
— security (police, protection against industrial espionage, fire brigades).

Tightening Budget Restrictions

The following consensual arrangements restrict the budgetary means received by the public administration.

1   Expenditures must be covered by normal tax receipts. When new expenditures are suggested the public administration must state precisely what current and future taxes will be required, or what other expenditures will be reduced. Running a deficit must not be permitted.

2   The tax base on which the public sector can draw in order to finance itself can be chosen so that it produces only limited tax income.

(These two rules will be further discussed in Chapter 8.)

3   The position of courts reviewing public expenditures can be strengthened by giving them the power to look into the *content* of the public administration's activities, and not just its formal correctness. It is important that the results of the inquiries be published in a form that is comprehensible to voters and parliamentarians. No great influence on the civil service can be expected, however, as long as the members of such courts are more or less part of the civil service themselves, because they will then have little incentive to make the inadequate activity of their colleagues known to outsiders. If the members of these courts were to be elected directly by the population, the institution would gain greater democratic legitimacy, and the members would have a stronger incentive to publicize the mistakes and shortcomings of administrative activities.

Tightening Political Constraints

There are institutions that reduce the discretionary scope of the public administration by strengthening the controls available to other politico-economic decision-makers, in particular the voters.

1   The direct influence of voters on the behaviour of public administrators can be increased by improving the information on the expected benefits and costs of bureaucratic activity and by enlarging the institution of *direct referenda*, especially on financial issues.

Empirical evidence

A study of the institutions of direct democracy in Swiss cities shows that, the less is the formal scope for direct voter participation, the more strongly will the policies actually undertaken deviate from the voters' preferences. This deviation can be attributed to the influence of the public administration, which pursues its own goals. For example, if there is the institution of obligatory referendum for all public expenditures (above some minimum limit), the discretionary power of public administration is small compared with those Swiss cities in which the institution of the referendum does not exist or where the referenda are optional.

The institution of an *ombudsman* can also be established. The population can complain to him about bureaucratic interventions. His influence should not, however, be overrated because he can intervene only in specific cases and then only partly, so that administrative behaviour as a whole will not be fundamentally affected. He may even serve as an alibi, allowing the public administration to take even less account of the population's wishes.

2   Public employees may not sit in parliaments because these decide about the budgets that will be at their disposition. The personal separation between the executive and the legislative should be strictly enforced. While this principle holds in some countries, it is strongly violated in others.

Example

In the Federal Republic of Germany, in the legislation period 1976–80 over 46 per cent of the members of the federal parliament (Bundestag) were public employees. In five of the eleven parliaments of the Länder (Landtage) the public employees had more than 50 per cent of the seats – a majority.

3   The use of *policy instruments* that require little bureaucratic intervention can be furthered. By social consensus a rule may be set that in all cases the application of instruments using the price system must be favoured. In particular, whenever the public sector takes over a new role, the rule can oblige the public administration seriously to consider the use of marketable licences, taxes or subsidies (see Chapter 14).

Example

Environmental policy can be undertaken by direct bureaucratic intervention, for example, by setting the maximum emission of pollutants per plant, or by checking whether any particular machine meets some environmental standards. The same goals can be reached by issuing licences specifying the maximum emission or by taxing the emissions. In these cases less administrative intervention is needed.

CONCLUSION

It has been argued that there is little possibility, in day-to-day political activity, of making the civil service fulfil the preferences of individuals, because decision-makers have neither the incentive nor the information actively to control bureaucracy's behaviour. The civil service can be made to conform more closely with the population's wishes only if the rules and institutions within which it acts are changed by social consensus. Possible rules are to introduce or increase competition between administrative units and with respect to private suppliers, and to enhance the possibility of voters' control by giving them more extended political rights, in particular by direct referenda.

FURTHER READING

A survey of the economic theory of bureaucracy is given by

William Orzechowski, Economic Models of Bureaucracy: Survey, Extensions, and Evidence. In Thomas E. Borcherding (ed.), *Budgets and Bureaucrats. The Sources of Government Growth.* Durham, North Carolina: Duke University Press, 1977, 229–59.

In this book edited by Borcherding there are a number of other, mostly empirically oriented, studies about the public administration and the relative efficiency of private and public production.

The two paradigmatic models of the public administration were developed by

William A. Niskanen, *Bureaucracy and Representative Government.* Chicago: Aldine, Atherton, 1971;

Oliver E. Williamson, *The Economics of Discretionary Behavior. Managerial Objectives in a Theory of the Firm.* Englewood Cliffs, New Jersey: Prentice-Hall, 1964.

Niskanen develops a model of budget maximizing bureaucrats, while Williamson concentrates on the discretionary scope within private and public administrations resulting from insufficient outside control.
Still relevant are the early books by

Gordon Tullock, *The Politics of Bureaucracy.* Washington: Public Affairs Press, 1965;

Anthony Downs, *Inside Bureaucracy.* Boston: Little, Brown, 1967.

Both books are almost exclusively concerned with the relationships within public administration.
The econometric study of refuse collection discussed is included in

Werner W. Pommerehne and Bruno S. Frey, Public versus Private Production Efficiency in Switzerland: A Theoretical and Empirical Comparison. In Vincent Ostrom and Frances P. Bish (eds), *Comparing Urban Service Delivery Systems.* Urban Affairs Annual Reviews, vol. 12. Beverly Hills: Sage, 1977, 221–41.

The influence of the various possibilities of using referenda in Swiss cities is analysed in

Werner W. Pommerehne and Bruno S. Frey's article cited in Chapter 3.

The capacity of public administration to survive even if the function for which it has been created no longer exists is well illustrated in the case of caring for the blind in the United States:

Donald A. Schon, The Blindness System, *Public Interest*, 18 (1970), 39–51.

CHAPTER 7

Decision-making by Economic Interest Groups

INTRODUCTION

Economic interest groups are the most important decision-makers in that area of the politico-economic system called the 'bargaining system', in which decisions are fashioned through the process of bargaining. Interest groups can have considerable influence in the current political process. The decision-makers at the level of the social consensus must consider whether they should, and how they could, restrict and control them. The economic advisers need to know the behaviour, possibilities and limits of organized groups in order to be able to suggest appropriate social arrangements.

Not all economic interests can easily be organized; stable interest groups can become established only under specific conditions. The influence of interest groups results from a variety of factors, and different avenues are taken in influencing the politico-economic process. The behaviour of interest groups can be analysed theoretically; based on this analysis, economic advisers can then suggest social agreements for controlling such groups and for limiting their influence.

7.1 RULES ABOUT INTEREST REPRESENTATION

The economic interests of the population are represented only in part by pressure groups in day-to-day politics. While some demands can be brought forward effectively by tightly structured groups, the interests of other groups of the population are difficult or even impossible to organize. Accordingly, the political influence of the various segments in the population differs strongly. It has already been pointed out that the interests of suppliers of goods and labour are dominant compared with those of consumers and taxpayers.

The decision-makers who set the rules and institutions under the social contract must consider the position to be accorded to the interest groups. Each individual must reckon with the possibility that he or his descendants belong to a segment of the population that will not be represented by pressure groups and whose demands will be overpowered by the strongly organized groups in the political bargaining process. In order to balance the various influences in the current political process, it is possible to introduce various rules and institutions. The decision-makers working towards a social consensus have to know the consequences of the various social arrangements in order to be able to take a well-reasoned decision. For this purpose the possibilities for the formation and the behaviour of interest groups have to be studied.

7.2   THE ORGANIZATION OF ECONOMIC INTERESTS

The Possibility of Formation

Common economic interests are a necessary but not sufficient condition for the organization of interests. Their activity – namely, influencing the voters, government and public administration – has the character of a public good, because all those with common interests are benefited without having to be a member of the organization.

Examples

The following activities of interest groups also benefit non-members:

— minimum prices for specific products (for example, the higher-than-equilibrium prices for agricultural goods benefit all farmers);
— tax concessions (for home owners, for instance);
— import duties and import restrictions on specific goods (such as for car manufacturers and workers employed in that industry);
— wage increases in an economic sector brought about by union pressure (which benefit all employees in that sector).

If the activity of an interest group consists of achieving the provision of a public good, there is little incentive for an individual or a firm to join the group and to carry the cost of the activity in the form of membership fees. The individuals and firms tend to act as *free-riders*. As this calculus applies to all, such interest groups are unlikely to form.

There are, however, three major conditions under which a stable organization of economic interest groups is possible.

1   In small groups, everyone knows that the activity in the common interest comes about only if there is no free-riding. In most cases, fairness rules and social pressure will lead individuals and firms to participate.

2   An interest group can establish itself by providing a private good as a by-product to its members only. There are various possibilities for such 'selective incentives':

— economic products and services of particularly good value may be made available to members only;
— the group may provide social and moral services to its members by, for example, organizing social activities, or by giving the feeling of belonging to an exclusive club.

The 'selective incentives' may also be negative; the individuals may be given an incentive to join because non-members are economically and socially discriminated against, such as in a closed-shop system.

3   An interest group can form and survive if individuals are forced to join. This can be done through public regulation: the government and public administration often find it advantageous to deal with an 'official' interest group in order to have an institutional addressee for its activity, and thereby to ease the execution of laws and regulations. In Germany and Austria, for example, such interest groups with public functions are of great importance.

Individuals with common interests, but to whom none of the three conditions just mentioned apply, constitute 'latent groups'. Important economic interests such as those of consumers or taxpayers are difficult to organize, because there is a great number of independently acting individuals and the possible activity has the character of a public good. It is not to be denied that in most countries interest groups of consumers and taxpayers do in fact exist. But their membership and financial means are quite limited compared, for example, with organizations of business and trade unions. The environmentalists constitute another pressure group that survives even though its activity clearly produces a public good. At the local level, where citizens' initiatives may form, their existence is due mainly to the small group interactions and to the moral benefits that go to the individual participants. At the regional and national level, environmental citizens' initiatives are difficult to maintain; they tend therefore to take the form of political parties competing for seats in parliaments. In various European nations such 'green parties' – though having only a small share of the vote – have gained some importance because they can be decisive for government formation.

The Most Important Interest Groups

In the United Kingdom, the main employers' organization is the Confederation of British Industry (CBI), which is the result of a merger in 1965 between the British Employers' Confederation (founded in 1919), the Federation of British Industries (1916) and the National Association of British Manufacturers (1915). The CBI has a membership of almost 11,000 companies and organizations, of which over 10,000 are industrial firms. The group fights mainly for the interests of manufacturing industry, although important banks and insurance companies as well as the nationalized industries have become members.

By far the most important labour organization in Britain is the Trade Union Congress (TUC). It comprises more than 100 affiliated unions with an overall membership of over 11 million people in 1976. The TUC represents the vast majority of the unionized population; the largest members – the Transport and General Workers' Union and the Amalgamated Union of Engineering Workers – have between 1 and 2 million members.

In the United States, the business interests are represented by organizations such as the National Association of Manufacturers and the US Chamber of Commerce, but also by the great many lobbies of the large firms active in Congress and the respective bureaus of the administration.

By far the most important labour organization in the United States is the American Federation of Labor and Congress of Industrial Organizations (AFL–CIO). It is the result of a merger, in 1955, of the AFL (founded in 1886), which is a craft union, and the CIO (founded in 1936), which is organized by the industrial sector. The AFL–CIO has more than 17 million members, with the Teamsters

TABLE 7.1   *Degree of Unionization in Various Countries, End of 1970s*

	%
Sweden	85
Austria	70–80
United Kingdom	44
Italy	33–40
Federal Republic of Germany	40
France	23
United States	22

Source: Own compilation from various publications.

Union, the United Steel Workers and the United Auto Workers having more than 1.5 million members. There are also organizations of professional people such as the American Medical Association, which are able to wield influence in the political process.

In the Federal Republic of Germany the business interests are represented by an employers' association (Bundesvereinigung der Deutschen Arbeitgeberverbände – BDA), by an organization of industrial firms (Bundesverband Deutscher Industrie – BDI), and by Chambers of Industry and Commerce.

The dominant German trade union organization is the Deutsche Gewerkschaftsbund – (DGB), with 7.4 million members, the largest industrial unions (IG Metall, union of public employees OeTV) having over 1 million members.

The degree of unionization differs strongly between countries, as is shown in Table 7.1. While Sweden and Austria are highly unionized (over three-quarters of the workers belong to a union), in the United Kingdom the share is below 50 per cent, in the United States it is below 25 per cent.

7.3   THE INFLUENCE AND BEHAVIOUR OF
INTEREST GROUPS

The particular weight of economic pressure groups can be attributed to three factors:

1   the government and public administration depend on the information provided by interest groups, who as a rule are well ac-

quainted with the facts about their economic sector; the interest groups, in exchange, receive services from the public sector;

2 interest groups may use their market power to influence voting groups: if they are able to disrupt the economic process, they can sometimes put pressure on government, because the voters often make the government responsible for the economic problems arising as a result;

3 interest groups can influence political decisions by granting or discontinuing financial support to political parties. Many parties depend heavily on financial contributions from economic organizations because they have only small incomes from membership fees.

Economic interest groups can make their demands felt at various stages of the political process. They have good opportunities to do so in the pre-parliamentary process and also completely outside the realm of parliament, because at this stage the superior information they possess is of particularly great importance. They can support candidates for parliament, and can arrange to have their representatives elected into the important parliamentary committees. Economic interest groups are also able to influence the outcome of referenda by supporting the propaganda financially and administratively. The most effective way for such organizations to influence policy outcomes is in many cases to collaborate with the public administration, which both prepares legislation and enacts it. Public officials normally welcome the participation of interest groups in both stages, because it makes their task easier to conduct.

Whatever their activity, interest groups use a typical pattern of strategic behaviour in order to reach their goals, the most important elements of which are as follows.

Vote Trading. Organized groups can achieve their demands in the political process by exchanging their votes. A group will abandon voting for a less important goal (say, pushing through a particular economic project) provided that one or several other groups will in exchange vote for a project deemed particularly important.

Example

Two pairs of alternatives, A and B, are to be decided upon. Consider two organized groups of voters, each of which has only a minority of the total number of votes. Group I is assumed to have a high preference for A and is weakly against B. Group II has a high preference for alternative B and is weakly against A. In this constellation, both groups find it advantageous to trade votes: Group I votes *for* B, provided that group II in exchange votes *for* alternative A. If the combined vote of groups I and II constitutes a majority, both alternatives A and B will be accepted after the vote trade, and both groups will have benefited.

One of the typical consequences of vote trading is that public expenditures are blown up above the level that would otherwise obtain. There is often an intensive preference for a project benefiting one's own economic sector, while one opposes projects undertaken in other sectors only weakly because one's tax burden (or the induced increase in inflation) is small or even imperceptible. Other negative effects are that the voters *not* participating in the vote trade are 'exploited' because the political externalities are imposed on them. It may happen, however, that all the groups are worse off after vote trading, even though each one of them finds it individually rational to participate (this is known as the 'paradox of vote trading'). This may come about because each group participating in vote trading may also belong to those being exploited when other groups exchange votes.

Selective Information.   Interest groups can gain at the expense of other members of society by making the positive and/or negative consequences of public activity for their own members known to decision-makers. Side effects on other segments of the population are, on the other hand, disregarded.

Partial Invisibility.   It is often profitable for interest groups to make their activities as little known as possible to outside observers in order to avoid opposition by other interest groups and the general voting population.

Putting Forward Weak Members.   The demands raised by an interest group are more easy to substantiate if the position of the economically weakest members of the group is stressed. But if their demands are met, the benefits accrue to *all* their members, including the higher-income recipients.

Example

Farm lobbies in very many countries have succeeded in getting internal food prices raised above the world market price with the argument of giving support to the needy farmers. However, this measure benefits *all* farmers, and particularly the most efficient, richer ones.

7.4   CONTROLLING INTEREST GROUPS

A social consensus about controlling pressure groups may well come about because, behind the veil of ignorance, individuals do not *know* whether their (or their descendants') interests will be represented by a strongly organized group. They have to consider that they may have preferences and demands that are difficult to organize and will tend to be neglected in the presence of well structured pressure groups.

Economic advisers can propose various social contracts by which the influence of interest groups can be restricted.

1   Pressure groups can be required to make their activities publicly known – for example, by registration as lobbies, by identification of representatives of group interests in parliament and by declaration of financial support. This obligation to publicize their activity enables the voters to counteract their demands. In referenda, the voters become informed of which pressure groups are urging alternatives. Interest groups would then find it more difficult to identify their own interests with the 'public good'. The effect of this rule should not be expected to be very great. At best, it would make it more difficult for the government and the public administration to support obviously unjustified demands. It may, however, lead interest groups to switch to activities that are more difficult to control.

2   Increased competition between the parties tightens the government's re-election constraint. The government is then forced to push back the demands of pressure groups, particularly when they are related to special interests of small minorities.

3   Competition between the groups can be intensified by creating 'countervailing powers'. This is especially needed in the case of the interests of consumers and taxpayers whose interests are otherwise

not effectively represented by an organization. A social contract may be formed to provide for financial support fo such 'latent groups'. In a direct democracy, for example, the public purse can pay part of the expenditure of a campaign.

4   The social consensus may also set rules about democratic representation within an interest group (including trade unions). This allows the members greater scope to reveal their preferences, and to have them implemented, and makes it difficult for the oligarchical leadership of the organization to pursue its own interests.

CONCLUSION

A social consensus on the rules regulating the existence and behaviour of interest groups is in the interest of individuals having to make decisions behind a veil of ignorance, because none of them knows whether his or her wishes will be represented effectively in the political process. Interest representation can be made to conform more closely with individual preferences by ensuring that information on pressure groups' activities is generally revealed and by establishing competition in the political process. As these rules may be only partially effective, there is a need to invent new forms of a social consensus concerning interest groups.

FURTHER READING

The economic theory of interest groups is mainly due to

Mancur Olson, *The Logic of Collective Action: Public Goods and the Theory of Groups*. Cambridge, Mass.: Harvard University Press, 1965.

Interest group activity has been analysed by

Peter Bernholz, Economic Policies in a Democracy, *Kyklos*, 19 (1966), 48–80;

Peter Bernholz, Dominant Interest Groups and Powerless Parties. *Kyklos* 30 (1977), 411–420.

Political science has a long tradition of studying pressure groups. For this approach in the English context see, for example, the classical study by

Samuel Finer, *The Anonymous Empire. A Study of the Lobby in Great Britain*, 2nd edn. London: Mall Press, 1966.

A newer text useful for factual information is,

W. N. Coxall, *Parties and Pressure Groups*. Harlow: Longman, 1980.

For the United States, a classical political science study is,

E. E. Schattschneider, *The Semi-Sovereign People*. New York: Holt, Rinehart and Winston, 1960.

An analysis of how organizations motivate their members to contribute and what makes some of them successful is given by

James Q. Wilson, *Political Organizations*. New York: Basic Books, 1973.

The exchange of votes, and in particular the vote trading mechanism, is analysed in

Steven J. Brams, *Game Theory and Politics*. New York: Free Press, 1975, Chapter 4.

CHAPTER 8

Allocation

INTRODUCTION

The following three chapters discuss how a social consensus can be attained in the three traditional economic spheres of allocation, income distribution and stabilization. Here it is no longer the decision-making mechanisms that are the focus of attention, but rather particular economic problem areas. By way of example, it is shown what the possibilities are for reaching a social consensus in these areas.

This chapter deals with allocation. Government activity increasingly determines how the resources available to an economy are used. For this reason, individuals and groups at the level of the social consensus will also consider how they can force the government and the public administration to take more notice of the population's preferences when deciding about the supply of goods and services. This goal can be achieved either by electoral constraints (in particular via popular referenda) or by appropriate rules of taxation. In both cases the public budget restriction has to be tightened. Social arrangements can be sought that limit the extent of taxation. Rules can be passed that government expenditures and receipts must balance; that the state has to be content with a narrowly defined tax base only; that taxes may not be regressive; and that taxes may be used for specific expenditures only. The possible arrangements regarding taxation serve only as illustrations of how fundamental rules may be determined in the area of allocation.

8.1 ALLOCATION AND THE PUBLIC SECTOR

The way the resources of a society are used depends heavily on the behaviour of the public sector. The government and the public administration use a number of instruments to influence allocation. Two of the most important are public revenues (taxes) and expenditures. In most industrial economies, these make up more than half of national income, and moreover show a strongly rising trend.

Empirical evidence

Table 8.1 shows the share of government expenditures in national income of Western industrial nations. Tax revenues exhibit a similar share and development. The table illustrates that, for a representative OECD country (one that is in the median with respect to the share of public outlays), the share of public expenditures in national income was about one-third in 1950. This share increased to over 50 per cent in 1974. Over the same period, the expenditures of the country with the lowest share increased from 22 to 29 per cent and of the country with the highest share, from 39 to 64 per cent.

TABLE 8.1   *Median and Range of Public Expenditures as Share of National Income in OECD Countries, 1950–74*

Year	Median	Range
	%	%
1950	31	22–39
1960	38	22–43
1970	48	24–57
1974	52	29–64

Note: The following members of the Organization of Economic Co-operation and Development (OECD) are included in this table: Australia, Belgium, Germany (FR), Denmark, France, Italy, Japan, Canada, Luxemburg, Netherlands, Norway, Austria, Sweden, Switzerland, United Kingdom, United States.

Source: G. Warren Nutter, *Growth of Government in the West.* Washington DC: American Enterprise Institute, 1978, Table 1.

The question arises whether the rapid growth of the share of public expenditures in national income, and therefore the increasing importance of government, reflects the population's wishes or is rather the result of insufficient control of the electorate over government and public administration. Did the population really want such an increase in the government's role in the allocation of resources, or is its growth due largely to autonomous decisions of public institutions which benefit from an increase in the public sector's influence over the economy?

One piece of evidence that suggests that many individuals are dissatisfied with the present mixture of taxation and public supply is the rise of an 'underground', or 'black' hidden economy. Taxpayers seem to feel unjustly burdened and thus have fewer moral qualms about not declaring part or all of their income for tax purposes. In this 'unofficial' sector there can be no tax regulation by the state; it is beyond the realm of government, but also beyond the realm of the rules and institutions established by social consensus. The existence and the growth of an underground sector may thus be interpreted as an indicator of the 'revealed preference' of individuals with respect to the extent of government activity and interference. The underground economy therefore merits special attention.

The underground economy

The undergound sector is defined as that part of the economy where value added is produced in the national income sense but is not contained in the official statistics. Hidden economies as such may encompass legal activities (for example, gardening) or illegal ones (if, say, heroin is produced).

The size of the underground economy is hard to measure because the participants do not declare themselves. There are five approaches to evaluating the size of this sector.

1 Interviews and surveys can be conducted on a voluntary or compliance basis (for example, by tax auditing).
2 A difference between officially declared income and observed expenditures (which are financed by both official and hidden incomes) may be taken as an indicator of underground activities. This approach is applicable at both the individual and the aggregate (national income) level.
3 A low and/or falling official participation rate may indicate that part of the population leaves the official economy and takes up work in the underground sector.
4 The most sophisticated approach looks at the development of monetary magnitudes. One such method assumes that hidden activities are transacted in cash; an increasing currency demand is then taken as an indicator of increasing underground activities. Another monetary approach is based on the quantity equation; an increasing demand for money (given the velocity of its circulation) indicates that total income has increased. The difference between this total and the official income measures the income created in the underground.

5   Yet another approach concentrates on the causes leading to the rise of
an underground economy, in particular the burdens of taxation and
regulation, tax morality and the potential for participation in the hidden
economy (in particular, the length of working time). These various factors are attributed weights (whose values are chosen on the basis of
outside information); this allows a ranking of the size of the underground economy between countries or over time.

TABLE 8.2   *Estimates of the Size of the Underground Economy
(percentage of officially measured GNP)*

Country	Year	Size (relative to official GNP)	Method of estimation	Author and year of study
		%		
United States	1976	6–8	Survey (tax auditing)	Internal Revenue Service (1979)
	1976	8–12	Currency demand	Tanzi (1980)
	1976	10–14	Currency demand	Gutmann (1977)
	1979	33	Money transactions	Feige (1979)
Canada	1978	14	Currency demand	Smith and Mirus (1981)
United Kingdom	1978	2.5–3	Difference between income and expenditure	Macafee (1980)
	1979	7	Difference between income and expenditure	Dilnot and Morris (1981)
Sweden	1978	7–17	Currency demand	Klovland (1980)
Italy	1978	30	Currency demand	Saba (1980)

Source: Bruno S. Frey and Werner W. Pommerehne, Measuring the Hidden
Economy: Though this be Madness, Yet There is Method in it? In Vito Tanzi (ed.),
The Underground Economy in the United States and Abroad. Lexington, Mass: Heath,
1982. The individual contributions are cited in this article.

Table 8.2 collects some estimates of the size of the underground economy in relation to official GNP. It shows that the estimates differ considerably between countries and years. Owing to the differences in method and the implied differences in the object measured, the results also vary for the same country and the same point of time. While, for example, the tax auditing and currency demand methods come to similar results for the United States in the year 1976 (between 6 and 14 per cent of officially measured GNP), the money transactions method yields a much higher estimate. The table also shows that a large underground economy – much above 10 per cent of official GNP – may be expected for Sweden and Italy. Overall, the estimates available suggest that the underground economy today is of considerable size in developed industrial economies.

Decision-makers seeking a social consensus will ask economic policy advisers to suggest rules and institutions that will take the individuals' preferences into account with respect to the allocation of goods and services. Such arrangements would also remove the basic causes and incentives for operating in an underground economy. One approach is to establish electoral constraints upon government, in particular via popular referenda. Such referenda have been used in various American states to limit taxation, California's proposition 13 (June 1978) being the best known. Another possible approach is to set rules of taxation by social contract designed to tighten the public budget constraints.

This chapter discusses some of these rules on taxation. Such rules induce public decision-makers to give greater consideration to citizens' preferences in the field of allocation. Indirectly influencing the behaviour of the government and public administration via rules on taxation, though, will be effective only if the budget is balanced at least in the medium and long run. Otherwise, the public decision-makers would not be restricted by tax revenues because they would finance their expenditures by credits and by printing more money. The approaches discussed here cannot exclude the possibility that the government and public administration increasingly resort to activities *without* major budgetary consequences – to intervention via regulation, for example. The approaches discussed below therefore are only able to restrict some types of public activities.

Three approaches for social rules will be discussed:

1   the tax base is fixed;
2   tax progression is determined;

3   tax receipts are made complementary to those public expendi-
    tures that meet the individuals' wishes.

I do not intend to present here a complete discussion of the rules
and institutions that may serve to force the government and the
public administration to comply with citizens' preferences. Rather, I
shall show by way of illustration how allocative decisions can be
steered by rules established by social consensus.

8.2   FIXING THE TAX BASE

The tax base determines the maximum possible tax revenue and
therefore the maximum level of public expenditure (provided the
budget is balanced). If the tax base is comprehensive, individuals find
it difficult to avoid taxation.

Example

If there is a tax on leisure besides the usual income tax – that is, if the total
capacity for earning income is taxed, an individual cannot avoid taxation
by working less. The maximum possible tax revenue is thus greatly increased.

If taxes are levied on a few specific objects only, it is easy for individuals to avoid taxation. The higher the marginal tax rate on labour
income, the larger will be the incentives to reduce work and to enjoy
untaxed leisure. An increase in the marginal (and therewith average)
tax rate, in this case, does not necessarily lead to higher tax revenue.
This can be seen in Figure 8.1, which shows the relationship between
the tax rate (marginal and average) and tax revenue, given the tax
base. This relationship is often called the 'Laffer curve'. The figure
demonstrates that the tax rate t^* maximizes tax revenue. Below t^*,
an increase in the tax rate raises tax receipts. Above t^*, an increase
in the tax rate reduces tax revenue because the potential taxpayers
increasingly avoid, or illegally evade, taxation.

The form of the Laffer curve depends on various conditions. The
more easily the individuals can avoid taxation, the lower is t^* and
the more rapidly the curve above t^* falls. This applies, for example,
to the taxation of goods that can easily be bought on the black
market.

In the case of many tax objects, however, individuals find it hard
to get around taxation. Often suitable (and less taxed) alternatives

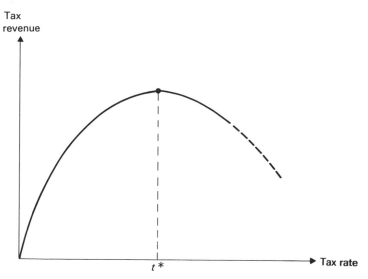

FIGURE 8.1 *Relationship between tax rate and tax revenue (the Laffer curve).*

are not available, or the cost of information is too high to make such behaviour worthwhile. In this case, tax revenue would steadily rise with an increasing tax rate.

If the public decision-makers are assigned a well defined and limited tax base that can be avoided if the individuals so choose, the government and public administration are more strongly controlled: their tax revenue depends more on the individuals' decisions. The rule of taxation shifts the decision power towards the individuals and forces the public decision-makers to take the population's wishes into account. If, on the other hand, the public decision-makers are accorded taxes that the individual cannot avoid, the tax revenue becomes independent of the decisions of the individuals and the public decision-makers receive financial discretionary power against which the individual can do little, as discussed in the previous chapters. Fixing the rules of taxation thus enables the individuals behind the veil of ignorance to influence the course of the day-to-day political and economic process.

Comparison with the traditional theory of taxation

In orthodox public finance, taxes are seen from a different point of view. Government is assumed to use taxes as a means of maximizing social welfare. The economic adviser is asked to develop a tax system that minimizes the distortions due to taxation (that is, the changes in the quantities of factors of production and goods) relative to a situation without taxation.

The theory of democratic economic policy assumes that the public decision-makers (like everybody else) pursue their own goals, and therefore that incentives must be set if the population's wishes are to be met. A comprehensive tax base favours behaviour of public decision-makers that does not take the population's preferences into account. A limited tax base that gives the individuals the chance to avoid taxation leads to a smaller distortion because the public decision-makers have an incentive to observe individuals' preferences.

8.3   DETERMINING TAX PROGRESSIVITY

The behaviour of public decision-makers can also be more closely monitored in the current politico-economic process if a rule is established about the admissible tax progressivity. The discretionary power of the government and public administration is again reduced by tightening the budget restrictions via limiting tax revenues.

Given the tax base (income on work), tax revenue is maximized when taxation of income is regressive. With increasing working time, the marginal utility of leisure rises or the marginal cost of earning income increases. For this reason, individuals will generally not be ready to increase work time if there are constant or increasing tax rates. If, however, the marginal tax rate on the extra income gained falls, there is a compensation: the falling tax burden compensates for the increasing cost of earning income. The government benefits from the higher labour supply by higher tax revenues. In order to prevent such a loosening of the budget restriction, a rule may be established by social consensus that the government may not impose regressive tax rates on high incomes. Such a rule limits the maximum revenues attainable in the current politico-economic process. This discussion presupposes that individuals are sensitive to changes in marginal taxation, in other words, that they make the division of time between work and leisure strongly dependent on taxation.

Existing econometric studies suggest that there are only weak disincentives of taxation on total labour supply with the tax rates presently existing in most industrial countries, except possibly for Britain and the Scandinavian countries. In many countries, it matters much more that, when individuals consider the tax burden to be too high, they supply labour in the hidden or underground economy, as was pointed out above. A high tax progression thus does not so much decrease the total supply of labour as shift the supply away from the official, taxed economy into the untaxed, underground economy. A social contract that constrains the tax activity of the public decision-makers through extending the possibilities and incentives of individuals to evade taxation (in the case here discussed, by not allowing regressive tax rates) runs the danger of creating an anarchical sector in society. Individuals are induced to switch to a sector outside all public rules in order to restrain government. The decision-makers at the level of the social consensus must balance the advantage of better control of the government and the public administration with the disadvantage of having an anarchical sector in which no collectively sanctioned rules exist.

8.4 COMPLEMENTARITY OF RECEIPTS AND EXPENDITURES

In daily politics, the government as well as the public administration can be assumed to pursue their own utility within the constraints imposed from the outside. The public employees, for example, will try to use as large a share of tax receipts as possible for their own purposes by granting themselves high salaries and all sorts of social security benefits and attractive working conditions (expensive buildings, nice offices, impressive chauffeur-driven cars and so on). As explained in previous chapters, there are several reasons why the individuals as voters and taxpayers do not have the information and incentives to prevent this. They are forced to tolerate the unnecessary outlays of government and public administrators as a side cost of the provision of public services. Do social contracts exist that induce public decision-makers to use a larger share of the tax receipts for the purpose of fulfilling the population's preferences?

Government and public officials will have positive incentives to observe individuals' preferences if they can simultaneously increase their own utility by increasing the population's utility. Such a coupling may be achieved if tax income and the goods desired by the population are complementary. If the public decision-makers supply those goods and services that the individuals desire, a rule must be set so that the tax base and tax receipts thereby increase. Government and public officials can, under such terms, extend their discretionary power only if they perform according to the wishes of the population. This rule, established by social consensus, has the purpose of making the interests of political suppliers and individual demanders consonant. The behaviour of the government and public administrators will be influenced by making it advantageous for them to take the individuals' wishes into account when using public revenues.

On the basis of these considerations, rules finding a social consensus can be derived. If tax receipts are earmarked – if there is a specific tax base allocated to each expenditure category – public outlays and public revenues become complementary. This presupposes, however, that for each expenditure category there is an unequivocal complementary tax base. If, on the other hand, tax revenues grow more or less autonomously, earmarking taxes for given expenditure categories may lead to unnecessary public outlays because the tax revenues may not be used for other purposes. The complementarity rule suggested leads to a positive incentive for government and public administration to fulfil individuals' preferences only if the tax revenues directly depend on the corresponding public good supply. The economic policy advisers will therefore suggest earmarked taxes only in those areas in which the required complementarity between revenues and expenditures is empirically well established.

Examples

The required complementarity applies, for example, in the following cases:

— the construction and maintenance of roads is financed by taxes on petrol and motor cars. If there are few and bad roads, there will – *ceteris paribus* – be less car traffic. If the public decision-makers expend money to improve roads that the individuals wish to use, there will be more traffic, thus increasing tax revenues.
— public radio and television can be financed according to how often the respective channels are used by the population. If a station is popular, that is, if the programmes meet the population's wishes, the station will have higher revenues.

An orientation of the tax system in the direction of complementarity between tax revenue and public services is closely related to charges and the equivalence principle. In the case of charges, the users pay for a specific public service; in other words, the supply by public decision-makers and the revenues they receive are completely complementary.

CONCLUSION

This chapter has dealt with the problem of what rules can be found to induce the government and the civil service to allocate resources according to the wishes of individuals. The existence and growth of underground economies is one indicator that the population is dissatisfied with the existing combination of public expenditures and taxes, as well as with other policies undertaken by political suppliers. It is shown that various rules exist that may contribute to the foundation of public policies that are in better accord with people's preferences. The rules that focus on taxation do, however, contribute only partly to this goal, because the government and the public administration may in response resort to more intensive regulatory actions to reach their goals. The rules discussed must therefore be seen in conjunction with other rules designed to force political suppliers to take greater notice of the population's preferences.

FURTHER READING

Various methods of estimating empirically the size of the underground economy are contained in

Vito Tanzi (ed.), *The Underground Economy in the United States and Abroad*. Lexington, Mass: Heath, 1982.

This volume contains examples for most of the methods mentioned in the text, in particular those based on the development of currency demand.

Electoral restrictions on the government and the public administration via referenda are discussed in

Helen F. Ladd and T. Nicholas Tideman (eds), *Tax and Expenditure Limitations*. Papers on Public Economics, vol. 5. Washington, DC: Urban Institute Press, 1981.

The discussion of the three non-electoral constraints on public decision-makers via taxation is based on

Geoffrey Brennan and James M. Buchanan, *The Power to Tax. Analytical Foundation of a Fiscal Constitution*. Cambridge: University Press, 1980.

The properties of the Laffer curve are discussed in

Arthur B. Laffer and Jan P. Seymour, *The Economics of the Tax Revolt: A Reader*. New York: Harcourt, Brace, Jovanovich, 1979.

Evidence that, at least in Sweden, a reduction of the tax rate may increase tax revenue is presented by

Charles E. Stuart, Swedish Tax Rates, Labor Supply and Tax Revenues. *Journal of Political Economy*, 89 (1981), 1028–38.

CHAPTER 9

Income Distribution

INTRODUCTION

There are many possibilities for introducing fundamental rules in the area of income distribution. These allow individuals and groups to assure themselves against bad luck and the aggressive behaviour of others.

Income distribution may be influenced on the income side by fixing minimum wages, and on the expenditure side by controlling prices. Both measures have turned out to be not very effective. Old age pensions can be looked at as intergenerational contracts; parts of the social security system may be interpreted in a similar way. Other rules concern the supply of public goods and services, in particular in the areas of education and health. The analysis shows, however, that in the current political process these approaches are not well suited to reaching the goals aimed at. More effective are a negative income tax and a property formation policy.

9.1 SOCIAL CONSENSUS AND REDISTRIBUTION

Individuals will always feel uncertain about their future income: they cannot exclude the possibility that it will fall – say, because of an accident – or that it will be greatly increased – perhaps by winning the pools. Groups of individuals are in the same position – members of certain occupations, for example, or inhabitants of certain economic regions. Insecurity can be caused by a great number of factors. Prospects of major change may be due to politics (wars, revolutions), to economics (recessions or crises, inflation, structural changes), to technological innovations, to natural catastrophes (earthquakes, floods) or to chance (accidents, lottery winnings). This uncertainty about the future can only partly be insured against by private insurance contracts, so risk-averse individuals and groups aim at insuring themselves against an unfavourable future income position by *collective action*.

People cannot ensure that they or their descendants will not be disadvantaged at some point in the future. To make sure of not falling into extreme poverty, they can agree that the poor will be supported by the better off sections of the population.

Economic advisers may try to bring about a social consensus on the 'maximin principle'. This principle first identifies that group of individuals which in all imaginable states of society has the lowest income (or more generally: the lowest utility level). Second, that state is chosen in which this *mini*mal income is *maxi*mized (maximin).

The properties of the maximin principle with respect to income distribution can be illustrated with the help of a numerical example.

Example

In a society the three economic states of the world, considered possible are shown in Table 9.1. According to the maximin principle, state B should be chosen because the poorest group of individuals (with 15 money or utility units) is better off there than in the other states. Following this principle, it does not matter that overall national income in state B is smaller than in states A and C, that the middle-income recipients have less in B than in A and C, and that the rich receive more in B than in A and C. This numerical

TABLE 9.1 *Hypothetical Social States and Income Distribution*

	Social states (the numbers indicate money or utility units)		
	A	*B*	*C*
Size of national income	200	180	220
Distribution of population:			
Richest 10%	30	37	25
Middle 80%	165	128	185
Poorest 10%	5	15	10

example shows that the application of the maximin principle may have doubtful consequences and that the individuals behind the veil of ignorance will not necessarily reach an agreement on it.

The maximin principle can be graphically compared with other welfare criteria – *egalitarian distribution* and the *potential Pareto optimum.*

Graphical Illustration

In Figure 9.1 two individuals are distinguished; the utility of individual I is represented on one axis, the utility of individual II on the other. The curve *NN* shows the utility frontier that can be maximally reached by the two individuals. The position and curvature is determined by the production possibilities in the economy considered. In the section in which the slope of *NN* is negative, the (maximum) welfare of one individual can be improved only if the other's (maximum) welfare is decreased. In the section in which the slope of *NN* is positive, incentive effects are prevalant: when individual II's utility is increased, so does the utility of individual I.

E shows the point of egalitarian distribution: both individuals reach the same level of utility. At point *M* the maximin principle is fulfilled, because the poorer individual I reaches his maximum utility. This point *M* lies on a

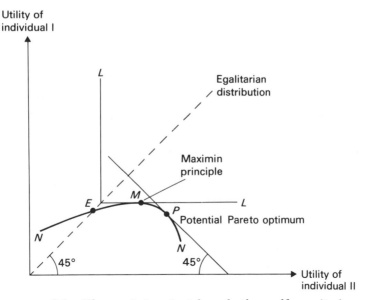

FIGURE 9.1   *The maximin principle and other welfare criteria.*

right-angled, lexicographic social indifference curve *LL*. At point *P* the *sum* of the utilities of the two individuals is maximized. The potential Pareto principle is fulfilled because no changes are feasible by which the gainers could compensate the losses.

Individuals may also reach a consensus about the desirable income distribution because a distribution considered 'unjust' can promote crime and can lead to social unrest and revolutions. One may have a personal interest that the income distribution currently taking place is not too unequal, in order to protect one's possibly high future income. A collective rule is required because an income distribution favouring social stabilization is a public good that an individual income recipient will not and cannot supply.

The following sections deal with various elements of a social consensus that can change the income distribution occurring in the current socioeconomic process. Sections 9.2 and 9.3 deal with intervention in the price structure (minimum wage, individual price controls); Section 9.4 discusses the intergenerational contract (old age pensions); and Section 9.5 deals with the public supply of goods and services for distributional purposes. The concluding two sections introduce the concepts of negative income tax and a property-creating policy.

9.2 MINIMUM WAGE

The minimum wage refers to *all* components of the wage income of the lowest group of workers. This effective wage comprises the implicit value of all sorts of protection (such as job security) and benefits (such as holidays and fewer working hours per week).

The minimum wage rate fixed by the government is intended to improve the position of those workers with the lowest income. The question is whether this goal is indeed reached by the institution of a minimum wage.

The consequences of the imposition of a minimum wage rate can be analysed by considering the market for labour, as shown in Figure 9.2. The figure shows that:

— the wage rate for those still employed rises above the market wage rate (W_0 increases to W_{min});

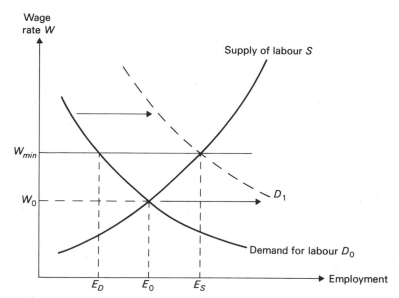

FIGURE 9.2   *Effect of the minimum wage on employment: circular flow effects on the demand for labour.*

— the number of employed falls from E_0 to E_D;
— the number of people seeking employment rises from E_0 to E_S;
— unemployment rises $(E_S - E_D)$.

These results of the partial (or single-market) analysis are relevant only if the minimum wage is restricted to a small sector of the economy. Usually, however, the minimum wage applies to large sectors or even to the whole economy. In this case, the repercussions throughout the circular flow of income must be taken into account. With an inelastic demand for labour, the imposition of a minimum wage rate increases the total wage sum. Moreover, a well-developed public support programme for unemployed workers increases the disposable income. In addition, increasing unemployment is likely to change the economic policy undertaken by government in the current politico-economic process. As mentioned above, a democratically elected government generally seeks to avoid unemployment in order not to endanger re-election.

These circular flow effects and the change in economic policy will increase the demand for labour. In Figure 9.2 the demand curve for labour shifts from D_0 to D_1, provided that the expansionary policy is undertaken in such a way as to re-establish full employment, and assuming that such a policy is feasible.

The introduction of a minimum wage is likely to hit those groups hardest that have the lowest labour productivity. Employers no longer find it worthwhile to hire them. In Europe and the United States, foreigners, non-whites, women and juveniles are the primary victims of minimum wage legislation. This effect has been shown in a great many econometric studies.

Empirical Evidence

The influence of minimum wages on the employment of various groups of workers has been analysed for the United States with monthly data for the period 1954–68. With the help of multiple regression, the influence of the general level of unemployment is kept constant. The minimum wage is defined relative to the general level of the wage rate ('standardized minimum wage'). The results of the regression analysis are shown in Table 9.2. The table shows that the standardized minimum wage has a significant effect on the unemployment rate of juveniles: the rate of unemployment for the age range 16–19 increases sharply (see the statistically significant parameter in column 2), with women being more strongly affected than men. The minimum wage does not, however, raise unemployment among the male adult workers (age 19–24) years. This group, on the other hand, is affected by the general level of unemployment (see the significant parameter of 1·8*), while the juveniles are not. This econometric study confirms that

TABLE 9.2   *Influence of the Minimum Wage Rate on Unemployment. United States, 1954–68 (regression coefficients)*

Dependent variable Unemployment rate	General unemployment rate (1)	Standardized minimum wage (as proportion of hourly earnings) (2)	$\bar{R}^2$ (3)
	Explanatory variables		
Females 16–19 years	0.5	86.7*	0.70
Males 16–19 years	1.5	68.6*	0.76
Males 20–24 years	1.8*	0.2	0.92

* Significantly different from zero at the 1% level.

Source: Thomas G. Moore, The Effect of Minimum Wages on Teenager Unemployment Rates, *Journal of Political Economy* 79 (1971), Table 1 (excerpt).

the groups with the lowest productivity and income – in our case juveniles and women – are most strongly burdened by a minimum wage.

The theoretical and empirical analyses suggest that:

— the overall effect of the minimum wage on employment is negligible;
— the minimum wage raises the unemployment among the *lowest-income recipients*.

The minimum wage is thus an inadequate instrument with which to reach the declared goal of improving the position of the economically poorest groups. The economic advisers can seek to bring about a social consensus on more effective instruments to change the income distribution in the current socioeconomic process in the direction desired by the individuals.

9.3 SPECIFIC PRICE CONTROLS

Income distribution can be influenced on the expenditure side by controlling specific prices. The prices of certain goods are fixed below the equilibrium price so that the poorer members of society can purchase more goods and services with their income.

Example

The application of individual price controls is very old. The Roman emperor Diocletian ruled in AD 301 that the maximum prices for almost all goods be fixed. Today we find publicly fixed prices particularly for so-called 'basic needs', among which the most important are foodstuffs (especially bread and milk), accommodation, transport (especially the prices of public means of transport), and credit (the fixing of maximum levels of interest).

It needs to be established whether and how specific price controls influence income distribution. Do they really benefit the lowest income recipients?

The main arguments raised in favour of price controls are rather obvious:

1 the immediate and assured effect;
2 'justice';
3 the need to intervene if the price system functions imperfectly.

The main arguments against price controls are as follows.

1   The functioning of the price system is impeded and the resulting distortions lead to high social cost. On the supply side, investment in sectors not subject to price controls becomes relatively more attractive, which tends to increase supply. On the other hand, the supply of goods in the controlled sector tends to fall. As the price control serves mainly to hold down the prices of goods consumed by the poor, expensive goods usually remain uncontrolled. In these categories the supply increases; in the case of rent-controlled property, a greater number of more expensive, non-controlled, flats and houses will be offered. On the supply side, therefore, there is a switch from the supply of goods of lower quality (which are therefore cheap, and subject to rent control), to more expensive goods of higher quality – to the disadvantage of lower-income recipients. On the demand side, the demand for the goods with controlled prices will be higher than the supply, as their prices are fixed below the equilibrium. The excess demand must be rationed by some mechanism, which may lead to high administrative costs and to discrimination in other forms.

2   The government can do little to mitigate the bad effects of price controls. The excess demand in the markets for controlled goods makes it profitable to get around the individual price controls. Black markets are likely to arise, because both suppliers and demanders are ready to undertake illegal transactions. If, for example, rents on housing are controlled, one must usually make a high payment when receiving the keys. Another way of evading individual price controls is by reducing the quality of the goods.

3   The rationing of demand in those areas with price controls is often arbitrary or ethically unacceptable. New criteria are often introduced; for example, one discriminates according to race and political views. When public administrations ration, one should not assume that the public employees involved act like 'benevolent dictators'.

4   Specific price controls are not an effective instrument for reaching the desired distributional goals. The low prices of controlled products also benefit, directly or indirectly (through the increased supply of higher quality products), the rich. On the other hand, not all the poor can benefit from price controls because, owing to the

restricted supply, they are not able to get hold of the controlled products.

The advisers can make it clear that individual price controls are rarely able to improve the position of the low-income recipients, and may even worsen it. The supply of the goods of inexpensive categories tends to be reduced, and it is by no means certain that the poor are privileged by rationing. Individual price controls are an ill-suited instrument to influence income distribution in the current social process to the benefit of the low-income groups.

9.4 REDISTRIBUTION BETWEEN AND WITHIN GENERATIONS: OLD AGE PENSIONS AND SOCIAL SECURITY

The intergenerational distribution has for a long time been the subject of a social consensus: the working population supports the no-longer-working population. There is an implicit or explicit contract that the present working generation will later be supported by the succeeding generation. It is a contract advantageous for all generations so that a consensus is possible.

Old age pensions have attained a considerable magnitude in industrial countries.

Empirical evidence

In many Western industrial countries, old age incomes arising out of pensions from the state and from firms almost reach the level of the net wage income before retirement. Table 9.3 shows that an average income recipient in Sweden, Switzerland and Austria receives more than 90 per cent of his last net income. For the Federal Republic of Germany and the Anglo-Saxon countries this share is only a little smaller – above 70 per cent, except for Canada with 62 per cent.

There is a similar consensus with respect to social security, which relates to income distribution within a generation. The working population pays for those not employed owing to illness, disablement or accident. The social security benefits in industrial countries today cover a high share of past net work income.

TABLE 9.3 *Retirement Income of a Married Couple, compared with average Income before Retirement: Various Countries, 1976*

Country	Retirement income as a percentage of last work income, net of taxes and social security contributions
	%
Sweden	132
Switzerland	96
Austria*	91
Federal Republic of Germany*	84
United Kingdom	82
United States*	71
Canada*	62

* Countries in which the retirement benefits of a company-provided pension scheme are not included (criteria: less than half of the employees are members of a company-provided pension scheme).

Source: Union Bank of Switzerland, *Social Security in Ten Industrial Nations.* Zurich, April 1977, Table 2 (selection).

TABLE 9.4 *Invalidity Income of a Family with Three Children if the Husband is Fully Disabled: Various Countries, 1976*

Country	Invalidity income as a percentage of previous income, net of taxes and social security contributions: Due to illness	Due to accident
	%	%
Sweden	135	137
United Kingdom	115	166
Switzerland	110	110
Federal Republic of Germany	97	134
United States	93	93
Austria	78	173
Canada	74	110

Source: Union Bank of Switzerland, *Social Security in Ten Industrial Nations.* Zurich, April 1977, Table 5 (selection).

Empirical evidence

Table 9.4 shows that in Sweden, the United Kingdom and Switzerland social security benefits in case of illness are higher than the work income received before, after deduction of taxes and social security contributions. For the other countries shown in the table, the share is above 90 per cent, except for Austria and Canada. The situation is even more favourable in the case of an accident: in all countries the social security benefits exceed 100 per cent of the net last work income except for the United States, where it is 93 per cent.

The great achievements of public old age pensions and social security schemes are obvious and need not be stressed here. But there are two problems of the social security system that are likely to become more important in the future.

Doubtful Distributional Consequences

A public old age pension does not necessarily redistribute income in the direction of the low-income groups:

— old age is *not* identical with poverty. The public old age pension is ineffective from the point of view of redistribution because the high-income recipients normally also get an old age pension;
— on the average, the rich live longer than the poor. This tends to redistribute income in favour of the high-income recipients, who benefit longer from the pensions paid out.

Heavy Burden on the Working Generation

The public old age pensions have continually increased in recent decades. In many countries they are connected with the rate of growth in the economy ('dynamic rents'). This means that the working generation has been increasingly burdened by social security contributions as well as by taxes. Figure 9.3 shows the rise in the share of social security contributions as a percentage of national income between 1960 and 1978/79. As can be seen from this figure, in all the countries shown the burden imposed on the working population in the form of social security contributions has increased rapidly. The rise is most dramatic in Sweden (an increase of almost 12

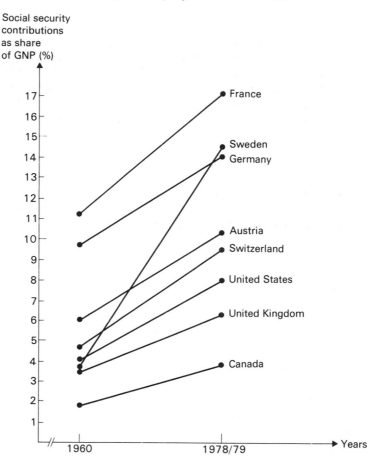

FIGURE 9.3 *The increasing burden of social security contributions as a percentage of GNP for various countries, 1970–78/79.*
Source: OECD, National Accounts Statistics of OECD Countries. Paris, various years.

percentage points over the period 1960–78); in France and Switzerland it is around 5 percentage points. In the United States the rise is smaller, somewhat below 4 percentage points, and in the United Kingdom it is somewhat below 3 percentage points.

If the burden on the working population continues to increase, two reactions must be expected:

— an *individual* adjustment on the part of the working population, who may switch to the untaxed underground economy or may reduce labour input and enjoy more leisure.

— a *collective* adjustment involving a breaking of the intergenerational contract because it is considered to be overly burdensome. If a new consensus is reached, the working generation will pay smaller contributions, and the social security benefits will also be smaller.

Today, there is certainly a consensus that the social security system should provide a floor for the poorest members of society. Economic policy advisers can be of help in giving thought to the conditions presently attained. They can suggest alternative ways of redistributing income in the current social process which are capable of coping with the changed conditions of social security.

9.5 PUBLIC SUPPLY OF GOODS AND SERVICES

Income distribution can be influenced if the government and the public administration provide for the supply of particular public goods free of charge (or at a reduced price). The most important of these goods are in the area of education and health.

Education

In all civilized countries citizens agree that the state should guarantee the population a minimum education. Such a basic education is advantageous to all because positive external effects are created. Lively democratic institutions require that the citizens be able to deal with political problems and, if they wish, to press their demands. Such activities require a minimum degree of formal education which is achieved by requiring that children attend school. Basic education is accordingly free of charge. The opportunity cost of school attendance can be compensated by granting scholarships and credits which must be paid back out of increased future income.

Such a social consensus on the public provision of education will not however lead to large distributional consequences, because the supply is not restricted to the poor but is available to all income groups.

Health Service

In a modern 'welfare state' individuals agree that the government has a special responsibility for the health of the population. Those who are ill should be supported by the rest of the society because illness is a misfortune that can hit anyone. An adequate provision of health services can be secured in various ways. Health insurance in the context of the public social security system, which guarantees everyone treatment largely free of charge in the case of illness or accident, has already been discussed. The direct public supply of health services is also of great importance. The government runs hospitals and other health institutions and charges prices that are lower than cost. Moreover, private health institutions are subsidized.

The public health policy has at least secured a minimum health standard of the population and has in particular prevented the outbreak of major epidemics (such as pestilence or smallpox). The growth of the public health system has, however, some disadvantages. The services only partly benefit the poor. To a considerable degree, upper-income recipients also benefit, so expenditure on health services is not a very effective means of redistributing income. In addition, inefficiencies have arisen in the health sector, leading to a *cost explosion*:

— the individual demand for health services is too high compared with the cost created because the public health system can to a large extent be used free of charge ('moral hazard');
— on the supply side, there are few incentives for reducing cost: the public hospitals are usually organized bureaucratically; the employees are not rewarded when they use the resources economically; the health personnel, in particular the doctors, have an incentive to use expensive appliances and medical drugs because in this way they can demonstrate their professional competence.

The existing system of publicly provided health services requires high financial contributions by the taxpayers but is not very effective in influencing income distribution. The rising financial burden may lead to a one-sided breakdown of the social consensus.

Economic advisers can suggest new possibilities for guaranteeing an adequate health standard. They can show under what circumstances the public production of health services can be given up and private competition admitted. They can check whether a consensus can be reached that a collective health insurance (with no retention) can also guarantee the desired level of health. The lowest-income groups could possibly be insured free of charge.

9.6 NEGATIVE INCOME TAX

Some of the measures for income redistribution discussed so far can be overcome by introducing a negative income tax. In this system, every individual whose income is below a politically determined level would automatically receive a public transfer which can be interpreted as a negative tax. The negative income tax system is often called 'guaranteed income', because it ensures that the lowest-income recipients receive a minimal income.

The functioning of the negative income tax is best shown with the help of an example.

Example

Table 9.5 shows the relationship between wage income, negative or positive taxes and the income disposable after redistribution. A person who has no income from work receives a transfer of 2000 monetary units. With an

TABLE 9.5 *Numerical Example of a Negative Income System*

Income from work	Tax	After-tax (net) income
	(monetary units)	
0	− 2000	2000
500	− 1750	2250
1000	− 1500	2500
1500	− 1250	2750
2000	− 1000	3000
2500	− 750	3250
3000	− 500	3500
3500	− 250	3750
4000	0	4000
4500	100	4400
5000	200	4800
5500	300	5200

income of 500 monetary units, the negative tax is only 1750 monetary units and the income after tax rises to 2250 monetary units. If labour income is 1000 monetary units, the negative tax is reduced to 1500 monetary units, and after tax income rises to 2500 monetary units. What matters is that, when income from work rises by 500 monetary units, the public support is not reduced by the same amount (which would imply a marginal tax rate of 100 per cent) but only by the smaller amount of 250 monetary units. The implicit marginal tax rate in the range of negative taxes is in our example only 50 per cent.

When income from work reaches 4000 monetary units, public support stops. With higher income a positive tax must be payed (the example assumes a marginal positive tax rate of 20 per cent).

A system of negative taxes is characterized by three parameters:

1   minimum income, i.e. the negative tax when work income is zero;
2   income when taxes are zero ('break-even point');
3   the marginal tax rate.

Only two parameters need be fixed; the third parameter follows by definition. These parameters determine the budgetary costs of income redistribution.

The negative income tax has a number of important advantages compared with other approaches to income redistribution.

1   Poverty in the form of low income is directly attacked by the public redistributive measures. The approaches so far discussed all use other criteria, such as old age or health. Because of its direct approach, the negative income tax is able to guarantee effectively an adequate material living standard for the poorest strata of society.

2   Administrative expenses are low. The negative income tax can replace a number of other social programmes. Nobody is required to decide who is 'needy' and who 'merits' public support. In a negative income tax system everyone with a low income automatically receives a transfer in the same way as everyone earning a higher income has to pay taxes. No new institution is required; the existing tax authorities can operate the negative income tax.

3   Work incentives are affected less, because the negative income tax implies a marginal tax rate of less than 100 per cent. This marginal tax rate should be compared with the practice existing today: for a recipient of social security benefits who makes an effort to earn more by working, public support is, as a rule, reduced by the same

amount. The income earned by one's own effort is thus taxed at 100 per cent: the lowest-income recipients are those who have to pay the highest marginal tax rates.

The negative income tax does however have some *disadvantages*.

1 It may be argued that the low-income recipients spend the monetary support received for the 'wrong' purposes, for example to buy alcohol or cigarettes. A 'wrong' use of the money received cannot, however, contrary to general opinion, necessarily be prevented by transfers in kind. The goods transferred can be sold on a black market or be substituted by reducing the outlays already made for these kinds of goods.

2 The negative income tax system (as well as many support programmes in terms of goods) does not attack the underlying causes of poverty. No account is taken of why somebody is poor, and therefore no effort is made to help these people to overcome the causes. It is, however, quite difficult to establish the true causes of poverty and to do anything about it within the framework of traditional social work.

The negative income tax system thus has positive and negative aspects – as has every other public intervention. Introducing negative income taxes requires a social consensus because it involves a fundamental socio-political decision. It seems feasible that individuals and groups agree on it behind the veil of ignorance, because this system is capable of effectively bringing about a redistribution of income and of protecting individuals against insufficient income. The principle is new and therefore seems to be 'utopian' in political discussions. Nevertheless, political advisers may introduce such new concepts into the discussion and may consider how to find agreement on it.

9.7 PROPERTY FORMATION POLICY

A redistribution of property in the current social process may be undertaken for various reasons.

1 Property may serve as a means of protecting the economic standard of living. This aspect is of little importance today because this goal can be reached more effectively by other instruments, in particular by the negative income tax.

2   Differences in property can be considered to be one of the principal reasons for differences in income between individuals. A redistribution of property can influence income distribution in three ways:

— property results in additional income from capital;
— the bargaining power of workers is increased if they can resort to income from their property in case of a conflict with employers;
— a rise in the savings rate of workers not only leads to increased property-holding in their hands, but, owing to the circular flow effect, also increases the wage share in national income.

3   A larger share of property in the hands of the workers results in 'people's capitalism'. The confrontation between 'workers' and 'capitalists' is reduced because the interests of both are now, at least partially, parallel. The politico-economic system becomes more stable, which is advantageous for all its members.

Property can be redistributed by expropriating owners and giving it to other individuals. Such a violation of private property is likely to have negative effects on savings, on capital accumulation, and therewith on economic growth. Most plans for 'people's capitalism' therefore seek to influence the distribution of newly formed property by raising the rate of savings among workers. This can be achieved by:

1   *voluntary saving*: individuals will consume a smaller share of their income if their saving capacity is raised (by increasing their income), or if they are given an incentive to save more out of a given income;

2   *coercive saving*: in the case of an 'investive wage', part of the wage sum (in the case of 'investive profit participation', part of the profits) is retained by collective agreement. Individuals can try to avoid coercive savings by substituting. The previous level of voluntary savings can accordingly be reduced so that the total amount of savings stays constant. Individuals who previously did not save can also avoid an increase in savings by borrowing money on the basis of the coercively accumulated property.

The capital accumulated by the saving policy can be invested in the firms in which the workers are employed. The money stays in the sector in which the wage income and property has arisen. Such an investment can result in a comparatively small rate of return if the sector is not profitable. The accumulated savings can also be invested in a national fund. If a saving policy is successful, a large centralized property is created within a short time. The institution deciding upon the use of this fund will have considerable power. Economic policy advisers should point out this consequence and suggest rules that control this accumulation of power.

A social consensus among individuals and groups to propagate the creation of property among broad sections of the population seems possible. This decision must be taken by overall agreement, because problems of public 'goods' and therefore free-riding arise which may endanger the success of a property-formation policy. Economic advisers can suggest to the decision-makers ways of reaching a social consensus about how to increase workers' savings most effectively. Neither plans for voluntary nor for coercive savings are certain to reach their goals. A public savings policy can also be successful indirectly by teaching low-income recipients the 'virtue' of saving.

CONCLUSION

Today, the existing social consensus on various aspects of income distribution seems to have been called into question. The present system of minimum wages, price controls, and in particular social security is a rather ineffective way of changing income distribution, and imposes increasingly heavy burdens on a part of the population that may be unwilling to stick to the social consensus. Alternative rules for effecting income distribution, avoiding some of the disadvantages of the existing systems such as the negative income tax and property formation, are available and may find a social consensus in the future.

FURTHER READING

General theoretical and empirical problems of measuring distribution are discussed in

Amartya Sen, *On Economic Inequality*. London: Clarendon, 1973.

The 'maximin principle' or 'distributive justice' (difference principle) has been developed by John Rawls whose book is quoted in Chapter 2.

The protection motive for and other aspects of redistribution are discussed in

Geoffrey Brennan, Pareto-Desirable Redistribution: The Non-altruistic Dimension, *Public Choice*, 14 (1973), 43–67.

Various applications of principles of justice to economic policy, in particular to taxation, are collected in

Edmund S. Phelps (ed.), *Economic Justice. Selected Readings*. Harmondsworth: Penguin, 1973.

The effects of minimum wages on employment are analysed by

George J. Stigler, The Economics of the Minimum Wage Legislation, *American Economic Review*, 6 (1946), 358–65;

A more recent empirical investigation is

Jacob Mincer, Unemployment Effects of Minimum Wages, *Journal of Political Economy*, 84 (1976), 87–104.

The effects of controlling specific prices are discussed and exemplified in textbooks on price theory, for example in

Jack Hirshleifer, *Price Theory and Applications*. Hemel Hempstead: Prentice-Hall, 1976.

A recent event is presented in

Stephen Chapman, The Gas Line of '79, *Public Interest*, 60 (1980), 40–9.

General economic analyses of social policy and redistribution in industrial societies are included in

Anthony J. Culyer, *The Economics of Social Policy*. Oxford: Martin Robertson, 1973;

Kenneth E. Boulding and Martin Pfaff (eds), *Redistribution to the Rich and the Poor*. Belmont, California: Wadsworth, 1972;

Dudley Johnson, *Poverty*. London: Macmillan, 1972.

The relationship between education and distribution are discussed with opposing views by

Christopher Jencks, *Inequality*. New York: Basic Books, 1972;

Richard Layard, Education versus Cash Redistribution: The Lifetime Context, *Journal of Public Economics*, 12 (1979), 377–86.

Current problems of health services are surveyed by

Victor R. Fuchs, The Economics of Health in a Post-Industrial Society, *Public Interest*, 56 (1979), 3–20.

The possibilities and problems of the negative income tax are discussed, for example, by

Jonathan R. Kesselmann, A Comprehensive Approach to Income Maintenance: SWIFFT, *Journal of Public Economics*, 2 (1973), 59–88;

Joseph A. Pechman and P. Michael Timpane (eds), *Work Incentives and Income Guarantees*. Washington DC: Brookings Institution, 1975.

The property formation policy has been influenced strongly by Kaldor's theory of income distribution, originally set out in

Nicholas Kaldor, Alternative Theories of Distribution, *Review of Economic Studies*, 23 (1956), 83–100.

New developments of this theory and its relevance for property redistribution policy are discussed in

Twenty-Five Years Kaldorian Theory of Distribution, *Kyklos*, 34 (1981), (in particular the article by Gottfried Bombach).

The basic problems of property and income distribution are excellently treated in

James M. Meade, *Efficiency, Equality and the Ownership of Property*. London: Allen & Unwin, 1964.

CHAPTER 10

Stabilization

INTRODUCTION

It is possible for the stabilization of prices and employment to be furthered through social consensus.

Rises in prices can be dampened if a consensus can be reached about an incomes policy. The actors, in particular the trade unions and big business, are largely autonomous in the current political process; the government cannot force them to forgo wage claims and price rises that threaten stability. In the state of uncertainty, however, individuals and groups may *ex ante* arrive at a consensus on income distribution which allows them to avoid the high social cost of distribution conflicts.

The price level can also be stabilized by controlling the supply of money. The money supply either can be made independent of the current politico-economic process and controlled by an autonomous central bank, or can be left to the competition of a sufficiently large number of monetary institutions (banks).

To secure full employment, social arrangements may be implemented that serve to increase the flexibility of the labour market, to distribute the work among more people, and to increase the number of jobs offered in the economy.

Both the price level and employment level can be stabilized by monetary incentives, for example by taxing price increases or subsidizing the employment of additional workers.

10.1 STABILIZATION OF THE PRICE LEVEL

Social Consensus on Price Stabilization

Conflict over the distribution of income is one of the basic causes of inflation. The aggregate monetary demands of the various social groups are larger than the national product available. Inflation may thus be seen as a means of making demand and supply compatible; in other words, it is a 'social mollifier'. The employers often find that the easiest solution of an industrial conflict is to grant the wage demands and to impose the cost on to their customers through price increases. The same applies to the government: it can 'solve' many conflicts by increasing public expenditures and granting tax reductions. The resulting price increases will occur only in the future; the politicians in power are little affected, if at all.

An increase of the price level constitutes a 'public bad'. All consumers are burdened by higher prices. No group is ready, however, to give up its income claims because each of them has to bear only a small part of the resulting price increases. For this reason, there is no contradiction between the cries for price stability on the one hand and the lack of readiness to agree to the necessary reductions in income claims on the other.

Empirical studies find, with few exceptions, that the costs associated with inflation are small compared with those of unemployment. Inflation has little effect on income distribution, particularly if the individuals and groups foresee and adjust to the price rises. Though the social cost of inflation is seen to be rather small, however, the population considers price stability to be important. This is visible, for example, in the econometrically estimated *popularity functions* as discussed in the first chapter of this book. Individuals are uncertain about the speed of future inflation (whether it will be creeping or galloping) and its distributional consequences. They realize that inflation must be combated by *collective agreement*, because only if all major social groups participate in the stabilization policy will it be effective.

An *incomes policy* arises out of a social consensus on how to fight inflation. The arrangements made between the various groups are, indeed, referred to as a 'social contract' in some countries. In addition to incomes policy, there are a number of more recent proposals for a wage and price policy which endeavour to hold down price rises through positive and negative incentives. One is the *tax incomes policy*; other proposals concern the *supply of money*.

Incomes Policy

This type of anti-inflation policy is based on two fundamental ideas.

1   Inflation is seen as the result of a conflict over the distribution of income.

Remark

This view does not necessarily contradict traditional theories of inflation. In particular, it is compatible with the monetarist view of the economy, according to which inflation is always caused by an over-extension of the money supply. The incomes policy approach, however, goes one step further than that of the monetarists. The supply of money is not seen as the ultimate reason for price rises; rather, it is the fight over income distribution that has an influence on the supply of money. If the trade unions demand excessive wage rises, for example, employers will attempt to shift the increased cost on to prices. The policy-makers can decide either to hold the money supply constant and to tolerate increased inflation (at least for an intermediate period), or to increase the money supply to prevent unemployment. In the latter case the price increases can be maintained by the producers because the aggregate monetary demand has grown.

2   Interest groups – in particular trade unions – are taken as an integral part of modern society. They are officially included in policy-making.

In all variants of incomes policy, a maximum increase of wages (and of other income) is fixed. Such guidelines usually take future productivity increases of labour into account. If the economy-wide average wage rate rises at the same pace as average real labour productivity, unit labour costs stay constant. The producers are then able to supply at constant prices, provided that their mark-up (on unit labour cost) is unchanged. In this case income distribution between 'labour' and 'capital' (the wage share) stays constant.

If economy-wide average real productivity growth is taken as the guideline for wage increases, various problems arise.

— All nominal wage rates rise at the same rate. This induces changes in relative prices (given constant mark-ups): in branches with below-average increases in labour productivity, prices will rise; in branches with above-average productivity increases, prices will have to fall. If these price reductions do not take place – if mark-ups rise – income distribution worsens for labour.
— The relative price changes induced are not necessarily compatible

with the demand for the various goods, leading to distortions in allocation.

— There has to be a consensus not only about distribution but also about maintaining the existing shares of production being devoted to consumption, investment, the public sector and net exports.

— The future development of labour productivity is difficult to predict. If its increase is underestimated, the wage share falls.

— A guideline is likely to be taken by all groups as a *minimum* for wage increases. This may result in raising, instead of lowering, aggregate wage demand.

Incomes policy can be indicative, co-operative or mandatory.

Indicative Incomes Policy. The behaviour of individuals and groups is indirectly influenced: no coercion is used. The policy may proceed in various ways.

1 *Moral suasion*, by which behaviour compatible with price stability is sought by an appeal to 'reason': however, it remains unclear why the various interest groups, trade unions and producers should participate in a policy of restraint if it is not in their own interest.

2 *Exemplary behaviour of the public sector*: this sector today is so important in magnitude that a restrictive wage and price policy there has a noticeable effect on the whole economy, in particular on the consumer price index. The government can pursue an incomes policy in the long run only if it is able to bind its own sector to the established guidelines. This is not easy, because trade unions often have a particularly strong position in the public sector, and politicians are reluctant to risk a conflict with them in view of the importance of public employees as voters.

3 *Official statements by the government concerning particular wage and pricing decisions*: by publicizing violations of the guidelines agreed upon, the government hopes to mobilize public opinion against the unions and firms involved. Such a policy has little effect, because the leaders of the respective interest groups depend on re-election by their members, and they would risk losing their members' support if they agreed to abandon or reduce their wage or price increases.

4   *Threatening with sanctions*: the government can try to apply the following sanctions against groups that violate the guidelines:

— cancelling subsidies;
— reducing government orders;
— facilitating imports by reducing tariff barriers;
— sharpening price and monopoly supervision;
— increasing supply by selling goods from public stocks.

The threat of applying sanctions may be a policy carrying considerable drawbacks. Sanctions are seldom effective against trade unions because they are directed against enterprises. In general, sanctions may be applied only once; for example, subsidies can be withdrawn only once. To make sanctions credible, however, they must be applied at intervals. Their use may result in a negative sum game in which all participants threaten each other and everyone is worse off in the end.

On the whole, an indicative incomes policy is unlikely to be successful, except in the short run.

Co-operative Incomes Policy.   In this variant, the interest groups concerned are integrated into the economic policy-making process. Ideally, all important groups should participate voluntarily and feel responsible for the outcome. The goal is to determine *ex ante* a distribution of the national product that is compatible with stable prices. The discussions may be informal or may lead to a consensus on guidelines to be observed by all.

Co-operative incomes policy is faced with two problems:

1   the participating groups have an incentive to break the rules, or guidelines, because – as already mentioned – price stability is a public 'good' which nobody supplies voluntarily;
2   the (already strong) power of interest groups is enhanced as they now form part of official economic policy-making. Latent groups such as consumers or taxpayers, on the other hand, are difficult to represent: the well organized groups are likely to profit at the cost of the unrepresented groupings.

A co-operative incomes policy may have several beneficial effects:

— information about the likely development of the economy may improve, which will help to avoid bad decisions.

— owing to the regular meetings, solidarity will arise between the participants in the co-operative incomes policy.
— the traditional conflict between 'labour' and 'capital' will be reduced because the general economic climate will improve and common problems will be discussed together.

Mandatory Incomes Policy: Wage and Price Controls. In this variant of incomes policy, a violation of the guidelines is punished by official action. Freedom of wage bargaining and price setting is suspended. For this reason, a mandatory incomes policy is resisted by many important political groups, particularly the trade unions, who fear the loss of a crucial part of their power.

A wage and price control policy has the following effects.

1 It demonstrates to the population how serious the situation is, and that the government is determined to fight inflation. This may pave the way for acceptance of the anti-inflationary measures by the population.
2 Individual's expectations about the future development of inflation may be revised; the inflationary mentality may be broken.
3 Time can be gained until the conventional fiscal and monetary policy becomes effective.

The main disadvantages of a mandatory incomes policy are threefold.

1 The controls are asymmetrical. It is relatively easy to monitor wages, but it is very difficult to control prices (because of quality changes and technical progress) and non-contractual incomes (profits). This dissatisfies the trade unions.
2 Incentives arise to get around the guidelines. It becomes more and more profitable for each group to break out. In order to maintain the incomes policy, the controls would have to be continually tightened. Simultaneously, political pressure mounts to grant exceptions from the guidelines. In such a situation, the government is usually forced to resort to voluntary incomes policy in order to save its face.
3 An activity that has hitherto been legal – say, the setting of wages and prices – is forbidden. As many violations occur, the danger of a criminalization of society arises. The public 'good' of public law is undermined, with the effect that all the members of society are worse off in the long run.

Empirical evidence

The effectiveness of all forms of incomes policy can be empirically captured by exploring how wages and prices would have developed in the absence of an incomes policy. It would be mistaken to restrict oneself to the development of *wages and prices* before and during the existence of an incomes policy, because other influences would not have remained constant. The increase of wages and prices may, for example, be smaller during an incomes policy because unemployment is high. On the other hand, it is perfectly possible that the growth of wages and prices is higher during the period of an incomes policy than before, although still smaller than without the incomes policy.

To capture the influence of incomes policy correctly, an econometric estimate of the determinants of wages and prices must be undertaken. Usually, an extended version of the Phillips curve is used, incorporating various factors in addition to the rate of unemployment. The effect of the incomes policy can be evaluated either by introducing a dummy variable for the period in which the incomes policy is in force, or by estimating wage and price equations separately for periods with and without incomes policy. In both cases, actual inflation is compared with the hypothetical development of prices that would have resulted if there had been no wage and price controls. Table 10.1 shows the effect of President Nixon's mandatory in-

TABLE 10.1   *The Effect of Wage and Price Controls on the Rate of Inflation, United States, 1971–75*

| | | Percentage change in the price index over the period indicated | | |
	Period	Actual rate of inflation	Hypothetical rate of inflation (no controls): estimated	Difference
		%	%	%
Initial effect	1971(2)–1973(3)	7.79	11.27	−3.48
Subsequent effect	1973(3)–1975(3)	15.40	11.88	+3.52
Total period		23.19	23.15	+0.04

Source: Robert J. Gordon, The Impact of Aggregate Demand on Prices, *Brookings Papers on Economic Activity* 6 (1975), Table 5, 641.

comes policy of 1971–74. The table shows that, according to the econometric estimates, the hypothetical price increase without controls between
1971(2) and 1973(3) would have been around 11.3 per cent, while the actual
inflation rate was 7.8 per cent. To the mandatory incomes policy may thus
be attributed a decrease in inflation of 3.5 per cent over these two years.
The decrease in inflation has, however, been nullified by the development
following the end of the price controls. In the two years between 1973(3)
and 1975(3) the actual inflation rate was 3.5 per cent higher than it would
have been without controls. Provided that the estimates are correct, after
the end of the mandatory income policy prices have been pushed up more
quickly than would have been the case had there been no controls. The
mandatory incomes policy has thus been unable to reduce inflation in the
long run.

Similar results are reported for other periods and countries. The government has either not been able to implement the mandatory incomes policy,
or has had to abandon it after a short-run success and has suffered higher
inflation thereafter.

The results of a great number of econometric studies of the effect of
mandatory incomes policies indicate that:

— in the short run, there is a modest dampening effect;
— in the long run, incomes policy is ineffective and may even lead to
  a surge of wages and prices.

Social Consensus on Incomes Policy.   The experiences with incomes
policy are not particularly encouraging. The basic idea should,
nevertheless, be pursued further. It is of great importance in a
modern society to integrate the organized groups into incomes
policy-making, and to reach a consensus about the distribution of
income *before* price rises have made excessive nominal demand compatible with supply. In a democratic society, an anti-inflationary
policy is not feasible in the face of opposition from the most important groups; in other words, a mandatory incomes policy is the
wrong way to approach the problem.

It follows that:

1   to stabilize prices, an incomes policy in the sense of an *ex ante*
    and *voluntary* agreement between the social groups is required.
    An incomes policy that seeks to reach an agreement in the cur-
    rent politico-economic process is doomed to failure. No group
    will participate seriously in a policy that is disadvantageous for it

in the mid and long run. The trade unions in particular will not conform to an incomes policy if they are asked to restrict wage demands, and it repeatedly turns out that the prices rise in any case and the wage share falls;

2 an effective incomes policy requires that each one of the groups concerned can expect to benefit. The social consensus must provide rules that improve the position of every group behind the veil of ignorance;

3 the welfare gains that can be reached as a result of the anti-inflationary policy must be distributed among the groups complying in order to ensure that they have an incentive to participate.

There are three kinds of incentives that may be set by social consensus in order to induce the groups to participate voluntarily in an incomes policy:

1 monetary incentives involving rewards to those obeying and fines on those violating the guidelines;

2 agreements about granting special incomes increases for those workers who manage to raise productivity more rapidly than is considered 'normal';

3 linking incomes policy with the benefits provided by other policies: the workers might, for example, be granted a larger share in property or increased co-determination if they are ready to keep to the rules of an incomes policy.

The types of arrangements that are able to induce the economic groups to participate in an incomes policy have so far been little explored. New inducements must be suggested. Some propositions regarding monetary incentives are discussed in the next section.

New Rules for a Wages Incomes Policy

Inflation can be considered as a negative external effect of the wage- and price-setting actions of various decision-makers. These externalities can be internalized by imposing monetary sanctions on those who violate the guidelines. As a consequence, the decision-makers have an incentive to comply with the incomes policy.

Two kinds of rules have been suggested.

Tax-based Incomes Policy (TIP).   Here, the tax system is used to penalize companies for price and wage increases exceeding the guidelines.

Example

Assume that the wage guideline is fixed at a (maximum) increase of 5 per cent per year. The basic corporate tax rate may be set at say 31 per cent. For each percentage point by which a firm's wage increase exceeds the 5 per cent standard, its tax rate might be raised by 15 per cent. A firm granting an overall wage increase of 6 per cent would thus have to pay a tax rate of 46 per cent; if the wage increase is 7 per cent, the tax rate would rise to 61 per cent.

The imposition of such a fine for 'inflationary' wage increases would motivate firms to take a harder stand against the wage demands of the trade unions. It is, however, quite unlikely that the entrepreneurial interest group would participate in such an incomes policy, because the rule is asymmetrical: when the wage increases are above the guideline, the firms are punished by higher taxes. If, on the other hand, wage increases are below the guideline, they are not rewarded. The enterprises can only lose by agreeing to such an arrangement. The co-operation of the firms would be secured only if the transfers were symmetrical, so that, if wage increases are below the guideline, the firms are rewarded by receiving a negative tax.

Market Anti-inflation Plan (MAP).   In this variant of decentralized systems of incentives, marketable licences are introduced to internalize external effects. The various groups first agree on the rate of inflation considered unavoidable for a given year, owing to foreign and exogenous influences. The government then issues a number of licences to firms in accordance with this inflation rate, in proportion to their value added. A firm is allowed to raise its prices only if it owns the necessary number of licences. If a firm reduces its prices it can sell its licences on a free market; an enterprise that wants to increase its prices more than the guideline permits has to buy the additional licences required. The firms thus have a monetary incentive for reducing their prices.

Example

Assume that the price increase deemed unavoidable is 2 per cent for a certain year. A licence unit is established that allows a price rise of 1 per cent per thousand monetary units of value added. A firm with a value added of 2 million per year thus receives 4,000 licence units (2,000 for each percentage point of inflation). If the firm wants to increase its prices by 3 per cent, it has to own 6,000 licence units: it has to buy the additional 2,000 units in the free market. The sellers of the licences can now increase their prices by 1 per cent *less* than they could have done otherwise. The overall target inflation rate is thus met.

This proposition is rather complicated, and introduces additional uncertainties into the private economy because the price of licences is variable. The goal of the policy is again to strengthen firms' opposition to wage increases. The firms are given new profit (or loss) opportunities by buying and selling licences. The entrepreneurial sector as a whole does not benefit because the price of the licences falls to zero when the demand is equal to or smaller than the supply – that is, when the overall price level rises by less than the guideline. Benefits arise only if the firms can sell unused licences to the government at a positive price. The entrepreneurial interest groups are thus likely to participate in such a market anti-inflation scheme only if such re-selling is guaranteed.

Influencing the Supply of Money

Inflation can be prevented in the medium and long run if the supply of money is controlled. A constant quantity of money constrains aggregate demand and makes it impossible for firms to maintain price increases. They will therefore oppose wage demands by trade unions.

Two approaches to controlling the quantity of money are discussed.

Fixing Money Supply by the Central Bank. Nominal national income rises at the same rate as the nominal quantity of money, given a constant velocity of circulation of money. If price stability is to be achieved, the quantity of money must not rise more rapidly than the expected increase in real GNP. The central bank has greater power to control the money supply under a regime of flexible exchange rates than with a fixed rate of exchange. In the current politico-economic process, however, the central bank cannot determine the quantity of money autonomously because the various social groups and the government will try to influence its policy.

Examples

Even the formally most independent central banks, the Federal Reserve Bank in the United States and the Bundesbank in Germany, are not, in fact, independent. The central bank must maintain a good relationship with the government, not least to ensure preservation of its autonomy. It risks being constrained by government-inspired laws if it conflicts too heavily with the democratically sanctioned executive. Econometric research for Germany has indeed shown that in the event of conflict the Bundesbank is ready to support the government's policy even if inflationary tendencies are thus created.

Steadying the supply of money by social consensus seems possible because this is advantageous for all behind the veil of ignorance. A price stabilization policy operating through a control of the money supply makes it possible to influence the economy indirectly; no direct intervention in the autonomy of groups is needed. For this reason it is conceivable that rules on steadying the money supply will be unanimously approved. Two kinds of rules (which may also complement each other) may be distinguished:

1 the growth rate of the money supply must be fixed in the constitution;
2 the central bank as established must be a completely autonomous institution which keeps its independence even in the event of conflict with the government.

Both social agreements serve to isolate the determination of the money supply from short-run and divergent interests of the current politico-economic process and to put it into the hands of institutions and rules that cannot be influenced in the short run.

A publicly determined supply of money – even if the public institution is the central bank – always runs the danger of becoming the puppet of special interests. The pressure imposed on it by the government and other social groups has often resulted in an excessive increase of the money supply and therewith in inflation. It can therefore be argued that prices can be stabilized only if the control of the money supply is taken out of the political sphere, a proposition that is advanced in the next section.

Private Money Supply.   Private competition in the supply of money exists when every bank has the right to issue its own money. Each bank has an interest in restricting its supply, because otherwise the value of its money will fall. The users of money prefer those sorts of money that preserve their value: the demand for a particular sort of money will be the higher, the less it depreciates in value over time. A money with a high value enables the issuing bank to make a profit when printing additional banknotes. The individual banks thus have to carry the cost of a loss in value of the money themselves – quite in contrast to the existing central bank institutions. Private banks therefore are not ready to support a government policy entailing moving to full employment via monetary expansion. They are not prepared to cover governmental budget deficits readily. This holds true, however, only if there is competition between the private suppliers of money, unrestricted by government intervention.

There are major problems connected with a competitive private supply of money:

— the individuals and firms are burdened with high transactions costs because they must continually compare and exchange the various sorts of money in circulation;
— the information costs are very high: everyone must know the relative prices of all kinds of money in order to avoid making losses. It is to be expected, however, that those banks that are not capable of keeping the value of their money constant will be put out of business quickly. The money supply will consist of a limited number of types only.

When a social consensus is to be reached, the individuals must consider whether the (possibly) lower rate of inflation is more important than the high transactions and information costs owing to the multitude of moneys within a nation. It does not seem likely that the advantages will outweigh the drawbacks of private money supply.

10.2 STABILIZATION OF EMPLOYMENT

Unemployment imposes a high cost on society: real output is smaller than it might be (production possibilities are wasted); the unemployed regard themselves as superfluous and can suffer high psychological damage; and many juveniles have no opportunity of entering working life and therefore run the danger of becoming dependent on drugs and alcohol, or of becoming criminals. Unemployment hits the lower-income groups worst, in particular those with little education, ethnic minorities and women.

Disadvantages are associated also with a level of employment that is too high. Overemployment reduces the flexibility of the labour market. Those looking for work do not devote sufficient time to finding jobs appropriate to their education and capabilities. Moreover, over-employment is a potent source of inflation.

In order to reach a social consensus on stabilizing employment, it is necessary not only that the employment situation of particular groups be improved (possibly at the expense of other groups), but that the state of employment be adjusted in a way that is Pareto-optimal. The demand for a public guarantee of a *particular* job with a *particular* employer (often raised in the current politico-economic process) is not likely to find a consensus behind the veil of ignorance. In an economy where the structure of goods and employment continually changes, such a guarantee greatly reduces flexibility and, in the long run, leads to stagnation and loss of jobs. A specific job guarantee pushes other employees out of their jobs, and prevents future job-seekers from finding work.

A social consensus seems possible in three areas:

1   increasing the flexibility of the labour market;
2   reducing the supply of labour;
3   setting incentives to increase employment.

These approaches are discussed below.

Job seekers can be helped in various ways to find an adequate place of work.

— A regional disequilibrium between the supply of and demand for labour may be reduced by increasing the *geographical mobility* of the workers. This can be achieved by granting public subsidies when workers change residence.

— Job seeking can be eased by *public employment agencies*, which offer information about the job market. It is also necessary to inform the workers about realistic wages in the various occupations and sectors. Unemployment is therewith reduced because the worker knows more quickly whether to accept or reject a job offer.

— The workers can be additionally *trained* so that they can adjust to new developments in the economy.

— The unemployed may be given *incentives* to find a new job as quickly as possible by, for example, reducing unemployment benefits when job offers are rejected without good reason.

Some of these approaches are already put into practice in industrial economies.

The employment situation may also be improved by enlarging the spectrum of jobs available. Such an enlargement improves adjustment to structural change in the economy. Part-time work can be offered to men and women at all levels of qualification. Two (or more) persons may share a job between them according to their own wishes ('job-sharing'). This allows them to work for a variable number of hours, days and weeks; the employees are given 'time sovereignty'. The same purpose serves the offer of early retirement (with some reduction in pension allowances) or unpayed holidays.

The *options* open to individuals on the labour market can be improved by various means.

— Positive incentives may be created to induce enterprises to offer flexible employment opportunities, for example by granting appropriate tax reductions.

— Government regulations that reduce flexibility can be abolished.

— The social security system has to be adjusted to the new conditions. Part-time workers are often more expensive to the firms because many social security benefits have to be extended to all employees to the same extent. With increasing part-time work, the decision-makers seeking a social consensus should reconsider whether this provision is still adequate.

In principle, employment can also be increased by distributing the available jobs among a greater number of persons. Such a redistribution makes sense only if the people presently employed are having to work longer than they wish individually. In many countries, the working time in most occupations is now severely restricted by law. If the work volume of present employees is reduced, therefore, the number of newly employed does not rise accordingly, because the shorter working time should lead to an increase in labour productivity, reducing the number of additional employees needed.

Finally, the supply of jobs can be increased by giving enterprises positive incentives to employ more persons. The firms can be granted a subsidy to cover part of the cost of employing additional workers. Such *employment subsidies* can take two forms:

1 the subsidy can be directed to *all* the employees of an enterprise. The relative cost of using the factors of production will then be changed: labour will become cheaper relative to capital; labour-intensive sectors and firms will become privileged, and employment will be reduced less quickly when aggregate demand lags;
2 the wage subsidy can relate to *additional* employees: the firms would receive a subsidy relative to the amount by which they increase the number of employees over the level at a given time.

The effect of wage subsidies depends strongly on the size of the grant. In a recession the firms will not hesitate to dismiss workers if the wage subsidy is only meagre.

The wage subsidy is an interesting attempt to stabilize employment by changing relative prices. The approach works with positive incentives and is goal-oriented; it is therefore more effective than the current policy of supporting loss-producing firms during recessions, as these measures do not reward employment-creating policies of the firms. The economic advisers may point out the advantages, and may bring about a social consensus on such rules for employment stabilization.

CONCLUSION

A stabilization of prices is possible if a social consensus is reached about the shares of national product to be devoted to various purposes and used by the major groups in society. Behind the veil of ignorance, an agreement on a voluntary incomes policy seems possible, because strife over the distribution of the product results in dead-weight losses reducing the income of all. The discussion has shown that it is difficult to reach an agreement on an incomes policy that all the relevant groups find advantageous to stick to. It is important to consider new rules, such as a tax-based incomes policy or a market anti-inflation plan, which overcome some of the problems of incomes policy as traditionally undertaken. There is also a need for a social consensus with a view of stabilizing employment; again, new rules have to be considered.

FURTHER READING

Modern texts on inflation and price stabilization include

John S. Flemming, *Inflation*. Oxford: University Press, 1976;

Helmut Frisch, Inflation Theory 1963–1975: A 'Second Generation' Survey, *Journal of Economic Literature,* 15 (1977), 1289–1317.

Both aspects of the stabilization problem are discussed in

Robert J. Gordon, Recent Developments in the Theory of Inflation and Unemployment, *Journal of Monetary Economics,* 2 (1976), 185–219.

The British experience with incomes policy is treated, for example, by

Samuel Brittan with Peter Lilley, *The Delusion of Incomes Policy.* London: Maurice Temple Smith, 1977.

The American experience is analysed, and econometric evidence presented by

Karl Brunner and Allan H. Meltzer (eds), *The Economics of Price and Wage Controls.* Amsterdam: North Holland, 1976.

Tax-based incomes policy (TIP) has been suggested by

Henry Wallich and Sidney Weintraub, A Tax-based Incomes Policy, *Journal of Economic Issues,* 5 (1971), 1–19.

The Market Anti-inflation Plan (MAP) is discussed by

Abba Lerner and David Collander, Anti-inflation Incentives, *Kyklos,* 35 (1982), 39–52.

A collection of various types of incentive-based price stabilization policies is to be found in

Michael P. Clandon and Richard R. Cornwall (eds), *An Incomes Policy for the United States. New Approaches.* The Hague: Martinus Nijhoff, 1981.

The necessity to steady the supply of money is one of the central propositions of the monetarists; see for example

Milton Friedman, *The Optimum Quantity of Money and other Essays.* Chicago: Aldine, 1969.

Private competition in money supply is suggested by

Friedrich A. Hayek, *Denationalisation of Money,* 2nd edn. London: Institute of Economic Affairs, 1978.

The modern theory of employment and its stabilization is discussed in

Edmond Malinvaud, *The Theory of Unemployment Reconsidered.* Oxford: Basil Blackwell, 1977.

The traditional approaches for reducing unemployment are discussed, for example, in

Daniel S. Hamermesh, *Economic Aspects of Manpower Training Programs.* Lexington, Mass.: D. C. Heath, 1971.

Incentive schemes for increasing employment are analysed by

Jonathan R. Kesselman *et al.,* Tax Credits for Employment rather than Investment, *American Economic Review,* 67 (1977), 339–49.

Experiences with this instrument in various countries are discussed in

John Bishop and Robert Haveman, Selective Employment Subsidies, *American Economic Review, Papers and Proceedings* 69 (1979), 124–30.

CHAPTER 11

Evaluation

INTRODUCTION

The last three chapters discussed applications of the social consensus
in the spheres of allocation, distribution and stabilization. The specific properties of such a democratic economic policy may best be
judged when it is contrasted with an alternative approach: the
'technocratic–elitist' theory of quantitive economic policy. This
theory may be criticized for various reasons: the imputed social
welfare function generally does not exist and cannot be determined
empirically; the policy measures derived are not in the interest of the
decision-makers and thus have little chance of being implemented;
the approach presupposes a 'benevolent dictator' and is therefore
inconsistent with consumer sovereignty; and, finally, this approach
does not allow us to derive optimal plans because rational actors
will incorporate such plans into their calculations, thus neutralizing
(at least partially) their effect.

Economic advisers have three tasks to fulfil in an economic policy
based on social consensus: they must work out productive arrangements, promote agreement and suggest rules and institutions that
help to maintain the social contracts in the current politico-
economic process. The derivation of economic policy based on a
social contract raises a number of problems because the conditions
for a social consensus are not usually met in full. These problems are
discussed, and it is shown that there are ways of overcoming the
difficulties.

11.1 SOCIAL CONSENSUS V. THE TECHNOCRATIC– ELITIST THEORY OF ECONOMIC POLICY

This part of the book has considered practical applications of agreements on rules and institutions. A social consensus has been characterized as follows:

— it is concerned with basic and long-run problems;
— individuals and groups are assumed to be behind a veil of ignorance about their position in the future;
— any decision is to be taken unanimously;
— mutually productive (Pareto-superior) arrangments must exist.

A particular social contract need not meet all these characteristics in full. Current rules and institutions may be beneficial to society even if the individuals and groups deciding whether or not to retain them are not completely uncertain about their future position in society; for example, a *partial* uncertainty with respect to the problems to be solved often suffices. The close connection between unanimity and the productivity of a social contract has been pointed out in Chapter 2: if unanimity exists for only a part of society, the social arrangement arrived at is less productive than if all had participated.

In order to see clearly the properties of economic policy derived from social consensus, it is useful to contrast it with the traditional 'technocratic–elitist' theory of economic policy.

The Technocratic–Elitist Theory of Economic Policy

The traditional theory of economic policy postulates a social welfare function that is maximized within the constraints imposed by the economic system. The economic advisers derive therefrom the optimal economic policy measures and propose them to government (and other decision-makers such as the central bank) for execution.

A typical variant of the technocratic–elitist approach is the *theory of quantitative economic policy*. An optimal policy is derived by maximizing explicitly a social welfare function, the constraints being represented by a macro- (and econometrically estimated) model of the economy. The relationship between the 'exogenous' variables – the instruments X and non-controllable variables N, and the 'endogenous' variables in the form of goals G and side-effects S, are shown in Figure 11.1. The goals G_1, G_2 ... G_n contained in the social welfare function W depend on the use of economic policy instruments X_1, X_2, ..., X_m *and the non-controllable variables* N_1, N_2, ..., N_q. The instruments and the non-controllable variables also influence other variables of the economic system, which are, however, irrelevant side-effects S_1, S_2, ..., S_r if they have no effect on social welfare.

The general formal maximization problem is:

$$\max W (G_1, G_2, ..., G_n)$$

subject to the constraints

$$G_1 = f_1(X_1, X_2, ..., X_m; N_1, N_2, ..., N_q)$$
$$G_2 = f_2(X_1, X_2, ..., X_m; N_1, N_2, ..., N_q)$$
$$\vdots \qquad \vdots \qquad \vdots$$
$$G_n = f_n(X_1, X_2, ..., X_m; N_1, N_2, ..., N_q).$$

The social welfare function $W(G_1, G_2, ..., G_n)$ is often defined as a *loss function*. It shows the welfare reductions that arise from a deviation of the value of G_i from the socially desired value $\overline{G}_i$, where i

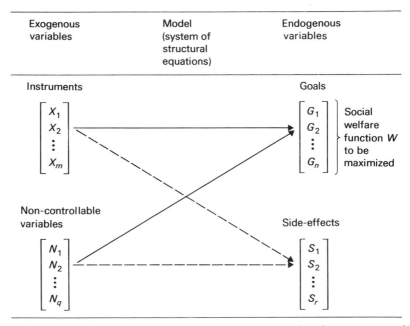

FIGURE 11.1   *The relationship between exogenous and endogenous variables in the theory of quantitative economic policy.*

runs from 1 to n. The loss function L is commonly formulated quadratically, $(G_i - \overline{G}_i)^2$, in order to capture deviations between actual and desired values of the goals in both directions, and to indicate that larger deviations lead to utility losses increasing at an accelerating rate, in other words that losses are more than proportional to the deviation $(G_i - \overline{G}_i)$. The economic constraints are often linearized to make the maximization problem more readily soluble. The procedure can be illustrated with a simple example.

Example

Social welfare is taken to depend on two variables, the goal variable G and the instrument variable X; in other words, it is assumed that the instrument use affects social welfare:

$$L = w_G(G - \overline{G})^2 + w_X(X - \overline{X})^2.$$

where $\overline{G}$ is the socially desired value of G, and $\overline{X}$ the socially desired use of the instrument X; w_G and w_X give the weights of the two arguments in the loss function.

The constraints imposed by the economic system are taken to be a linear function that relates the value taken by G to the value of X:

$$G = b + cX.$$

Introducing this equation into the loss function,

$$L = w_G(b + cX - \overline{G})^2 + w_X(X - \overline{X})^2.$$

Minimizing this function with respect to the instrument X gives

$$\frac{dL}{dX} = 2w_G c(b + cX - \overline{G}) + 2w_X(X - \overline{X}) = 0.$$

After some manipulation, it follows that:

$$(X^* - \overline{X}) = -\frac{cw_G}{w_X}(G - \overline{G})$$

where X^* indicates the welfare-maximizing (loss-minimizing) value of instrument X. The optimal use of the policy instrument X^* (or its deviation from the desired value $X^* - \overline{X}$) depends on the utility weights w_G and w_X, the parameter of the economic model c and the size of the deviation of the goal from its desired value $(G - \overline{G})$.

Once the economic advisers have calculated the optimal use of instruments and have proposed this to the public decision-makers, their task is completed according to the theory of quantitative economic policy. It is therefore appropriate to call it 'technocratic'.

This approach has been applied to many areas in economics. It has recently been used in public finance to devise *optimal taxes*, where an exogenously determined tax revenue is to be raised with a minimum welfare loss. This is achieved by keeping the distortions in the allocation of goods and factors of production brought about by taxation as small as possible. Formally, a social loss function is minimized subject to the usual economic constraints and to the requirement of raising a given tax revenue.

Closely related is the *theory of optimal pricing of public enterprises*. The problem here is to set the prices of publicly produced goods and services so that the economic distortions are minimized and social welfare maximized. This variant of the technocratic–elitist theory of economic policy thus seeks to determine the socially optimal pricing policy of public enterprises. The economic advisers' task is again fulfilled when the optimal prices (in the simplest case, marginal cost prices) are devised and communicated to the decision-makers. How this optimal policy is to be implemented is not analysed. In particular, nothing is said about what incentives the managers have (or as a rule: do *not* have) to put the policy into action.

Critique of the technocratic–elitist theory of economic policy*

The approach just discussed has a number of shortcomings, of which the five most important are discussed here.

1   *Problem of aggregation.* A social welfare function consistent with individual preferences can be derived only under very restrictive and unrealistic conditions. This applies particularly when the alternatives to be decided upon involve various *dimensions*. It follows that the social welfare function presupposed by the technocratic–elitist theory of economic policy either does not exist or contains a dictatorial element. The concept is therefore not suitable for economic policy-formation in a democracy.

2   *Empirical emptiness.* A social welfare function is rarely, if ever,

---

* The criticisms raised here are directed against the approach as a form of economic policy, but not against the mathematical instruments used. As will be shown in Part III, this instrument has a useful role to play in the context of a theory of democratic economic policy.

econometrically estimated. The concept – at least in the stringent form required for the theory of quantitative economic policy – is in practice a non-operational concept.

3 *Missing incentives.* The 'optimal' policies derived are unlikely to be put into practice, because no decision-maker has an incentive to maximize social welfare, but prefers to pursue his own goals (the government, for example, aims at receiving sufficient votes to be re-elected). It is therefore not surprising that the theory of quantitative economic policy is not applied in practice.

4 *Methodological contradiction.* Western (neoclassical) economics presupposes that the consumers know their preferences best. In the case of decisions at the level of the whole society, the individuals' sovereignty is, however, dismissed. The government is assumed to maximize social welfare, which is an inadmissible application of the utility calculus from the individual to society as a whole. The technocratic–elitist theory of economic policy thus presupposes the existence of a 'benevolent dictator' in the form of government. It is based on an 'elitist' conception of policy-making. This contradicts the basic tenet of democracy that the preferences of individuals, both as consumers and voters, must be respected.

5 *Inconsistency of optimal plans.* The 'optimal' plans derived by maximizing a social welfare function may become inconsistent once allowance is made for the reactions of individuals and groups to the plans. In the extreme, private decision-makers base their expectations of the government's future actions on a full use of the information available to them (so-called 'rational expectations'). The consequences of this knowledge about the government's plans for the actions of individuals and groups are not incorporated when the 'optimal' plans are derived.

The shortcomings of the technocratic–elitist theory of economic policy could be overcome by taking into account the mutual reactions of the private and public decision-makers. This would mean that each actor would be assumed to pursue his own goals and that the total outcome would be the result of the actions of a number of individuals and groups. The approach of maximizing a social welfare function would be given up and the view of politico-economic modelling (as shown in Chapter 1) adopted. This leads to a *theory of democratic economic policy*.

11.2   THE ECONOMIC ADVISERS' TASKS

The differences between an economic policy based on social contract and one based on the traditional view have considerable consequences for the role of the advisers.

In the technocratic–elitist theory of economic policy, in particular in its quantitative variant, the economic advisers' task is to *apply* economic theory. The only difference from pure theory is that the outcomes are formally evaluated with the help of a social welfare function. The advisers have to fulfil a mainly technical task; they must be capable of solving the maximization problems. This requires asking 'well-defined' questions – with the danger that technical aspects become dominant and the analyses socially irrelevant. The advisers' task is not to inquire how the 'optimal' solution can be put into reality.

Economic advisers have a quite different role in the theory of democratic economic policy: they must endeavour to bring about a social consensus. This involves three activities.

1   The advisers suggest *productive arrangements* that are advantageous to all. Individuals and groups may lack the appropriate information, or the transactions cost of agreeing spontaneously on a social contract may be too high. The advisers may then supply the necessary information and thereby reduce the transactions cost, and they can also point out innovative solutions (such as have been discussed in previous chapters).

2   The advisers can look for ways and means to bring about a social consensus on rules and institutions. For that purpose, they can cite the advantages of the social rules discussed, and explain to the individuals that, because future developments are unknown, they have to decide behind the veil of ignorance (for example, by discussing possible scenarios of the future). On the other hand, advisers may inform individuals and groups about the possible negative consequences for them if an agreement is not reached. The advisers may also further the process of finding a consensus by suggesting various forms of compensation schemes to those individuals and groups who otherwise expect to lose and would not co-operate, and may offer their help as negotiators to promote an agreement.

3   A social contract can be productive only if it is maintained over a sufficiently long period. Economic advisers must devise institutions that register violations of rules and punish them. Courts may be established for that purpose. Ways must also be found to prevent the rules being broken by well organized minorities or majorities. The advisers would do well to suggest only social contracts that have a chance of surviving in the current political process. Rules that lead to strong conflicts are likely to be violated. On the other hand, some tension cannot be avoided because otherwise the rules would not be productive. The goal is to influence the behaviour of the decision-makers in the current politico-economic process, and this is not possible without imposing some adjustment cost.

These three tasks can be fulfilled only if the economic advisers accept the interests of the individuals and groups involved. They must appeal to the individuals' self-interest in order to reach productive arrangements. Such advisers are required to participate actively in the political discussions and negotiations. The economist as policy adviser does not remain in isolation, and his contribution is not restricted to technocratic aspects. While the advisers participate in the political discussions, they cannot impose their will on the individuals and groups: the collaboration is voluntary and the decisions are taken by consensus.

Economic advisers will fulfil their task only if they have an incentive to do so. This aspect will be discussed in the final part of the book.

11.3   APPLYING THE SOCIAL CONSENSUS

Undertaking an economic policy based on social consensus is easy if the conditions mentioned at the outset of this chapter, in particular the ignorance of the individuals about their future position in society, are fully met. It may not be assumed, however, that this is always the case. Normally, individuals and groups do have some ideas about their likely future position, so that they do not decide behind the veil of ignorance. The practical application of an economic policy based on social consensus is therefore confronted with several problems.

1   Only if it is possible to separate *decisions on rules and institutions* by consensus from *everyday political decisions* will the economic

policy approach suggested here be fruitful. Social agreements have to stay unchanged for a certain length of time, so that individuals can adjust to them and the rules and institutions introduced become productive for society as a whole. If, however, the rules and institutions remain immutable over too long a time period, they run the danger of becoming unproductive because they are no longer related to the actual problems confronted by society. A rigid social consensus is a vain attempt to solve social problems in one stroke. The more basic are the rules arrived at by social consensus, the less they should be changed; less basic rules can be changed more often without destroying the character of the social consensus.

2   It may be doubted whether the agreements reached by social consensus can be maintained in the current social process. There has so far been little research on the exact conditions under which rules and institutions survive in everyday politico-economic conflict. Experience suggests that a considerable part of the rules is indeed maintained. Even in times of strong conflict between the various groups in society, the basic social agreements are usually observed and can therefore exert their long-run productive effects.

Example

A particularly important case in which social contracts in democracies are maintained even in the face of intensive conflict is when there is a change of government as a result of an election: most governments would have the means to use the police, the military and the judicial system to prevent having to give up power.

   True, in many countries in the world election forgeries, the wielding of illicit political influence and even campaigns of terror can be observed. In such nations there is no basic consensus on the part of the decision-makers that a voluntary change in power is beneficial for all in the long run. Even in authoritarian countries, in which the individuals' preferences are disregarded, there is a type of consensus betwen the competing groups. The implicit rule may obtain that overthrown politicians are exiled. Such an agreement is beneficial for all potential participants, compared with a situation without rules in which overthrown politicians are killed.

3   Assuming that social contracts are of increasing importance in future economic policy formation, individuals and groups have a stronger incentive to increase their influence at the level of the social

consensus. This may lead them to distort information. In order to prohibit such a distortion, economic advisers can suggest various means of reducing the dependence of the decision-makers on possibly biased sources of information. With the help of social agreements, the interest groups may be subjected to competition, or public institutions may be founded and given an incentive to provide objective information.

4   A social consensus is viable only if all individuals and groups involved agree. Narrowly interpreted, this would mean that all individuals would have to participate in the social consensus, because every rule affects every individual directly or indirectly. Because of the decision cost arising, however, it would not make sense to include weakly affected groups. Social rules are already productive when those *principally involved* take part. What matters is that the interests of the individuals who are weakly affected, but large in number, are adequately represented. Rules may be established by social consensus that motivate the economic advisers to look after the interests of these 'latent' groups. It is sometimes difficult to identify such groups; nevertheless, latent groups have a better chance of making their interest heard on the level of the social consensus than in day-to-day politics. Social contracts that relate to a specific problem are rarely and discontinuously formed. It is therefore easier to activate a latent group for this particular purpose than is the case in the current political process, where a continuous activity is required.

5   Individuals and groups who have an idea about their future position may have an incentive to misrepresent their true preferences in order to reap special benefits. Such *strategic behaviour* is to be expected, especially when a compensation scheme has to be devised: everyone will try to exaggerate his losses when he participates in a social contract in order to get compensation that is as high as possible. Owing to this exaggeration of the cost, a Pareto-optimal improvement seems impossible, though it could occur if the preferences were correctly revealed. Economic advisers must have thorough knowledge of the true preferences in order to prevent strategic behaviour. (The corresponding methods are discussed in Part III below.) One way to ensure that preferences are revealed properly is to approach them from two sides: situations in which there is a tendency to exaggerate such preferences can be combined with situations in which they are concealed.

Example

The willingness to pay for a public good is exaggerated by individuals if the contribution to the cost of providing the good is determined completely separately from the revelation of the preferences. The 'demand' will, on the other hand, be (at least partly) concealed if the cost contribution is fixed in relation to the preference revealed ('free-riding'). If the willingness to pay is established with and without relating it to cost contributions, the true preferences may be determined, within a range.

The basic principle of this procedure may be exemplified in the case of an evaluation of the monetary value of a private good, say a house. If the house is to be expropriated, the owner will indicate a high value; if the same house is to be taxed, the owner will indicate a low value. The true evaluation of the house by the owner can be determined if there is a rule that the owner must be prepared to sell the house to the government for the tax value he himself indicates. In this case he will make an effort to indicate a value that is neither too high nor too low.

6   A social consensus can best be reached if the individuals and groups have not yet taken a firm position, but are ready to consider new information and to negotiate. In such a situation, the incentive for reaching a social contract may, however, be low because the problem does not seem pressing. If, on the other hand, the decision-makers have taken their positions because they are aware of the importance of the problem to be regulated, it may be difficult to find an agreement. The chances for a social consensus seem to be best when the economic advisers make proposals for possible rules and institutions early. It is not unlikely that the competing individuals and groups will converge on such an early proposition once they see the importance of the problem to be solved. An agreement will also be facilitated if economic advisers keep the discussion open as long as possible and prevent positions from hardening. For this purpose they can try to increase the diversity of information and to describe possible future developments with the help of scenarios.

CONCLUSION

By finding a social consensus about rules and institutions, economic policy can provide a quite different approach from that used in the traditional (quantitative) theory of economic policy. This requires giving up the convenient but futile idea that public decision-makers listen and follow advice based on social welfare maximization. Instead, it must be accepted that all actors pursue their own interests in day-to-day politics, but that their behaviour can be influenced significantly by setting adequate rules and institutions. There is thus little room for the traditional role of the economic adviser suggesting particular policies. Rather, one has to consider what rules will induce decision-makers to act according to the preferences of individuals. One of the main problems is to create and sustain the veil of ignorance necessary for a social consensus to be reached, and to find procedures to maintain the rules in day-to-day politics (where they may come up against the short-run interests of powerful groups). While this approach presents a useful alternative to the prevalent way of thinking about economic policy, it is only a beginning, and much work still has to be done along these lines.

FURTHER READING

The aspects of the social consensus discussed in the chapter are rarely treated in the literature. Some basic, more philosophical than practical, ideas may be found in

James Buchanan, *Freedom in Constitutional Contract*, cited in Chapter 2.

Worth mentioning is the attempt within mathematical game theory to start from an 'original state' and to derive the institutional arrangements that will emerge as a result of given preferences and technical (economic) conditions. This approach is at its very beginning; see

Andrew Schotter, *The Economic Theory of Social Institutions*. Cambridge: University Press, 1981.

The theory of quantitative economic policy has been developed mainly by Ragnar Frisch. Leading representatives of this variant of the 'technocratic–elitist' theory of economic policy are

Jan Tinbergen, *Economic Policy: Principles and Design*. Amsterdam: North Holland, 1956;

Henry Theil, *Optimal Decision Rules for Government and Industry*. Amsterdam: North Holland, 1968.

A demonstration that the theory of quantitative economic policy is not applied in practice may be found in

Leif Johansen, The Report of the Committee on Policy Optimisation – UK, *Journal of Economic Dynamics and Control* (1979), 101–9.

A survey of the theory of optimal taxation is given, for example, by

David F. Bradford and Harvey S. Rosen, The Optimal Taxation of Commodities and Income, *American Economic Review, Papers and Proceedings*, 66 (1976), 94–101.

The theory of optimal pricing of public enterprises is discussed, for example, by

Dieter Bös, *Economic Theory of Public Enterprise*. Lecture Notes in Economics and Mathematical Systems. Berlin, Heidelberg, New York: Springer, 1981.

The problem of inconsistent 'optimal' technocratic planning is developed by

Finn E. Kydland and Edward C. Prescott, Rules rather than Discretion. The Inconsistency of Optimal Plans, *Journal of Political Economy*, 85 (1977), 473–91.

The differences between the level of the social consensus (constitutional contract) and the current politico-economic process (post-constitutional) is dealt with in

Dennis C. Mueller, Constitutional Democracy and Social Welfare, cited in chapter 2.

The conflict between the two levels and the necessary adjustments in the agreements is discussed in

James M. Buchanan and Winston Bush, Political Constraints on Contractual Redistribution, *American Economic Review, Papers and Proceedings*, 64 (1974), 153–61.

PART III

Policy-making in the Current Politico-economic Process

In this part of the book it is assumed that the fundamental rules of society have been determined. The various actors now try to reach their goals within the limits set by these rules.

Economic advisers have limited influence on the current politico-economic process. They can only help the actors to reach their own goals as well as possible by providing them with information that enables the actors to become aware of the possibilities they have in the current politico-economic process and to use these opportunities to the maximum extent. This is achieved primarily by informing the decision-makers about the kinds of instruments at their disposal and about how they function.

Chapter 12 deals with the possibility of influencing behaviour in the current politico-economic process through the provision of information. It also analyses how information can be disseminated to individuals and interest groups and what kind of information will be sought. Methods for collecting information on the preferences of the population for the institutionalized decision-makers (government, parties and public administration) is discussed in Chapter 13. In Chapter 14, the multitude of economic policy instruments at their disposal is emphasized. Chapter 15 discusses the most effective means for applying economic policy.

CHAPTER 12

Influencing Behaviour through Information

INTRODUCTION

Information provided in the current politico-economic process can influence the behaviour of the various decision-makers – individuals, groups and government – each of which pursues its own goals. Behaviour changes as the preferences, and the constraints on fulfilling them, are perceived more clearly or in a different way.

The politico-economic actors demand information up to the point where the cost of additional information is greater than the additional benefit derived from it. The actors will therefore endeavour to be optimally, and not fully, informed.

If all the decision-makers were completely informed, economic advisers would be unable to influence the current politico-economic process. The course of policy would be determined by the rules and institutions set by social consensus and could not be influenced from outside. But obviously no actor is fully informed. Economic advisers can supply information on economic and social relationships on the basis of their specialized knowledge. The decision-makers can use such information profitably in order to fulfil their preferences in the current politico-economic process.

12.1 APPROACHES TO CHANGING BEHAVIOUR

The information supplied by economic policy advisers covers two areas:

1   the decision-makers can be made aware of their own preferences: this entails demonstrating what economic policy can achieve – explaining the range and the effects of the instruments available;

2   the decision-makers may be advised about the best strategies by
    which they can achieve their goals.

Informing the actors in the current politico-economic process will
lead to a better fulfilment of *all* individuals' preferences only if rules
and institutions have been established by social consensus that
ensure that the selfish behaviour of individuals does not result in
their mutually harming each other. The social contracts thus are of
prime importance, as they determine the framework within which
the decision-makers in the current politico-economic process can act.
If these rules and institutions are inadequate, the information provided by economic advisers to the decision-makers can result in
some actors profiting at the expense of others.

Example

Economic advisers can inform the government and the public administration of how to reach their goals efficiently, for example by suggesting to
them the use of cost–benefit analysis (see Chapter 15). However, this instrument for increasing efficiency will be used by government to pursue its own
goals at the cost of the population if the government is insufficiently controlled, in particular if the re-election constraint does not exist or is not
sufficiently developed. The public decision-makers could then, for example,
use cost–benefit analysis to favour an extension of public expenditures that
mainly benefit themselves and are of little value to the population at large.
    This example illustrates that, in general, when basic rules are inadequate,
organized groups can increase their influence at the cost of latent groups
because the use of instruments often requires knowledge and information
not available to unorganized groups.

This illustration demonstrates the importance of *social rules*. Individuals must ensure by social consensus that their preferences are respected. Social agreements that guarantee basic rights such as
freedom of expression are essential. If the supply of information is
monopolized, individual preferences can be articulated but inad-
equately. The following rules can help to prevent a monopoly of
information.

— Radio and television may be state-controlled to guarantee a diversity of opinions. In the case of other media, such as newspapers, diversity may be secured by publicly supporting
  unprofitable enterprises. The decision to control the media thus

must be determined by social consensus, because in the current politico-economic process there is always a tendency for the government to employ the mass media for its own purposes.

— Competition, and therewith a diversity of opinions, can be achieved if licences to run a radio or television station are sold on the free market. However, such an arrangement runs the danger that the 'educational' role of the mass media is neglected and that only opinions that are held by well-financed persons and institutions are propagated. The use of the licences could thus be coupled with the imposition of a duty on private owners of mass media to supply a given number and type of 'educational' broadcasts.

The existence of both public and private supply in the mass media ensures that the public stations experience competition from the outside that is likely to increase the diversity of opinions catered for.

12.2   DEMAND FOR AND SUPPLY OF INFORMATION

The information demanded by the decision-makers is determined by the relationship between the *benefits* and the *cost* of information. The benefit, or utility, gained consists in avoiding mistakes in decision-making owing to insufficient knowledge. This utility is, however, difficult to determine beforehand. The cost consists in collecting, assembling and evaluating the information. This requires both time and money (as, for example, in buying newspapers and acquiring specialized means of information).

The marginal utility of information is likely to fall, while the marginal cost of searching for and evaluating information are likely to rise. Figure 12.1 shows the development of these marginal curves. The figure illustrates, that under the assumptions mentioned above, it is worthwhile to inform oneself to a certain extent. To be totally uninformed is unwise because at first additional information yields more benefits than cost. It is beneficial to avoid grave mistakes owing to insufficient information. The figure also demonstrates that it is not worthwhile to be fully informed because the additional cost of collecting and evaluating information becomes prohibitive. The intersection of marginal utility and marginal cost determines the optimal amount of information.

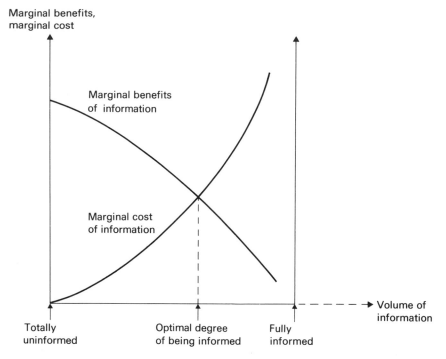

FIGURE 12.1   *Determining the demand for information.*

The benefits and cost of information are different for each person and situation. In many cases a small amount of information is optimal; in other cases it is worthwhile to absorb more information. This means that the decision-makers in the current politico-economic process do not have a strong interest in obtaining full information; only part of the knowledge offered by the economic advisers yields them a positive net benefit. The more important and the more easily understandable the information offered to the actors is, the more likely it is to be assimilated. The amount of information optimal from the point of view of one individual is possibly non-optimal from the point of view of others; there may be external effects of informing oneself. This will particularly be the case if the information that forms the basis for a collective decision has consequences for other individuals and groups. If, for example, an individual decides in an election between the government and the opposition without being adequately informed, all the other voters have to carry the possibly negative consequences.

Measures may be instituted by social contract to ensure that such distortions in information are avoided. For example, it is possible to offer information free of charge or to reward the assimilation of it.

12.3   THE IMPORTANCE OF INFORMING THE POPULATION

Information helps individuals to recognize their own preferences and abilities and thereby to better attain their goals in the current politico-economic process. Information on economic policy is demanded by the individuals for three different purposes:

1   in *referenda*, the consequences of the issues must be known in order to make a well-reasoned decision;
2   in most nations, the *elections* of the legislative and/or executive authorities are the most important chance for the individuals to influence economic policy. The voters must be informed about the government's past performance so that they can evaluate whether to give the vote to the politicians in office or to those in opposition. They can be advised to what extent the (good or bad) state of the economy is due to the government's actions, and to what extent it is due to other influences, such as the economic conditions in foreign countries;
3   the government's and the public administration's actions can also be influenced in a number of other ways. Individuals can try to push their demands through by themselves by, for example, writing letters to important decision-makers or going to court. They may also try to receive help from actors independent of government, such as ombudsmen or the mass media. An individual can also act together with others, for example by joining a political party, interest group or citizens' initiative.

The information provided by the economic advisers is useful only if it is not confined to policy alternatives; it should also specifically show how the decisions made in the current political process can be influenced, and which actions are the most promising.

Individuals who are well informed about matters of the economy are able to react quickly to economic policy actions. Such a reaction is possible, however, only if the corresponding markets allow adjustments, that is, if there are no forces that prevent or hinder them from reacting to the policy actions. Individuals who act on the basis of such information as is available to them can sometimes make economic policy measures ineffective by pre-empting them. This result of the so-called *theory of rational expectations* can be illustrated by way of examples.

Examples

If a government considers additional government expenditures for construction, the informed employees will demand higher wages, and the producers will set higher prices because they know that their action will be supported by the announced increase in demand. In the extreme, the additional government expenditures will have no effect on the real economy at all but will only result in inflation.

If an expansionary policy is undertaken by reducing taxes, well informed economic actors will recognize that the resulting budget deficit will have to be covered by higher taxes in the future. They will therefore not increase their consumption and investment expenditures, and the initial tax reduction will not produce any expansionary effect.

Government interventions thus can be effective only if they are not fully foreseen by the population. It is therefore necessary that new economic policy measures are continually introduced. Economic policy actions have a real effect only if the individuals adjust with a time lag, for example because wages and prices are fixed for a specified time period.

The theory of rational expectations assumes that the population is well-informed: it knows the structure of the economic system (at least as well as the government does) and can therefore predict the government's policy measures as well as the exogenous variables of the economic system. Such a high level of information implies that the cost of information is low. This, however, is unrealistic: as will be shown in the next section, the population rationally informs itself only poorly about economic problems.

When the economic advisers improve the information of the population, economic policy measures tend to become less effective. This deterioration in 'technical' efficiency of economic policy instruments is, however, not important within a theory of *democratic* economic policy. What matters is that the individuals may better fulfil their preferences as a result of the improved information.

12.4   THE POPULATION'S LOW LEVEL OF INFORMATION

The Individual Demand for Information

The low level of information on economic policy matters in the population is the result of an unfavourable cost–benefit relationship.

— The *benefits* of information for an individual lie in his possibility of influencing the current politico-economic process in his own favour as a result of his possessing the information. His subjectively evaluated utility of the outcome of the decisions is weighted with the probability of his being able to change the outcome on the basis of his own information intake (for example, that his vote will result in another party forming the government, or in an alternative issue winning in a referendum). This probability is extremely small where there is a large number of voters; it matters only where the electorate is small. The value attached by the voters to *general* information on economic policy is therefore rather low; the utility of *specific* information on the economic and political problems directly affecting an individual, and which he believes he can influence, is, in comparison, much higher.

— The *cost* of information consists of the effort expended, and resources used, to collect and evalute it. To inform oneself intensively on matters of economic policy would require an extremely high input of time and material.

This comparison between benefits and cost shows that it is not worthwhile for an individual to collect and evaluate much information about general economic policy questions. The respective political decisions made by individuals are therefore based only on superficial knowledge.

Empirical evidence

An analysis of election and popularity functions (see Chapter 1) suggests that the voters make their decisions almost solely on the basis of the state of the economy in the election year. They thus disregard:

— the economic conditions in previous years in which the government was in power;

— the contribution of exogenous influences, such as those emanating from foreign economies;
— the difference it would have made had the opposition party been in power.

In order to facilitate their decision-making in particular cases, a large number of voters resort to ideological views. An ideology enables the voters to capture and evaluate difficult relationships more easily, and thereby to save information cost.

Mass Communication

Much information on matters of economic policy is received from television, radio and the press. Social psychologists have studied the process of the transmission of information from the mass media to the population both theoretically and by controlled experiments. In the case of mass communication, the content of the information is: emitted indirectly (there is a distance between sender and recipient); one-sided (the information always comes from the same side); and public (the recipients are not personally addressed).

Individuals have a strong tendency to avoid contradictory pieces of information which would throw them into internal conflict (this is referred to as the *theory of cognitive dissonance*). This makes them choose their sources of information selectively, and also to store and interpret the content of such information selectively, so as to make the information compatible with their own views and interests.

The information is often transmitted not directly, but rather indirectly, by opinion-leaders such as well-known writers, sportsmen or scientists who have proved their competence in other areas. Opinion-leaders form their own opinions on the basis of information available to them via the mass media and other sources, and in turn influence other people by direct contacts (two-stage communication).

The main effect of this type of information is that existing views are strengthened. The mass media cannot change opinions in the short run because individuals want to avoid cross-pressures and to keep their own decision costs low. New information is most easily accepted if it is supplied jointly with already accepted opinions.

The results of social psychological research indicate that economic advisers inform the population of those economic policy matters about which there are no preconceived opinions. This relates not only to new problem areas (such as environment and energy at the beginning of the 1970s), but also to new aspects of traditional problems (such as the difficulty of financing social security in the face of a growing share of the non-working population). The transmission of information will be the more successful, the more the economic advisers are able to discuss questions that are important (or will soon be) and about which opinions are still open.

12.5 ADDRESSEES OF INFORMATION

Economic advisers can inform the population with the help of opinion-leaders or by directly addressing themselves to the public. The level of information and the way it is transmitted will thus vary considerably according to the desired audience.

It is not always simple to identify the persons who constitute the opinion-leaders on a particular matter. With respect to economic policy, there are 'specialists' who claim to fulfil this role, but it is not certain whether the population really accepts them as such and follows their judgements on economic policy. It is rather the journalists who can be considered as opinion-leaders in this field. It is they who inform the population on television, on the radio and in the press about economic facts and relationships, who criticize the government's economic policy and indicate alternatives. Professional economists may also be opinion-leaders, *if* they are able to apply abstract economic theory in a way that is relevant to practical policy problems.

Economic advisers can inform the opinion-leaders on a fairly technical level, because the latter usually have a background in economics. The information can then be transmitted on a lower level in the form of informal discussion, scientific seminars and conferences, scientific books and articles that are reasonably easy to understand, and official or unofficial advisory groups.

Informing the general public is difficult, however, because individuals have few incentives to absorb information that is of little relevance from their own point of view. Moreover, economic advisers compete with many other sources of information and entertainment, which all distract the attention of the public. For this reason the economic policy information must be offered in a way that suits the users: it must be easy to understand with respect to form and content, and, above all, it must specifically relate to the interests of the individuals as voters.

Example

The information that a particular infrastructural project (say, a road) will cost $1.8 billion over the next twenty years is of little use for the population. The information must be made more concrete – by, for example, computing by how much the yearly tax burden of an average voter would be reduced if the project were not undertaken, and which specific advantages particular groups of the population may expect from the project. Such information enables the citizen to compare the cost imposed on him with the expected benefits.

Individuals must be made aware of the unavoidable trade-offs.

Nowadays, a considerable share of total information is supplied by television. Programmes dealing with economic policy problems are particularly difficult to present because their contents are hard to adapt to this medium. The topics presented on national television are often of little interest, because only a small part of the information offered can be directly relevant to any one prospective viewer. In this respect, the radio and the press have some advantages because, owing to the larger number of programmes and newspapers, they are able to discuss regional issues whose benefits and costs are likely to affect the individuals more directly.

In many cases the economic sections of newspapers are ill suited to inform the average reader about problems of economic policy. The articles therein are often directed exclusively to business people and stock market speculators, and present the material in the specialists' jargon; all in all, too much basic knowledge is required to grasp the text.

When economic advisers address themselves to interest groups, they would do well to differentiate clearly between organized and latent groups. Officials of organized economic pressure groups have an incentive to demand information relevant to the interests they represent. They will also be ready to assimilate more general information about the economy, as this may be useful for the purpose of vote-trading. Accordingly, the information supplied can be on a higher level, similar to that used when addressing opinion-leaders. In contrast, the non-organized groups usually know little about economic policy and are not aware of the possibilities for having their demands observed in the current political process. The limited demand for information (rational from the point of view of an individual) and the subsequent lack of knowledge about economic policy problems are the main reasons why these latent groups have a weak position in the politico-economic process. Economic advisers can try to offer information that facilitates the organization of a group, and can thereby indirectly help these sections of the population to have their views or interests taken more seriously.

12.6 INFORMATION AND PREFERENCE CHANGE

As long as the economic advisers restrict themselves to giving the decision-makers explanatory information, problems for a theory of democratic economic policy do not arise. The preferences of the population are accepted. If, however, the economic advisers go further and influence the *preferences* of the population, a basic problem of legitimacy arises: who has the right to influence the wishes of the people? The danger arises that economic advisers will become 'benevolent dictators', who tell the individuals what is good for them. It may be denied that a problem of legitimacy exists by assuming that preferences are immutable. But this position is difficult to maintain: it is almost impossible to distinguish empirically between a change of preferences and a change of the individuals' opportunity set. If one accepts that preferences are, in principle, changeable, the problem of legitimacy can be overcome by ensuring, through social contract, that the economic advisers compete with one another. None of them then will have a monopoly with which he can influence the preferences of individuals in the direction he desires. Rather, the individuals have the chance of selecting between various sources of influence: such a choice restores their sovereignty at a higher level. It is likely that part (or even all) of the attempts to influence the preferences neutralize each other.

CONCLUSION

Economic advisers can help individuals to realize their preferences more fully in the current politico-economic process. Information allows people to make more reasoned political choices in elections, referenda and other forms of political participation. The problem is that individuals demand little information; choice and perception are selective, and the information actually consumed serves mainly to strengthen views already held. The leaders of organized groups, on the other hand, have an incentive to absorb and use information. To provide information to latent unorganized groups is again particularly difficult. In order to have an effect in that case, information must both have an immediate appeal to the individuals' interests and be easy to understand.

FURTHER READING

The economic theory of information has been mainly developed by

George J. Stigler, The Economics of Information, *Journal of Political Economy*, 69 (1961), 213–25.

This article and other useful contributions on the economic approach to information have been collected in

Donald M. Lamberton (ed.), *Economics of Information and Knowledge*. Harmondsworth: Penguin, 1971.

The role of information in modern economic theory is discussed by

Jack Hirshleifer, Where are We in the Theory of Information? *American Economic Review, Papers and Proceedings,* 63 (1973), 31–9.

The relationship between information and uncertainty is treated in

Jack Hirshleifer and John G. Riley, The Analytics of Uncertainty and Information – An Expository Survey, *Journal of Economic Literature*, 17 (1979), 1375–1421.

The reasons for the low level of information of individuals in the politico-economic process are analysed in

Anthony Downs, *An Economic Theory of Democracy*. New York: Harper & Row 1957.

A survey of the determinants of the political participation of the population is given by

Lester W. Milbrath and M. L. Goel, *Political Participation. How and Why Do People get Involved in Politics?* 2nd edn. Chicago: Rand McNally, 1977.

The observation that voters base their election decision on little information concerning the government's performance is empirically supported by, for example,

Ray C. Fair, The Effect of Economic Events on Votes for President, *Review of Economics and Statistics,* 60 (1978), 159–73.

Various contributions on the effect of information in the political sphere are discussed in the collection of essays by

David G. Tuerck (ed.), *Political Economy of Advertising.* Washington DC: American Enterprise Institute, 1978.

The social psychological research on mass communication is summarized, for example, in

Joseph T. Klapper, Effects of Mass Communication. In David L. Sills (ed.), *International Encyclopedia of the Social Sciences,* New York: Macmillan, 1968, vol. 3, 81–9.

CHAPTER 13

Investigating Preferences

INTRODUCTION

The 'political suppliers' in the current politico-economic process – namely, the government, political parties and the public administration – consider only that information which is useful for their own purposes. If there is enough political competition, the political parties (including government) are forced to consider the population's preferences in order to win elections.

This chapter considers methods of finding out about the preferences of the people. These methods can be used by economic advisers to inform the political suppliers about the wishes of the population, or they can be directly employed by the political suppliers themselves. It is shown that the preferences can be revealed by direct methods such as surveys and referenda, by observing behaviour and by performing experiments.

13.1 POLITICAL COMPETITION AND THE POPULATION'S PREFERENCES

Once the rules of the political system are established through social consensus, political competition forces the government and the parties in opposition to take the preferences of the individuals into account in day-to-day politics. Economic advisers who advise the political parties of how they can best win the forthcoming elections (within the boundaries set by the constitution) by their action promote the competitive democratic process that results in the voters' preferences being realized in the political process. The better informed a political supplier is, the better are his or her chances of winning the election. As this information is available to all parties, political competition is improved, and this forces each party to take the voters' preferences more fully into account.

Remark

The view advanced here – that the economists' role is to advise the political parties – is in severe contrast to the traditional theory of economic policy, in which it is categorically rejected that the economic policy advisers should promote the interests of particular political parties; their task is rather to advise the government, the representative of the 'common good'. The traditional view is based on the concept of a benevolent dictator. Political parties are seen as representatives of particular interests which commonly are in conflict with the general interest. Economic advisers should therefore rise above the 'dirty' fights of party politics; they should not be partial. The difference between the views of the theory of democratic economic policy and the traditional theory of economic policy is particularly clear on this point.

As mentioned earlier, economic advisers can influence the behaviour of the public administration in the current politico-economic process only by offering information that is of interest to the public officials themselves: information that is counter to their interests will be ignored or rejected. The discussion of the behaviour of the public administration in Chapter 6 has clearly shown that the government bureaucracy does not depend directly on the preferences of individuals. Only rules imposed by social consensus can compel it to act in the interest of the population. Once these rules are adequately established, economic advisers can work, indirectly, towards the fulfilment of the population's wishes.

The various political suppliers demand different sorts of information from the economic advisers:

— the *political parties* (including the government's), which aim at winning the election in the context of intensive political competition, are interested in knowing the individuals' preferences: they want to know how they can accurately determine the voters' preferences;
— the *government and the public adminstration* require knowledge about the economic policy instruments available; they will further be interested in the most suitable strategy for applying these instruments.

Three types of method for revealing individual preferences will be distinguished:

1   *direct approaches*, on the basis of surveys, referenda, and popularity and election functions;
2   *indirect approaches*, relying on 'revealed preferences' in the political sphere or in the market;
3   *experimental approaches*, where the conditions in which the preferences are revealed are controlled.

13.2   DIRECT APPROACHES

Preferences cannot be observed and measured directly; people must always be induced in one way or another to reveal them. The 'direct' approaches make an effort to come as close as possible to the preferences; in other words, the transmission process is kept as short as possible.

Surveys

Revealing preferences by interviews and questionnaires is a well developed method in empirical social research. Surveys are relatively easy to undertake and can almost always be adopted to the topic of study. They usually enable a wide range of information to be acquired on a representative sample of persons. For this reason the approach is fairly popular and has been applied to many economic areas. Surveys on the voters' preferences about expenditure programmes are of great interest to politicians, because they yield direct information about those economic policy measures likely to win votes.

The approach commonly used in empirical social research is, however, deficient because the budget constraint is neglected. The questions are asked without taking the monetary opportunity cost of the expenditure programme into account, in particular as it would affect the level of taxation. It remains unclear what ideas respondents have about the tax consequences when they answer – or whether they think at all of the effects of the expenditure on their tax burden. As is shown in Figure 13.1, the answer given to questions about goods supplied by the government (that is, public expenditures) depends essentially on the expected tax price – in other words, on the addi-

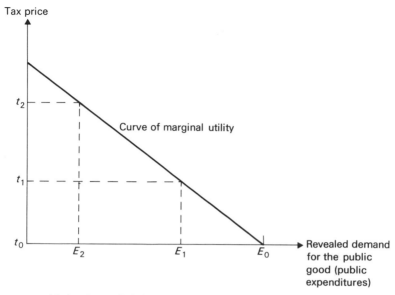

FIGURE 13.1   *Revealed demand for public goods depends on tax price.*

tional tax burden expected by the individual asked. If the person questioned believes that the public expenditure programme envisaged will have no effect on the amount of tax he will have to pay – if he assumes his tax price to be zero (t_0) – he will reveal a demand for public expenditures E_0. This corresponds to that expenditure level which brings him the maximum utility from the goods supplied; in other words, the marginal utility is zero. On the other hand, if the person questioned thinks that the expenditure programme will lead to a higher tax burden for himself, he will reduce the demand revealed. At an expected tax price of t_1 he will reveal a public expenditure demand E_1; at tax price t_2, the demand E_2.

Newer survey approaches, developed mainly by economists, explicitly do take tax prices into account. It is made clear to the interviewed person that the total budget is restricted and that the supply of a unit of the public good involves a particular cost (or price). (See also the 'budget games' discussed below.)

Surveying has various disadvantages:

— the persons questioned tend to give superficial answers because they do not understand how they will have to bear the consequences. Often they are badly informed about the properties of the publicly supplied goods and services in question. In some cases the knowledge is acquired through the questions asked by the interviewer, who thus influences the answers and imparts systematic bias.

— the respondents tend to give strategic answers in order to promote their own wishes. This applies particularly to public goods where everyone has an incentive to act as a free-rider.

Some of the disadvantages of surveys can be overcome with the help of specially designed experiments. This, however, involves substantially higher cost.

Referenda

The individuals cast their votes in a referendum for that alternative from which they expect to derive the relatively highest net benefit. It is therefore possible to infer the underlying preferences on the basis of the results of the vote. The income and price elasticities of the 'goods' to which the referendum refers can be estimated empirically by regressing the average incomes and tax prices on the share of approval found in the various vote districts. Referenda are commonly used only in Switzerland (on all federal levels) and in some American states, particularly with respect to the financing of state school expenditures. For example, a referendum was held on the property tax rate in a Californian school district. In American community school districts, expenditures are financed principally through the property tax levy. An approval of the proposed increase in the property tax rate (in our example from $1.78 to $2.05 per each hundred dollars of assessed property evaluation) can therefore be interpreted as an approval of an increase in public expenditures for schools. The estimated income and tax price elasticities are shown in Table 13.1. The estimates in the table indicate that the voters in the Santa Barbara school district are, *ceteris paribus*, more likely to support a property tax increase, and therefore school expenditures, the higher their income is. (The income elasticity is statistically significant and positive: 1.85). On the other hand, given constant income, the voters are more likely to reject such a referendum, the higher their tax price is. (The elasticity with respect to the expected tax cost per child is significantly negative: -0.99).

The interpretation of referenda allows us to reveal the preferences of voters in a simple and inexpensive way. There are, however, simi-

TABLE 13.1 *Income and Price Elasticities for School Expenditures (Property Tax Rate) in the School District of Santa Barbara, California, February 1971*

Explanatory variables (*elasticities*)	
Mean family income	*Expected tax cost per child*
1.85*	−0.99*
(3.89)	(−7.10)

Note: The *t*-statistic is given in parentheses. The asterisks indicate that all elasticities are statistically significantly different from zero with a 99% probability.

Source: Anthony J. Barkume, Tax-Prices and Voting Behavior: The Case of Local Educational Financing, *Economic Inquiry*, 15 (1977), Table 1, p. 581.

lar problems as for surveys: the results can be biased because the voters may be badly informed about the issues, and because strategic voting cannot be excluded; those people who vote do not constitute a representative sample of the total population; finally, for practical reasons the citizens can choose only between a proposition and the status quo. A negative vote therefore can simply mean that the voter is dissatisfied that he cannot express his preferences in a more differentiated way.

Popularity and Vote Functions

It has been suggested various times in this book that the individuals' preferences can also be revealed by surveys on the government's popularity and by election results. In particular, these allow us to capture the consequences of business cycle policies. The effect of changes in the most important macroeconomic variables (unemployment, inflation and income growth) on government popularity and election outcomes is quantitatively evaluated. This makes it an interesting source of information for the government. It is well established that in all democratic Western countries an increase in the rate of unemployment and in the rate of inflation has, *ceteris paribus*, a negative effect on the voters' evaluation of government performance. The positive effect of an increase in real income growth is statistically significant in only a few countries. The results must, however, be interpreted carefully. The estimated economic influences are rather unstable over time.

13.3   INDIRECT APPROACHES

Methods Based on Political Behaviour

The following two methods for revealing the preferences of individuals are based on behaviour in the political sphere.

Party Programmes.   The preferences of the voters can be deduced by analysing the programme of the political party that has won the last election. It is assumed that the winning party had adjusted its programme to the preferences of the voters, and has therefore been elected.

Table 13.2 shows the relative importance attached to various macroeconomic goals by parties of the left, the centre and the right in Europe. The ranking of the goals by left-wing and right-wing parties is almost inverse: while left-wing parties attach highest priority to full employment and a just income distribution, these goals are given lowest priority by right-wing parties. Price stability, on the other hand, is given top priority by right-wing parties, and low priority by left-wing parties.

This approach for revealing the voters' preferences is problematic. No distinction is made between those parts of the programme that reflect the government's ideology and those that seek to capture the preferences of the voters. It cannot, for example, be distinguished whether the left-wing parties attach highest priority to full employment for ideological or for vote-winning reasons. The party programmes are, moreover, usually quite general, so that it is not possible to infer anything very specific about voters' preferences.

Government Behaviour.   Voters' preferences can be studied by analysing the relationship between government activity (in particular public expenditure) and objectively measurable determinants of the decision of the voters. This approach can be applied to institutions of both direct and representative democracy.

Direct Democracy.   In a democratic system in which public expenditures are determined by simple majority and in which the suggested size of the budget can be varied from the floor of a voters' assembly,

TABLE 13.2   *Macroeconomic Goals of Parties: Synthesis for Eight European Countries, 1964*

Ranking of the goals	Political party		
	Left-wing	*Centre*	*Right-wing*
Dominating	Full employment Just income distribution	Price stability	Price stability
Important	Satisfactory growth	Satisfactory growth Full employment Just income distribution	Balance of payments equilibrium
Little importance	Price stability Balance of payments equilibrium	Balance of payments equilibrium	Satisfactory growth Full employment
Unimportant			Just income distribution

Source: Etienne-Sadi Kirschen *et al., Economic Policy in Our Time.* Vol. I: *General Theory.* Amsterdam: North Holland, 1964. Table IX.2, p. 227 (selection).

in equilibrium it is the *median voter* who will be decisive. The median voter model permits the estimation of the income and tax price elasticities of the various expenditure categories. The procedure is similar to the one used in the case of referenda. The yearly public expenditure per capita is regressed on the income and tax burden of the median income recipient (as well as on so-called ecological variables, such as age, of the voters in the various political entities). The approach has been applied mainly to American and Swiss communes. Table 13.3 provides an illustration for the case of directly democratic Swiss municipalities (that is, districts that decide in a voter assembly) which have the institutions of obligatory and optional referenda. The table suggests that, with the tax burden held

TABLE 13.3   *Median Voter Model: Income and Price Elasticity of the Demand for Various Categories of Public Expenditures: 32 Swiss Municipalities with Direct Democracy and Obligatory and Optional Referendum, 1968–72*

Expenditure category	Demand elasticity with respect to:	
	Median income	Median tax share
General administration	1.4*	−0.7*
Education, recreation, sports	0.9*	−0.3*
Health, hospitals	3.9*	−1.3*
Social assistance	1.3	−0.6*
Municipal roads	2.0*	−1.1*
Environmental protection	2.0*	−1.1*
Aggregate	1.4*	−0.7*

Note: The aggregate includes municipal expenditures for civil defence, police and fire protection and interest payments on debt. An asterisk indicates that the respective coefficient is statistically different from zero with a 95% probability.

Source: Werner W. Pommerehne, Institutional Approaches to Public Expenditure: Empirical Evidence from Swiss Municipalities, *Journal of Public Economics*, 9 (1978), Table 4 (excerpt), 268–9.

constant, when income increases voters desire above all larger expenditures for health and hospitals (income elasticity of 3.9), roads, and environmental protection (income elasticity of 2). When the tax burden rises and income is kept constant, however, the voters desire above all reductions in the same expenditure categories. The table indicates that, *ceteris paribus*, with rising income voters want more public expenditures of all categories, and with tax price rises voters want less.

The conditions of the median voter model are rarely met. In particular, it is usually unrealistic to assume that the government will fulfil the voters' wishes in a completely passive way, and that it has no discretionary power.

Representative Democracy.   In the past the ruling party has undertaken economic policies that have enabled it to stay in power until the next election, and possibly to be re-elected. Voters' preferences can therefore be inferred indirectly from the government's behaviour. This is the obverse of the approach used in the theory of quantitative economic policy, where a social welfare function is maximized subject to the economic constraints, and an optimal policy is derived. Here, on the contrary, it is assumed that the economic policy actually undertaken *is* optimal. The importance that the government assigns to the goals in its preference function ('inverse optimum principle') can then be determined.

This method, which relies on the econometric estimation of reaction functions for the government (and the central bank), is quite problematic. It is impossible to distinguish between policies undertaken because of the government's specific ideology or because of the vote-winning motive. Another difficulty is that the preferences of the government are difficult to separate from the parameters of the economic system. It has to be assumed that the government has based its decisions on exactly the model of the economy specified in the analysis.

Methods Based on Economic Behaviour

The preferences of individuals can be revealed by analysing how they act in the economic sphere.

Cost Incurred Reflects Utility. Private goods offered in a market are evaluated by the consumers with the help of the willingness-to-pay curve. It indicates the marginal utility – and thus the maximum amount the consumers would be prepared to pay – for alternative quantities of the good. As the quantities and the prices of private goods can be observed on a market, the curve of marginal willingness to pay can be estimated econometrically. In the case of public goods for which no price is demanded (say, in the case of parks or open spaces), no such curve can be directly observed. The cost that consumers are prepared to incur in order to consume the public good in question reflects the minimum value attributed to the good (because otherwise the cost would not be incurred). The higher the cost in terms of monetary expenses and time that the individuals are prepared to carry in order to visit a natural park, the more highly the park is valued (and the higher is the marginal willingness to pay). Considering the various visitors who have to cover different distances – and therefore to incur different costs – to visit the park, a synthetic 'demand curve' for the public good can be constructed and the overall consumer net benefit can be estimated.

This approach has been used to estimate the benefits of environmental amenities such as natural parks. As the cost carried mainly consists of the travel expenses, the approach is often referred to as the 'travel cost method'. It is based on some rather restrictive assumptions. In particular, only the minimum benefit is captured, and the travel cost undertaken must refer solely to the particular park considered. Travelling itself may not yield benefits, and the trip must serve no other purpose. The approach based on *actual* behaviour is moreover unable to capture two important sources of benefits:

1   the *option value* derived from the possibility of being able to consume the public good (visit the park);
2   the *existence value* derived from the knowledge that the public good (the park with its plant and wildlife) is not destroyed.

Market Price of Real Estate.   Public goods supplied free of charge by the government increase the utility of the individuals; this is reflected in price increases of real estate.

Example

If the quality of air in a particular region is improved owing to environmental measures by the government, the value of the land and houses in this area, *ceteris paribus*, rises. The buyers are prepared to pay a higher price for real estate because of the improved natural environment. A deteriorating air quality tends, on the other hand, to decrease the market value of real estate in the area affected.

The change in the value of real estate can be taken as an indicator of the preferences (willingness to pay) of individuals for government activities, provided the other determinants of the land and house prices (the size and the location) are kept constant. When all the factors determining particular house prices are included, for example by multiple regression, individuals' evaluation of a change in the supply of a public good such as air quality can be captured by measuring the induced change in the market value of real estate.

This approach is confronted with various problems. In particular, it is assumed that the real estate market functions perfectly, so that the individuals' evaluations of the public good are fully reflected in property price changes. Option and existence values are again excluded. It has proved difficult to isolate the effect of changes in public goods supply from other influences on real estate prices; the individuals' evaluations derived are accordingly quite unstable and depend on the specific formulations.

13.4 EXPERIMENTS

There are two kinds of experiments that can be used to determine the preferences of individuals for economic policies. In *laboratory experiments* the environmental conditions are set by the researcher. The change in the behaviour of individuals can then be attributed without error to the variable changed, provided disturbing influences are indeed excluded. *Social experiments* are undertaken in an environment not controlled by the researcher, so that disturbing outside influences are more likely. They have, however, the advantage of being more realistic.

Laboratory experiments have been used in two main forms to reveal the preference of individuals for public goods.

Budget Games

Individuals can be induced to reveal their relative evaluation of public goods in an experimental setting when they are given the chance to 'buy' various kinds and quantities of such goods within a given budget. Publicly supplied 'goods', such as a reduction in noise, an improvement in the conditions of the natural environment or the construction of roads, can be demanded by paying a unit 'price' which corresponds to the budgetary cost. The individuals are forced to account for economic scarcity because they have to stay within a given budget. By choosing an allocation of the budget among the various competing alternatives, they reveal their marginal rates of substitution for the corresponding public goods. Individuals may change the allocation until they are indifferent between pairs of goods, within the constraints of the budget. The experimenter may change the budget prices and the budget level, one at a time, in order to derive price and income elasticities of the demand for the various public goods.

Example

Each individual participating in the laboratory experiment is given 15 coupons which correspond to the additional budget considered. Thus, the reaction to a *change* of the historical budget allocation is analysed. The coupons may be allocated either to additional public expenditures, to a tax reduction, or to both. Table 13.4 shows the percentage allocation to the various expenditure categories of the budget of North Carolina, and the implied percentage increase compared with the status quo. The table indicates that the participants in this budget game *allocate* 68 per cent of the coupons to additional government expenditures and 32 per cent of the coupons to reduction in taxes. The additional outlays are mainly for health and social services (27 per cent) and schools (19 per cent), while little is

TABLE 13.4   *Budget Game: Individuals' Allocations of Coupons to Expenditure and Tax Reduction Categories, North Carolina, 1973*

Category	Percentage of of coupons allocated	Percentage increase in budget
	%	%
Spending category		
Schools	19.1	4.3
Health and social services	26.9	28.5
Motor vehicles and highways	6.1	6
Other (resource development, agriculture and collection systems)	16.0	39.7
Total	68.1	
Tax reduction category		
Turnover tax	10.4	3.7
State personal and corporation income tax	10.8	2.8
Local property and inventory tax	10.7	
Total	31.9	

Source: Own calculations based on Robert P. Strauss and G. David Hughes, A new approach to the demand for public goods. *Journal of Public Economics,* 6 (1976), Table 1 (excerpt), 195.

allocated to motor vehicle controls and highways (6 per cent). The tax reduction is allocated equally to the three categories distinguished. Considering the percentage increase of expenditure over the historical level, the residual expenditure category including resource development, agriculture and the collection system profits most (+40 per cent), followed by health and social services (+29 per cent).

The allocation of the coupons can be related to such characteristics as age, sex, education and income. This allows the political suppliers to know which group of voters has a special preference for which kinds of expenditure extension or tax reduction.

Experiments with budget games are a good method of revealing the preferences for public goods, including taxation. They can help the government to offer a supply of public goods that is favoured by the population. It should, however, be recognized that individuals participating in the experiment may not be familiar with the alternatives, the prices and the budget, or that they do not take the game seriously enough. Care must therefore be taken before generalizing the results of the experiments (This is referrred to as the 'problem of external validity').

Manipulation of Cost Expectations

The preferences revealed by individuals for public goods depend to a large extent on their cost expectations: if the individuals believe that they will have to bear the cost to the amount of (or proportional to) the marginal willingness to pay revealed, they have an incentive to indicate a willingness to pay that is lower than what is actually true. If, on the other hand, they assume that the good has not to be financed by themselves, they have an incentive to indicate a higher marginal willingness to pay than is true. This strategic behaviour of individuals makes the empirical measurement of the preferences for public goods difficult.

The contrasting behaviour in the case of the two cost expectations just mentioned makes it possible to undertake an experiment that reveals the area within which the 'true' willingness to pay for the public good considered lies. In a first situation the contribution to the cost of providing the public good is fixed according to the revealed individual willingness to pay. The individuals will then reveal a low willingness to pay. In a second situation the public good is

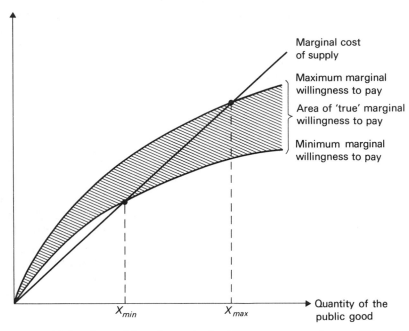

FIGURE 13.2   *Area of 'true' marginal willingness to pay for a public good.*

provided free of charge; this induces individuals to indicate their maximum willingness to pay. The corresponding curves for these extreme values of the willingness to pay, and the area in between, are shown graphically in Figure 13.2. The figure indicates what the minimum quantity X_{min} (intersection of the marginal cost curve with the curve of the minimum willingness to pay) and the maximum quantity X_{max} (intersection of marginal cost with maximum willingness to pay) of the public good are expected to be.

The experiment performed helps a political supplier to determine that quantity of the public good (lying between X_{min} and X_{max}) which corresponds to the preferences of the population.

CONCLUSION

The chapter has shown that there are a great many different methods available with which the preferences of the population can be revealed. Each one of these methods has specific advantages and disadvantages; depending on the purpose at hand, the method (or methods) best suited must be chosen.

FURTHER READING

Various approaches to the discovery and measurement of individual preferences are discussed in

John A. Sinden and Albert C. Worrell, *Unpriced Values. Decisions without Market Prices.* New York: John Wiley, 1979.

Paul Davidson, The Valuation of Public Goods. In Robert R. Dorfman and Nancy S. Dorfman (eds), *Economics of Environment*, 2nd edn. New York: Norton, 1977, 345–55.

Similar methods are also used in cost–benefit analysis. See for example

Edward M. Gramlich, *Benefit–Cost Analysis of Government Programs.* Englewood Cliffs, NJ: Prentice-Hall, 1981.

The travel cost method has been developed by

Marion Clawson and Jack L. Knetsch, *Economics of Outdoor Recreation.* Baltimore: John Hopkins University Press, 1966.

The market price of real estate method is treated in

A. Myrick Freeman, Hedonic Prices, Property Values and Measuring Environmental Benefits: A Survey of the Issues, *Scandinavian Journal of Economics*, 81 (1979), 154–73.

CHAPTER 14

Economic Policy Instruments

The government and the civil service can use various types of economic policy instruments in order to influence people's preferences and possibility sets. Moral appeals to the public would be effective only under very specific circumstances, such as in times of emergency. *Global instruments* in the form of fiscal and monetary policy mainly attempt to influence the budget constraint, or income, of individuals and firms. *Incentive-oriented instruments* of economic policy can influence the behaviour of individuals, groups and institutions by changing the relative advantages offered by the available courses of action – in other words, by changing relative prices. Among these methods are incentive taxes, incentive subsidies and marketable certificates. Finally, the course of the economy can be influenced by *direct intervention regulations*. It is important to distinguish between formal, or intended, and actual effects.

14.1 EFFECTS OF VARIOUS ECONOMIC POLICY INSTRUMENTS

The effects of economic policy depend on the behaviour of the decision-makers involved. According to the economic model of behaviour based on utility maximization subject to constraints, policy instruments may change behaviour by changing either the *preferences* or the *possibility sets*. The possibility set is determined by the constraints imposed. The most important restriction on behaviour from an economic point of view is the budget constraint. The decision-makers' behaviour depends not only on the level of the budget (that is, of one's income and wealth) but also on relative prices. The possibility set can also be influenced by direct government intervention such as regulation.

The economic model of behaviour applies not only to individuals but also to institutional decision-makers. Indeed, it is often the intention of economic policy to affect the behaviour of institutions such as interest groups, trade unions, public enterprises and other government entities such as local governments.

14.2 TYPES OF ECONOMIC POLICY INSTRUMENTS

Influencing Preferences

Preferences can be changed by two kinds of instruments:

1 *moral appeals* (moral suasion), which can be expected to have a short-run effect only;
2 *education*, which can be used to change preferences in the long run. The publicly run schools play a central role in this process. This instrument has been used, for example, to develop an 'environmental ethic'.

The effect of moral suasion and education on the behaviour of individuals has been little analysed. Certainly, these instruments are effective only if the population is ready to behave in the way demanded. The socio-psychological theory of mass communication, as discussed in Chapter 12, suggests that otherwise the selective choice of sources of information would prevent individuals from changing their preferences. Moral suasion is certainly unsuited to change the behaviour of institutions such as firms and interest groups. If they are subject to competition they cannot afford to follow the politicians' moral appeals. To further their image in public, institutions will seemingly consent, but will at the same time look for ways and means of maintaining their behaviour. There are many such possibilities.

Experience with moral appeals suggests that the instrument has little effect when generally applied.

Empirical evidence

— Five communities in various American states have undertaken voluntary programmes for reusing glass bottles and paper. Households were expected to wash the bottles, to bundle the papers and magazines, and to transport the whole to a depot. The appeals for voluntary co-operation had little effect: in this way not more than 8 per cent of the total solid waste was collected in any area. When the local authorities issued a compulsory regulation to process their waste in that way, 80 per cent of the refuse was collected.

— Moral appeals do not seem effective to save energy, either. In the state of Oregon, noted for its environment-minded population, the governor appealed for a reduction in electric energy by using massive propaganda and his personal authority. In the first month thereafter electricity consumption in the private sector fell by 2 per cent; later no effect at all was visible. (The electricity saving within government institutions, for which the governor issued regulations to the same effect, amounted to 20 per cent.)

Moral appeals have a large-scale effect only in the case of emergencies and catastrophies. Under these circumstances, the population can be motivated to participate in voluntary action. This behaviour can be explained by an implicit consensus according to which mutual aid is advantageous to all in times of trouble.

Examples

In many countries calls to donate blood are successful provided that the population is informed about its urgency.

In New York in the mid-1960s an appeal to save water voluntarily had a considerable effect during an extended period of drought. Water use sank by 4–6 per cent.

Whether preferences can really be changed in the long run through education is open to debate. It is not even sure whether preferences can be changed in the desired direction. Not infrequently, young people subjected to certain kinds of education do exactly the opposite of what has been intended (consider, for example, the student revolts in the West in 1968, and the failure of many educational measures in Communist countries). On the other hand, education may be effective in the long run if it is related to damage caused by *many* small activities of *many* isolated individuals.

Example

The number of forest fires has strongly declined since American children (and adults) have been advised about the damages caused by careless behaviour with the help of the symbolic figure of 'Smoky Bear'.

The great advantage of moral appeals is that they require few resources. This instrument can be applied by the government very rapidly, and no legal and administrative obstacles have to be overcome: no laws need to be changed, and the public bureaucracy need not participate. The disadvantage of this instrument is that it is to a large extent ineffective. Economic advisers should advocate its use only in times of emergency, or to supplement the use of other instruments. Long-run education measures are warranted when other instruments are too expensive or ineffective.

Global Instruments

These instruments affect the behaviour of agents mainly through the circular flow of income, that is, through the level of the budget constraint pertaining to each actor. The application of these instruments also changes relative prices (in other words, it rotates the budget constraint line), but this is only a side-effect. The main global instruments are fiscal and monetary policy. They are not treated here because their nature and effects are thoroughly discussed in textbooks on macroeconomics, as well as on public finance, and in more specialized textbooks.

Incentive Instruments

The behaviour of actors can be influenced by changing the relative prices of the alternatives available, inducing *substitution effects*. The processes of substitution extend over long time periods because incentives are created to introduce innovations that correspond to the change in relative scarcities.

Remark

The substitution effect is based on a basic theorem in economics: if a price rises relative to other prices, the demand for the more expensive good falls relatively, provided that the accompanying income effect is compensated: the compensated demand curve has a negative slope.

The substitution effect is usually established on the basis of a utility calculus. Figure 14.1 illustrates the relationships graphically. In the initial situation the individual consumes at point P_0, where the budget line AB touches the indifference curve U_0 of the two goods X_1 and X_2. It is now assumed that the relative prices of the two goods change by rotation about

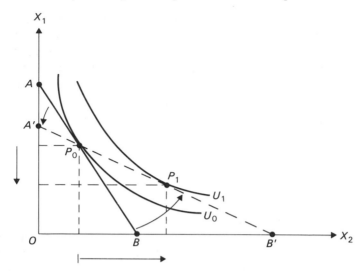

FIGURE 14.1   *Explaining the substitution effect through the utility calculus.*

point P_0 : good X_1 becomes more expensive (the maximum possible consumption of this good falls), and good X_2 becomes cheaper (the maximum
quantity consumable increases). If the individual stays at point P_0 he will
not fully exhaust his consumption possibilities. He could increase his utility
by consuming at point P_1, reaching the indifference curve U_1. At P_1, more
of the cheaper good X_2 and less of the more expensive good X_1 is consumed.

The substitution effect can also be explained with the help of a change in
the consumption possibility set. This approach has the advantage that the
basic theorem can be derived without using any information about utility
and indifference curves. The change in the consumption possibility set (a
rotation of the budget line) is usually easier to observe than movements
along indifference curves. The approach is illustrated graphically in Figure
14.2. Initially, the consumption possibility set is given by the area OAB. The
representative individual may consume along the efficient combination AB
or within the possibility set. It is again assumed that the budget line rotates
about point P_0. The resulting change in the consumption possibility area
has two effects: consumption in the hatched area $A'AP_0$ becomes unfeas-
ible, because the income available would be insufficient; consumption in the
area BP_0B' becomes feasible. The arrows in the figure indicate the changes
in the consumption of the two goods to be expected as a result of random
movements away from the initial points of consumption. There is a tendency for the consumption of good X_1 to decrease, and of good X_2 to
increase.

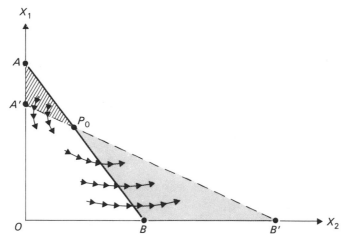

FIGURE 14.2   *Explaining the substitution effect through a change in the consumption possibility set.*

Relative prices can be changed by applying

— incentive taxes;
— incentive subsidies;
— marketable certificates.

These instruments will be discussed in the following sections.

Incentive Taxation.   Undesired goods and/or activities can be taxed in order to increase their relative price. The change in relative price gives an incentive to reduce the consumption and/or the activities concerned. The goal of incentive taxation is not to increase tax revenue, but rather to *change the relative prices*, and to therewith motivate individuals and firms to change their behaviour.

A simple demand and supply diagram illustrates how an incentive tax changes the demand for a good (see Figure 14.3). The equilibrium of demand and supply is initially at point *B*. The introduction of an incentive tax per unit of output makes the taxed good more expensive: the marginal cost curve of each producer, and therefore the supply curve of the whole sector, shifts upwards. Price is increased, and demand is reduced, to point *C*.

An incentive tax is able to reduce producing activities; this is, for example, the purpose of an *emission tax*. This tax is imposed on those activities that damage the environment – for example, on a firm that pollutes the air and water. If the emissions are taxed, the

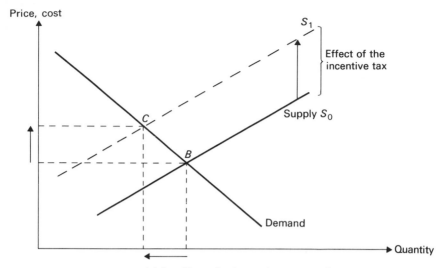

FIGURE 14.3   *How the incentive tax works.*

polluter changes his calculus: an activity that up to now could be undertaken free of charge (pollution) now leads to costs (the payment of the emission tax). The polluter has an incentive to evade these costs as far as possible. There are two possibilities of doing so:

1   the environmental damage can be directly lowered by reducing the pollution emitted per unit of output produced: this will be achieved, for example, by using filters or new production techniques;
2   the structure of production can be changed by reducing the output of those goods whose production causes high environmental damage, and instead supplying goods whose production is less harmful to the environment.

The producer can also try to shift the emission tax by charging higher prices. But if the prices of the goods whose production causes heavy pollution rise, this will induce consumers to shift to alternative goods. Because of falling demand, production will become less profitable and the resources (labour and capital) will increasingly be used for other purposes. The goods causing pollution lose in importance compared with goods that are less harmful to the natural environment.

   Incentive taxation can also be used to influence consumption patterns. The use of energy provides a good example. Assume that the government wants to reduce the energy consumption (particularly of oil) of the population. For that purpose, it may impose an energy tax on the oil sold to the final consumer. The use of oil becomes more expensive compared with other products, thus giving consumers an incentive to consume less oil. Private households have a number of possibilities for substitution, including:

— reduction of heating and wearing warmer clothing;
— better insulation of houses and apartments;
— installation of heating systems based on alternative energy sources (such as solar energy);
— use of public means of transport instead of the petrol-intensive private motor car;
— purchase of cars with more efficient motors;
— driving in a petrol-saving manner.

What matters is that individuals have a personal interest in devising and using these and other ways of saving energy – no regulations to that end are needed.

Incentive taxes not only affect existing activities but also encourage the introduction of technological and social innovations. When the consumption of conventional energy sources (oil, electricity, coal) is taxed, it becomes worthwhile to look for alternative energy sources.

The institution of incentive taxation has a long history.

Examples

In ancient Rome Cato, who was elected censor in 184 BC, made an effort to defend the Roman traditions of discipline against the Greek influence of luxury. He introduced a luxury tax on those properties connected with the Greek way of life. While ordinary property was taxed by 0.1 per cent, the luxurious properties were taxed 30 times as much, by 3 per cent.

Taxing bachelors has an equally long tradition. The Emperor Augustus raised this kind of incentive tax to fight against the increase of the number of those not marrying and having children, which was endangering the existence of the Roman empire. At the beginning of our century, bachelors were taxed more heavily than family fathers in most European countries, again for the purpose of increasing population growth.

A very special kind of incentive tax is due to Peter the Great. In order to accelerate Russia's process of adopting European customs, he imposed a tax on beards; at that time, not wearing beards was a sign of being progressive.

Incentive taxes can be used for a great many purposes. The following list serves to demonstrate the wide applicability and is arranged according to the sectors affected.

1   Population
    — birth tax (to lower the rate of births);
    — bachelor tax;
    — tax on foreigners;
    — immigration and emigration taxes.
2   Natural environment
    — effluent charge: a tax on the pollution emitted into the air and water. Such a tax corresponds to the 'polluter-pay principle';
    — energy tax;
    — tax on exploiting natural resources.
3   Change in the structure of production
    — import and export taxes;
    — job tax;
    — service tax – for example, the 'selective employment tax' in the United Kingdom, which served to lower the proportion of employees in the services sector.
4   Change in the structure of consumption
    (With respect to traffic):
    — car park tax;
    — congestion tax (contributing a price for the use of too-heavily-frequented roads);
    — noise pollution tax.
    (With respect to health:)
    — alcohol tax;
    — tobacco tax;
    — dog tax (with the purpose of reducing their excrements on the pavements).
    (With respect to 'good morals':)
    — luxury tax;
    — advertising tax;
    — pornography tax.
5   Changing global economic activity
    — tax on wage increases (this proposition has been discussed in Chapter 10);
    — tax on price increases;
    — investment and consumption tax.

A large number of empirical studies have shown that incentive taxes are very effective. Only a few examples can be presented here.

Empirical evidence

— A careful study analyses the options available to clean the Delaware River in the United States. The cost of achieving an exogenously determined quality standard is analysed by requiring (1) a uniform reduction of emissions by all polluters, and (2) a uniform effluent charge per unit of pollutant emitted. Table 14.1 compares the cost of these alternatives with a 'medium' water quality desired. The cleaning cost for the whole society amounts to $2.4 million per year if an effluent charge is used, and to $5 million per year if a uniform reduction is required. The cost savings when using the incentive tax amounts to 52 per cent. If a 'good' water quality is desired, the cost saving amounts to 40 per cent.

TABLE 14.1 *Cost of Using Alternative Instruments for Cleaning Water*

Water quality standard desired	Uniform reduction of pollution	Effluent charge	Cost saving of effluent charge compared to uniform reduction
		($ million per year)	
Medium	5.0	2.4	52%
Good	20.0	12.0	40%

Source: Edwin L. Johnson, A Study of the Economics of Water Quality Management, *Water Resources Research*, 3 (1967), p. 297.

— The sulphur emissions of coal electricity plants lead to high environmental damage. A study concludes that with even a low emission tax (which raises the electricity price by 7–19 per cent) there would be a reduction of sulphur emissions between 85 and 90 per cent.

— A study on the energy consumption of private households in the United States concludes that an increase of the electricity price by 10 per cent leads to a reduction in consumption by more than 10 per cent.

Economic advisers can point out remarkable advantages of incentive taxes to the government and the public administration.

— Set goals can be reached efficiently. Individuals and firms are given clear signals in the form of relative price changes which in turn give the incentive to change the behaviour in the desired direction.
— The administrative costs are often quite small. It suffices to fix the level of the incentive tax; no direct intervention into the individuals' and firms' decision-making is necessary.

The advisers must also indicate the negative consequences that the use of incentive taxes may have for the government and the public administration. It is very likely that their application will be strongly resisted by three important political decision-makers.

1   The population will find incentive taxes hard to understand because they are not accustomed to the steering function of relative prices. People often argue that an effluent charge is ineffective because the use and the destruction of the environment is simply paid for and that, moreover, the tax is simply passed on to the consumer. Economic advisers can help to overcome these erroneous assertions. Also, the population often has moral qualms about the application of incentive taxes such as a birth tax. But the most important reason why the introduction of incentive taxes is opposed is that they are considered 'anti-social': the poor are assumed to be worst hit by this tax and/or by the resulting price increases. Economic advisers may show that other instruments that are used for the same purpose (in particular, prohibitions) may have similar 'anti-social' consequences. The best response of the advisers to this assertion is to suggest how the negatively affected (lower-) income groups could be compensated for the loss in welfare.

2   Interest groups are often opposed to introducing incentive taxes precisely because they *do* believe them to be effective.

Example

Effluent charges on air and water pollution have been discussed in many countries, but they have only rarely been seriously applied because the industries affected put up political resistance (together with the corresponding trade unions, who want to maintain jobs). The interest groups obviously assume that they have to adjust less, and that the costs imposed on them are lower, when other instruments are used.

3　The public administration rejects incentive taxes because its discretionary power is reduced. It prefers non-price instruments such as regulation, which requires extensive administrative activities, thus increasing the importance of the sector in the political process.

Incentive Subsidies.　Subsidies can give a positive incentive to behave in a desired way. The compensation given depends on the extent to which the behaviour is changed. The principle of the incentive tax is thus reversed, because that instrument punishes undesired behaviour. In both cases, however, the relative prices that confront individuals and firms are changed; similar behavioural reactions can therefore be expected.

The main difference between incentive subsidies and incentive taxes lies in the fact that subsidies give a strong motivation to behave strategically: the potential recipients of subsidies can try to manipulate the initial level at which a change in behaviour is rewarded. For example, when they are expecting an incentive subsidy to be introduced, they will be inclined to take up the undesired activity in order to be compensated for giving it up again.

Incentive subsidies intended to reduce a certain activity, such as the pollution of air or water, have another disadvantage: the subsidy received tends to increase the profits in the subsidized sector, which gives firms an incentive to move into this sector. Though an incentive subsidy leads to a reduction of the activity (pollution) *per firm*, the *number* of firms in the sector is likely to increase. Part of the beneficial effect of the subsidy is thereby lost. An incentive tax has a contrasting effect: the number of firms affected decreases owing to falling profits, so that the relative price effect is strengthened.

Psychological experiments dealing with the effects of external rewards on behaviour suggest a possible third disadvantage of incentive subsidies (which are a typical case of 'external rewards'). If a certain activity has already been undertaken for its own sake, external rewards can devalue and thereby destroy this intrinsic motivation. An external reward in the form of a subsidy under certain circumstances may not lead to the expected effect because the underlying intrinsic motivation to act in the desired way has been reduced.

Incentive subsidies should be clearly distinguished from subsidies that do not change the relative prices, but rather increase income. In general, incentive subsidies are more effective in changing behaviour in the desired direction because strong incentives are set. The difference in the effect of the two kinds of subsidies is illustrated graphically in Figure 14.4. The horizontal axis shows the activity (or good X) that should be expanded with the help of subsidies. The vertical axis shows all other activities (or goods) Z. Initially, the budget constraint is $P_0 P_1$, and the quantities X_0 and Z_0 are 'consumed' at point A. It is now assumed that a subsidy is given which enables an increase in activity X by the distance $X_0 X_s$, or AB. A subsidy just leading to a rise in income shifts the budget curve in a parallel way outwards to $P_0' P_1'$. The relative price of X and Z remains unaffected. Owing to the higher income, a higher indifference curve U_2 can be reached than before (U_0), and at point C both activities are larger. The increase of the subsidized activity X is smaller, namely $X_0 X_1'$, than would seem possible on the basis of the amount transferred ($X_0 X_s$).

If a subsidy of equal size is introduced that changes the relative prices in favour of activity X, the budget line rotates about point P_0. The amount of subsidy is larger, the greater activity X. The new budget line is $P_0 P_1''$, going through point B in order that the same size of subsidy AB is expended relative to the initial situation A.

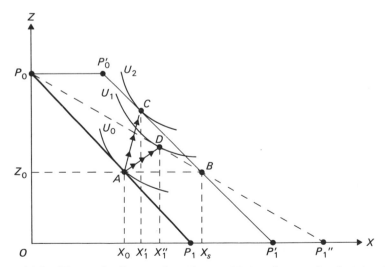

FIGURE 14.4   *How subsidies work with or without changes in relative prices: X is a good or an activity; Z refers to all other goods or activities.*

Owing to the relative price change, this kind of subsidy leads to a 'consumption' at point D. Owing to the relative price effect, the desired activity X is greater (increase from X_0 to X_1'') compared with the other type of subsidy (where the increase was $X_1 X_1'$). The actual subsidy paid out is, moreover, smaller.

In principle, incentive subsidies can be applied in all those areas in which incentive taxes can be used. Some examples are:

1　*environment:* the reduction of the emission of pollutants into the air and the water can be subsidized;
2　*production structure:* reducing the cultivation of agrarian products (which are in excess supply) can be subsidized;
3　*infrastructure:* in this area the most important kind of incentive subsidies are the *matching grants.* A higher-level federal unit pays part of the cost of an infrastructural project provided that the rest is carried by the lower-level federal units directly benefited. For that unit, the matching grant changes the relative cost of the infrastructural project compared with other uses of the money. Such subsidies are often given to build roads or purification plants.

Economic advisers can suggest the use of incentive subsidies, in particular, when incentive taxes are difficult to introduce owing to the opposition of those affected. Incentive subsidies are somewhat less efficient and lead to administrative problems and control costs because of the strategic behaviour of those who potentially benefit. They do, however, change the relative prices in the desired direction so that the behaviour is influenced in an effective way.

Marketable Certificates.　Certificates allow the pursuit of certain activity. The number of certificates issued determines the overall extent of the respective activity, because one certificate allows an exactly determined extent of the corresponding activity. The certificates, sometimes called *licences*, can be bought and sold on a free market, the market price being determined by supply and demand. The price of the certificate, and therefore the implicit 'tax' on engaging in the activity, are a reflection of the number of certificates supplied, given the demand.

There are two main advantages of marketable licences over incentive taxes:

1   a given activity can be steered more simply because its extent can be determined directly by fixing the number of certificates issued. There is less uncertainty about the results. In the case of incentive taxes (and incentive subsidies), the reaction of the individuals and firms affected can only be conjectured;
2   when the number of economic producers, national income and the price level change, no adjustments need to be made. If, for example, the price level increases, the price of the certificates also rises; if the number of producers increases, the price of the certificates will tend to rise because the demand for the activities regulated by the certificates is likely to increase. In the case of an incentive tax, on the other hand, the tax rate must be adjusted in both cases in order to keep the extent of the activity constant.

Marketable certificates can be introduced in all those areas in which incentive taxes are possible. Some examples include:

— environmental certificates, to allow an exactly specified emission of pollutants into the environment;
— baby certificates, to control the birth rate;
— certificates for controlling price increases (see the discussion in Chapter 10).

Marketable certificates are closely related to the *voucher system*. This regulates areas in which consumption is enforced but where competition between various suppliers is to be newly introduced. For example, schooling is compulsory for children until a certain age. The parents can be given vouchers which entitle them to send their children to any school they wish. The schools get their income only in the form of the value of the vouchers they receive. This fosters the competition between suppliers of education, and this is likely to improve quality. Vouchers can be used in many different areas.

Marketable certificates are rarely used in practical economic policy. They are resisted by those potentially affected, probably because they are known to be effective in influencing behaviour. There is also a certain dislike of introducing the price system into new areas, partly because the public often does not understand how prices influence behaviour. Stiff resistance against marketable certificates will be raised especially by the civil service because it fears the loss of the possibility to intervene into the economy, resulting in a loss of influence.

Economic advisers will recommend the use of marketable certificates to the government and political parties only under especially favourable conditions. The instrument has a chance of being used in the current politico-economic process only when the civil service does not vehemently oppose it. In areas that have to be newly regulated and in which the civil service does not have to defend established positions, there might be a chance for introducing this type of regulation. If this should occur, the public has to be informed about the working of certificates. In particular, it has to be told what their advantages are compared with direct administrative controls. The latter reduce the discretionary power of citizens much more and lead to annoyances owing to government tutelage. In many cases it is advisable to make suggestions about how the expected losses may be compensated in order to increase the political support for the introduction of the marketable certificates.

Direct Controls

Behaviour can also be influenced by the use of direct controls. The consequence of disregarding regulations, orders or commands are legal sanctions, which may range from small fines to imprisonment (or even to death penalty).

Direct controls are possible everywhere; there is indeed an uncountable number of public regulations. The 'flood of regulations' observed almost everywhere is an immediate consequence of the tendency for governments to intervene directly.

Empirical evidence

The United States Federal Register, which was established in 1936 to record all the regulations, hearings, and other matters connected with regulatory agencies, contained 2,599 pages. Twenty years later, in 1956, the Register contained 10,528 pages, and ten years later (1966), 16,850 pages. In 1978 it contained 36,487 pages. The size grew from six inches of shelf space (1936) to a ten-foot shelf.

Direct intervention can be applied to three areas:

1 *price controls*, for example fixing the price of food and rents;
2 *quantity controls*, for example fixing the maximum amount of emissions of air pollutants or by restricting quantitatively emigration or immigration;

3   *quality controls*, for example supervising the characteristics of food or drugs or limiting entry into a profession to those having a certain diploma.

Direct quantitative and qualitative interventions are of utmost importance in practical economic policy. Space does not permit a listing of all the areas in which they are applied.

The public regulations can be either *generally* valid, that is, applicable to all situations and all individuals and firms concerned, or *specifically* for particular situations. In the latter case the resources required are much higher because each case must be judged on the basis of the special circumstances.

Example

Emission standards for the protection of the natural environment can prescribe that all firms (and possibly all households) must reduce the emissions of a particular pollutant (say, sulphur dioxyde) by the same amount. Similarly, in order to save energy all users of oil can be ordered to reduce consumption by the same percentage rate. Specific regulations would, in the case of emission standards, take into account which costs a firm has to carry in order to reduce emissions, and how threatening the environmental deterioration in the region concerned is. The prescriptions on the quantitative reduction of oil consumption, may take into account the substitution possibilities and the 'importance' of the good therewith produced (for example, food stuffs v. luxury goods).

The effectiveness of direct controls is determined on five different levels.

1   *Formulation of the regulation.* The government succeeds in having parliament accept only vague and general regulations. Anything more specific would immediately be opposed by the pressure groups. As long as the norms are sufficiently indeterminate, interest groups have little reason to oppose them; they know that they can still become active when the bargaining process over the practical application of the regulations starts.

2   *Control of the regulations.* Regulations can be effective only if the individuals and firms affected accept that they have to bear negative sanctions when they violate them. In general, the marginal cost of control increases quickly, so that a comprehensive enforcement is impossible. The controls often require a great amount of technical

knowledge which the controlling public institutions do not always have. They therefore depend often on the co-operation of the 'controlled'. This opens the way to mutual bargaining.

3 *Accusation.* Those who infringe regulations, and are caught, are not necessarily brought to court. In general, the controllers have little interest in creating conflicts with those not sticking to the regulations because they depend on them for future co-operation. Moreover, they fear the risk of losing before the courts because of the often insufficient evidence. This would result in a loss of prestige and power for the controllers, so on all levels they will rather try to reach an 'amicable agreement'; they are satisfied if the regulations are partly followed. The effect of regulations is increased if their violation is actionable by the individuals negatively affected. If only those directly affected can bring the case to court, individuals often have little motivation to do so because the success is uncertain and the cost may be high in terms of money, time and annoyance. Moreover, a suit has the characteristics of a public good because all others in the same or similar situation profit directly or can thereafter more easily win their own case because of the precedent. The possibility for accusation is greater when organizations can go to court in the name of all those negatively affected (collective complaint). This is particularly important for environmental regulations.

4 *Conviction.* An accused person is not necessarily convicted, because the evidence is often insufficient and the accused will bring forward counter-arguments. The odds of this happening are high, because the violaters of the regulation usually have a particularly good knowledge about the substantive issues involved. Large firms and institutions can afford to have specialized attorneys, which make conviction less likely.

7 *Punishment.* A convicted person is not necessarily really punished. Often, special circumstances can be adduced so that the degree of punishment and its execution will be relatively small compared with the severity of the violation. In many cases, those responsible for infringing regulations do not even have to bear the consequences themselves because their organization or firm will pay the fines.

Direct intervention through public regulations will be effective only if action on all five of these steps is guaranteed, *and* if the expected actual punishment is higher than the utility of violating a

regulation. The individuals and firms undertake a cost–benefit calcu-
lation. Often, the advantage of infringing a regulation is immediate
and clearly visible while the expected costs are uncertain, because it
is doubtful if the five steps leading to actual punishment will be
realized. The normal result will be that the regulations are not perfectly followed but, depending on the specific circumstances, will be
observed only to some degree. The commonly held notion that it is
sufficient to issue laws is certainly mistaken; the fact that a regulation exists does not mean that it is observed and that it has the
desired effect on behaviour.

The more restrictive a regulation, the larger, *ceteris paribus*, are
the incentives to get around or to violate it.

Example

Price controls designed to keep down the prices of specific goods lead to a
reduction of the supply in the official market. Instead, an illegal black
market will arise with higher prices and sufficient supply. Historical experience tells us that such a development cannot be prevented even if large
resources are put into fighting it: increasing controls and imprisoning black
market suppliers may be able to restrict supply on the black market in the
short run, but the resulting price increase gives an incentive for *new* suppliers to enter the illegal market, so that the original supply situation tends
to be re-established.

Economic advisers can make suggestions to the government and to
the public administration on how to make regulations more effective.
Owing to the reaction of the affected and administrative problems,
however, they must be aware that it will never be possible to make
direct intervention fully effective.

Example

A study for the United States shows that in those occupations subject to the
minimum wage law in 1973 only 65 per cent of the employees received at
least the legal minimum wage. When a rise of the legal minimum wage was
introduced in 1975, the share of legal minimum wage recipients dropped to
55 per cent.

The compliance rate to regulations can be increased through unex-
pected controls, undertaken on a random basis. They should be
directed to those areas in which the benefits of violating the law are
large compared with the control cost. If the resources for control are

applied in this way, the rate of compliance can be sizeably increased. The punishment effected must be so high that the expected present value of the punishment – the probability of being caught, accused and convicted, multiplied by the severity of punishment – is higher than the expected benefits of not keeping to the regulations. Only in this case does punishment have a deterrent effect.

Remark

The *economic theory of crime* has empirically shown that increasing punishment, *ceteris paribus*, leads to a statistically significant reduction in crime. The marginal effect of higher punishment is, however, not very large. This result has been found on the basis of cross-section and time series analyses carried out for many different countries and periods.

To remain effective, the level of punishment must not be raised to very high levels, for a number of reasons. The size of the punishment must be in a reasonable relationship to the severity of the violation of the law; it must be possible to intensify the punishment when a violation of greater consequence occurs. (If you condemn a plain thief to death, how do you punish a murderer adequately?) Another basic problem is that the law should be morally 'just' in order to be respected. The potential violators calculate (at least implicitly) the *probability* of being punished; therefore the punishment as specified in the law must be heavier than its (mathematically) expected value (size of punishment times its probability).

Example

Assume that the probability of being caught when parking unlawfully is 10 per cent, and that the corresponding punishment considered to be 'just' is £10. The expected value of the punishment thus is £1. This low value may induce many drivers to disregard parking regulations. If the fine is raised to £100, the expected value would be £10, but the legal punishment for those convicted would be considered too high compared to the rather minor violation of the law.

Economic advisers will suggest direct interventions to the political suppliers in the following circumstances:
— when rapid changes of behaviour are required;
— in critical situations (for example in case of an imminent poisoning of the air or water);

— when the reaction of individuals, firms and independent public authorities is uncertain if other policy instruments (such as incentive taxes) were used;
— when the application of other instruments is very costly or impossible, or if it is rejected by the population on moral grounds.

One of the main advantages of the application of regulation from the point of view of the government (and the political parties) is that this instrument is accepted by the most important political groups, quite in contrast to incentive-oriented instruments:

— the *population* is used to regulations and is therefore better able to adjust (whereas the fluctuating prices of marketable certificates, for example, is more difficult to get used to). Direct interventions are often interpreted as indicating that the government has decided to act; their use may therefore be advantageous for the government even if the effects are small or non-existent ('symbolic behaviour'). The public likes direct intervention because it believes that its effects are 'socially just' (even if this is not really the case).
— The *public administration* prefers regulations to all other instruments because their application augments bureaucracy's own role and influence. Direct intervention gives it greater scope for discretionary behaviour such that it can better pursue its own goals.

CONCLUSION

It has been argued that efforts to change people's preferences, particularly by moral appeals, work only under very limited circumstances. More effective are incentive instruments, which can be applied in the form of taxes, subsidies or marketable certificates. These are difficult to introduce because they are resisted by the civil service as well as by interest groups. The actors prefer direct controls, whose effectiveness is, however, often rather low. The various instruments have particular strengths and weaknesses. A good economic policy therefore seeks to combine them in such a way that the goals to be attained are served best.

FURTHER READING

A general survey of the main instruments used in the various countries is given by

Etienne-Sadi Kirschen (ed.), *Economic Policies Compared; West and East*. Vol. I: *General Theory*. Amsterdam: North Holland, 1974.

Fiscal and monetary policy and their interaction, and the difference between a Keynesian and a monetarist view of the world, is ably discussed in many modern textbooks on macroeconomic theory: see for example

Robert J. Gordon, *Macroeconomics,* 2nd edn. Boston: Little, Brown, 1981.

The interpretation of the substitution effect as a change in the possibility set was introduced by

Gary S. Becker, Irrational Behavior and Economy Theory, *Journal of Political Economy*, 70 (1962), 1–13; reprinted in his collection of articles: *The Economic Approach to Human Behavior*. Chicago and London: Chicago University Press, 1976, 3–14.

The analysis of the effects of instrument use is based on the economic model of human behaviour which is quite compatible with socio-psychological views. See

Herbert A. Simon, Rationality as Process and Product of Thought, *American Economic Review, Papers and Proceedings, 68* (1978), 1–16;

Wolfgang Stroebe and Bruno S. Frey, In Defense of Economic Man: Towards an Integration of Economics and Psychology, *Schweizerische Zeitschrift für Volkswirtschaft und Statistik*, 116 (1980), 119–48.

Incentive taxes, incentive subsidies and marketable certificates are theoretically discussed, and empirical evidence for the case of environmental protection is cited, in

William J. Baumol and Wallace E. Oates, *Economics, Environmental Policy, and the Quality of Life*. Englewood Cliffs, NJ: Prentice-Hall, 1979.

Psychological studies analysing the effect of external rewards on intrinsic motivation can be found in

Kenneth O. McGraw, The Detrimental Effects of Reward on Performance: A Literature Review and Prediction Model. In: Mark R. Lepper and David Greene (eds), *The Hidden Cost of Reward: New Perspectives on the Psychology of Human Motivation*. New York: Erlbaum, 1978.

An interesting account of the practical experiences with introducing educational vouchers is given by

Davis K. Cohen and Eleanor Farrar, Power to the Parents? The Story of Educational Vouchers, *Public Interest* 48 (1977), 72–97.

The evidence cited on the application of the minimum wage laws in the United States is based on

Orley Ashenfelter and Robert S. Smith, Compliance with the Minimum Wage Law, *Journal of Political Economy,* 87 (1979), 333–50.

CHAPTER 15

Applying Economic Policy

INTRODUCTION

Economic advisers can help the government and the public administration to improve their decision-making capacity. For this purpose, they can use their knowledge of economics and of interdisciplinary approaches, such as systems analysis and policy science. Various techniques are applicable and useful in different circumstances – for example, econometric models, planning methods and implementation procedures.

It may be useful for the government and the public administration to dissect a decision into several stages in order to be able to advance step by step, and not to get lost in the complex decision-making process. The following stages of a decision process may be distinguished:

— formulation of the problem;
— collection of the underlying facts, enumeration of the instruments available and evaluations of their general effectiveness;
— analysis of the specific effects of the instruments in view of the defined problems and the given situation;
— interpretation of the results;
— comparison of the results with the problem formulated;
— suggestion of specific policy actions;
— *ex post* evaluation of the procedures, the measures and the effects of the instruments.

15.1 ECONOMETRIC MODELS

The specific results of applying particular instruments can be analysed by *econometric models*. In such models, the relationships between the variables are theoretically specified and econometrically estimated. In the macroeconometric models, which intend to capture the overall relationships existing in an economy, the estimates are, however, often based on rather *ad hoc* assumptions instead of clear theoretical hypotheses. As yet it is very difficult to base these macro-models on a micro-theory of behaviour. In addition, the specific kinds of theoretical views have a considerable impact on the formulation and the properties of macroeconometric models. This applies in particular to business cycle models, in which the opposing views of the Keynesians (fiscalists) and the monetarists are well visible.

Empirical evidence

The sequence and size of the multipliers contained in the modern macroeconomic models essentially depend on the decision of whether a Keynesian or monetarist model is to be used. Consider the public expenditure multiplier. It measures the change in real GNP when real government expenditures are increased by a given amount. In the Keynesian type the corresponding multiplier is very high and positive; in those of the monetarist type it is at best positive at the beginning and then becomes increasingly negative. The reason lies in the crowding out of private expenditures owing to the increase of public expenditures.

The change in the size of the public expenditure multiplier is illustrated in Figure 15.1 for four modern macroeconometric models of the United States. The temporal sequence of the cummulated multiplier is shown for 12 quarters – three years. The econometric models of the Brookings Institution, the Wharton School and the University of Michigan are of the Keynesian type. The multipliers are large, considerably exceeding the value of 1 and often surpassing the value of 2. In the case of the Wharton model the multiplier rises continually over the 12 quarters; in the case of the Brookings and the Michigan models the multipliers fall somewhat after having reached a maximum (after seven and two quarters, respectively).

The econometric model of the Federal Reserve Bank of St Louis is of the strict monetarist type. The public expenditure multiplier is very small, reaching its maximum of 1 in the second quarter, and becoming even negative after the fifth quarter.

Macroeconometric models have recently come under attack from the 'rational expectations' school of thought. This argues that, once the decision-makers use their knowledge of the effects of the intended policy measures, they will adjust to them and will therefore antici-

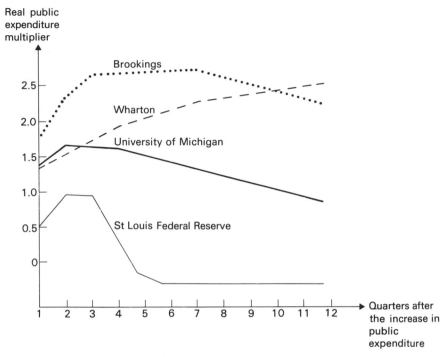

FIGURE 15.1 *The temporal sequences of the real public expenditure multiplier in macroeconometric models of the United States of the
Keynesian and monetarist type.*
Source: Gary Fromm and Lawrence R. Klein, A Comparison of Eleven Econometric Models
of the United States, *American Economic Review, Papers and Proceedings*, 63 (1973), table 5
(excerpt), 391.

pate them. The structure of a macroeconometric model is not constant but changes when an attempt is made by the government to
use its knowledge about the economic system in order to influence
the real price corrected variables of the economic system. This finding that it is a complete impossibility to affect the real economic
system by applying policy instruments, however, depends on a
number of highly restrictive assumptions, for example that economic
policy-makers and the decision-makers in the private sectors have
the same 'rational [or rather, consistent] expectations' about the
economic system. As these assumptions are seldom fulfilled, applying
economic policy instruments does have an effect on the real variables
of the economy, though the effects are probably smaller than was
expected in the heyday of Keynesianism.

Econometric macro-models can be extended by incorporating election and popularity functions, which capture the influence of the instrument use on the evaluations by the voters. With the help of such *politico-economic models*, economic policy advisers can inform the government and the parties about how economic policy measures will affect their re-election chances.

15.2   PLANNING TECHNIQUES

The best possible use of economic policy instruments can be derived with the help of formalized planning techniques. A complete discussion of these procedures may be found in the textbooks on public finance. Here, they are put into the context of the current politico-economic process. There are four important planning techniques.

1   *Cost–benefit analysis.*   This method makes an effort to take into account the monetary as well as the non-monetary, the short-term as well as the long-term, consequences of economic policy measures. The government uses the cost–benefit analysis as a planning instrument which captures the advantages and disadvantages of the policy measures on its own goals in quantitative terms. The quantification helps to compare competing policy actions. The government is also interested to know the distributional consequences as they are of great importance to the voters. A cost–benefit analysis can help the government to find out whether a project is potentially Pareto-optimal; whether it is, in principle, possible to improve the position of some individuals and groups without harming others. This knowledge, however, is not sufficient to determine the political consequences of a project. It may well be that a project that is not Pareto-optimal brings more votes: the vote gain from few citizens being greatly favoured may well exceed the vote loss from the remaining population, which experiences but a small reduction in its utility. The Pareto optimality as the cornerstone of traditional cost–benefit analysis will interest the government solely in so far as the economic advisers can suggest an income redistribution that is politically advantageous to the government. The government is also interested to know the consequences of a project for its chances of re-election. The 'politically' defined benefits and costs may differ markedly from those 'economically' defined. In a given region, the resource input for a project often yields political benefits because the

additional government expenditures increase employment, the profits of the private enterprises that receive orders, and the tax receipts. If such 'economic' costs become local 'political' benefits, the optimal size of such projects from the government's point of view lies above the economically optimal size.

Example

The Pareto-optimal, or 'economically' efficient, size X of a public project is achieved when maximizing the net benefit NB, in other words, the difference between the gross benefit and the total cost of the project. This 'economically' optimum size is indicated in Figure 15.2 by X_{ec}. X_{ec} is defined by the equality of marginal benefits and marginal cost of the project. The figure assumes for simplicity that the cost rises linearly, i.e. that the marginal costs are constant.)

The total cost C can be split up into that which yields political *benefits* in the local community (C_1) and that which yields nothing but cost (C_2). The government maximizes the difference between the total benefits of the project $B + C_1$ and the project cost $C = C_1 + C_2$. The political net benefits of the project are $B - C_2$. The government thus considers only the politically relevant cost C_2 when it determines the size of the project. The equality of marginal benefits and politically relevant marginal cost determines the politically optimal size of the public project, X_{pol}. As may be seen from the figure, the size chosen by the government is larger than is 'economically' efficient (Pareto-optimal): $X_{pol} > X_{ec}$.

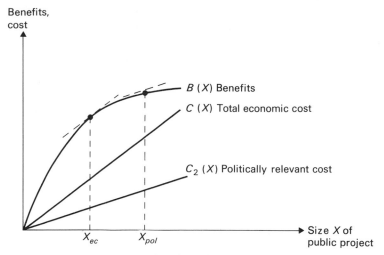

FIGURE 15.2 *'Economic' and 'political' optimum size of a public project.*

2   *Goals achievement analysis.*   This method systematically evaluates the benefits of the outcome of a policy measure, or project, on
the basis of a set of criteria by attributing utility quantities, called
'utiles'. The criteria are then attributed relative weights, and finally it
is calculated which project yields the highest sum of utiles. Economic
advisers will suggest and apply this planning technique, especially
when the government wants to pursue several independent goals,
because this method will enable it to get a good view of the overall
interdependence between instruments and goals. Once the effects of
the various measures or projects are determined, the technique can
be applied quickly and with little cost and is therefore well suited for
economic policy in the framework of the current politico-economic
process. One of the major disadvantages of this method is that the
results strongly depend on subjective evaluations and will therefore
differ between advisers.

3   *Cost effectiveness analysis.*   This method allows us to find out
how a given goal can be reached at least cost. For the government, it
is not the total economic cost but that cost attributed by the population to the government that is relevant. A cost effectiveness analysis allows the government to save costs and to use the money for
other purposes.

4   *Budgeting planning techniques.*   Various methods exist in this
area. *Financial planning* over several years is superior to the traditional yearly budget, because the long-run cost consequences can be
taken into account. This information is important for the government because it determines the future possibilities for spending
money. The *planning–programming–budgeting system* (PPBS) goes
one step further: the planning phase is followed by a programming
phase in which the benefits and the cost of the projects are compared, and only then follows the determination of the financial consequences. In this planning method, cost–benefit analysis is
combined with financial planning over several years.

15.3   OPTIMIZATION

The optimal combination of the various policy instruments can be
found with the help of formalized decision models. Various techniques of analysis are available:

— the methods of the theory of quantitative economic policy;
— optimal control theory, which is an extension of the static optimization theory to dynamic problems;
— the theory of risk and uncertainty, which takes into account the fact that decision-makers are never fully informed about the functioning of the economic system and about the effects of the policy instruments.

These optimization techniques can help to combine the various policy instruments so that the government's own utility (ideological benefits, re-election) are maximized within the given constraints. The formalized optimization procedure requires, however, a considerable knowledge about the quantitative relationships in the economic system. In the framework of *soft modelling* an effort is made to derive results even if the properties of the underlying economic system are not exactly known.

There is not much to say in general about the optimal use of the instruments. It depends on the specific conditions, in particular on the characteristics of the economic system and the state of the business cycle. The application of formal optimization procedures is often limited because of the lack of information and because there is no adequate macroeconometric model available. Moreover, the application requires considerable expenses, and the results are not always clear enough to be really useful to actors in day-to-day economic policy-making.

There are three basic principles to be observed when using economic policy instruments:

1 each instrument is to be applied according to its comparative advantage, that is, where it has the relatively largest effect;
2 the instruments have a diminishing marginal effect, unless the opposite is proved: this means that an instrument should not be applied so strongly that it loses its potency. Careful use also prevents the creation of economic fluctuations. An effect cannot be expected instantly; some time has to pass before an instrument is productive;
3 several instruments should be used simultaneously so that they supplement each other. Economic advisers can also point out that new instruments may be particularly potent because the decision-makers affected do not know yet how to anticipate and thus nullify their effect (by rational expectations).

15.4 INFORMATIONAL REQUIREMENTS

As has been stressed, economic policy-making requires considerable information about the present and the probable future state of the economy. Economic policy advisers can help the government and the public administration by improving the techniques for a diagnosis and prediction of economic conditions. There are a great many indicators available that intend to picture business cycle movements or structural conditions, such as the distribution of income between persons or regions. The social indicators have the more ambitious goal: to summarize the conditions of society as a whole. This information is important to the government because the population's voting decision depends not only on the state of the economy but also on general social conditions.

The social indicators have three particular features:

1 they cover market as well as non-market areas: the various aspects are not evaluated in monetary terms;
2 they encompass everything that is important for the wellbeing of the population;
3 they seek to capture the output, and not the input: for example, the state of health of the population is measured, rather than the number of hospital beds or of doctors.

These social indicators supplement national accounting and GNP, which is ill suited to measure the welfare of the population.

The future economic and social development can be forecast by different methods. The higher cost in terms of money and time required for the more sophisticated forecasting methods must be compared with the benefits gained by taking a larger number of relationships and aspects into account. The following methods are the most popular.

1 *Trend extrapolation.* It is assumed that the future development is essentially determined by the past. This is certainly true for most (aggregated) time series variables. This method has the advantage of being easy to apply: a trend extrapolation can be roughly done by hand or with a simple regression. The method fails, however, when new developments arise which lead to structural breaks and to a deviation from the former trend.

2 *Surveys.* In forecasting business cycles, surveys are often used to find out the expectations and plans of the various decision-makers. This method is quite successful for short-term forecasting.

3 *Scenarios.* The likely future states of society are described by showing up the various possible developments and their consequences. Scenarios belong to the *heuristic forecasting methods*, which include subjective elements to evaluate the future.

Example

The future demand for oil depends on the four variables: growth of real GNP, energy price (relative to the other prices), possibilities of substituting other energy sources, and the possibility of saving total energy. Making various assumptions about plausible developments of these variables yields scenarios whose likelihood can be subjectively evaluated.

The great advantage of scenarios is that many different developments can be analysed. This allows us to gain a notion about the possible future. A disadvantage of this method is the heavy use of subjective evaluations, which makes it difficult or even impossible to check the quality of the analysis.

4 *Delphi method.* This heuristic forecasting technique operates by questioning a group of experts anonymously in various rounds. The results of each round of inquiry are analysed statistically and communicated to the experts before the next. This feedback is built in to bring about a convergence of the experts' opinions. The anonymity of the questioning avoids the danger of the experts being pressed to conform. Each participant receives additional information during the process because each has to explain in written form if he or she holds extreme views about the future. This increase in information can be a motivation for the experts to participate actively. The disadvantages of the Delphi method are the slow learning process and the length of time required to reach a result (four rounds take about six months). There is, moreover, a tendency to make rather conservative projections of the future so as not to be forced to explain one's opinion in written form.

5 *Econometric and politometric forecasting models.* The forecasting capacity of econometric models can be checked by two procedures:

— In *ex post forecasts* the exogenous, or unexplained, variables of the model are given the actual, or realized, values and it is queried how well the model is able to trace the endogenous, or explained, variables. Such 'forecasts' are used to analyse the quality of the established model. They do not deal with the problem of how the exogenous variables can be predicted.

— *Ex ante forecasts* rely on information, or data, of the past only. The model is estimated for a base period, which precedes the forecasting period, and the future values of the endogenous as well as of the exogenous variables are predicted. This allows a true test of an econometric model's predictive capacity compared with other forecasting techniques.

CONCLUSION

Economic advisers can propose a variety of approaches and techniques with which the governmental actors, including those in the public administration, can improve their decision-making capacity. These decision-makers will use this knowledge to promote their own utility. As has been demonstrated with the example of cost–benefit analysis, the decisions made by a particular actor are based on the benefits and costs to himself, so that, in general, the decision is not the optimal one from the point of view of society as a whole. The decision-making techniques, as well as the instruments of economic policy, are 'converted' to a private use; they should not be considered to have any objective character (as is often thought to be the case from the point of view of the traditional theory of economic policy). This conclusion points again to the importance of the rules and institutions that set the framework within which the decision-makers act.

FURTHER READING

For a comparison of macroeconometric models, see for example

Econometric Models, *American Economic Review, Papers and Proceedings*, 63 (1973), 385–411.

The distinction between economically and politically relevant cost in benefit–cost analysis is used in

Barry R. Weingast, Kenneth A. Shepsle and Christopher Johnsen. The Political Economy of Benefits and Costs: A Neoclassical Approach to Distribution Politics, *Journal of Political Economy*, 89 (1981), 642–64.

The optimal use of policy instruments for business cycle stabilization in the case of risk and uncertainty is treated by

Stephen J. Turnovsky, *Macroeconomic Analysis and Stabilization Policies*, part III. Cambridge: University Press, 1977.

Various aspects of economic policy applications are discussed by

Alfred E. Kahn, Applications of Economics to an Imperfect World, *American Economic Review, Papers and Proceedings*, 69 (1979), 1–13.

PART IV

Economic Advising

This last part of the book discusses the conclusions for economic advising to be derived from the theory of democratic economic policy. The tasks of economic advisers differ according to whether they are offering information for reaching and maintaining a social consensus, or are advising the decision-makers in the current politico-economic process. Advisers have sufficient incentives to inform the political decision-makers, since they receive an income for doing this; for advice to the electorate, on the other hand, it is necessary to create the adequate incentives. The population's preferences will be disregarded if the advisers develop into 'benevolent dictators' who try to put through their own preferences. Such a development can be prevented by encouraging competition and mutual criticism among economists.

Economic advisers have to deal with the problem of applying their theories to practical economic policy. Different economists hold varying views about economic theory and policy, so their advice may differ; however, the area of consensus within economics is quite large. Another problem is the fact that the pragmatic theory directly applicable to economic policy does not always concur with the complex theorems of 'pure' economics. Suggestions are made to help overcome this problem.

There is a great number of institutions through which economic advice can be issued, ranging from individual scientists to councils and specialized research institutes.

Chapter 16 considers the position and the task of the economic advisers, the incentives necessary to bring about effective advising, and the various institutions of economic advising. Chapter 17 sketches the relationship between abstract economic theory and its application for the purpose of economic advising. The final Chapter 18 recapitulates the essence of democratic economic policy.

CHAPTER 16

Institutions and Incentives

INTRODUCTION

There are two levels of advising. On the level of the social consensus, the advisers can suggest economic alternatives, help to bring about their acceptance, and secure them against violation in the current political process. This advice is addressed to the general public and to interest groups, and can be undertaken only by advisers who are not directly involved in the current political process and who are independent of the government.

In the current politico-economic process, economists help the various decision-makers (in particular the government and the opposition parties) to reach their own goals as far as possible. In this position the advisers work for particular actors and thus become an endogenous part of the politico-economic process.

Economic advisers will offer services only if they have adequate incentives for doing so. In most cases the advisers of government, public bureaucracies and organized groups are hired at a market salary. Advice for the general population about productive social rules and the most effective behaviour in the current politico-economic process will, however, be offered only if incentives have been set by creating appropriate institutions by social consensus. Rules must be established that make sure that a 'dictatorship of advisers' cannot emerge.

There are many institutional forms of advising, including individuals, councils and specialized research institutes. The Council of Economic Advisers in the United States and the Council of Economic Experts (Sachverständigenrat) in Germany are two such advisory councils.

16.1   LEVELS OF ADVISING

Economic advisers help to further the preferences of the population by offering information. It is useful to distinguish between advising at the level of the social consensus and in the current politico-economic process.

Advice Concerning Social Consensus

The economic policy advisers who want to contribute to the formation of social contracts are confronted with three tasks (as pointed out in Chapter 11).

1   *Reaching consensus:* advisers can persuade and educate; suggest compensation schemes; use political mechanisms such as vote trading and activate latent groups in order to give incentives to participate in a social consensus;

2   *Introducing social innovations*: it is particularly important to find new rules and institutions to guide the behaviour of the decision-makers:

— the policy advisers can reveal unused possibilities for Pareto-optimal improvements;

— as the decision-makers often have not yet taken firm positions concerning innovations, it is easier to find a consensus on mutually productive social arrangements. Innovations are likely to be potent because their effects are probably not weakened by countervailing expectations and anticipating actions;

3   *Preserving the social contracts in the current politico-economic process*: economic advisers must make sure that the established social rules and institutions are not destroyed by a majority or by strongly organized minorities when they find it advantageous. The defence of social contracts requires establishing adequate institutions. Economic advisers can make a useful contribution to the formation of social agreements only if they themselves are situated *outside* the current politico-economic process. They must stand above the short-term and interest-dominated demands. This external position corresponds to the role of a referee in a football game.

Advice in the Current Politico-economic Process

This level is characterized by conflicts between the demands of actors who all pursue their *own* interests. The economic advisers will supply only that information which helps the respective decision-makers to reach their goals. In order to be listened to and applied, the information must deal with practical problems of policy-making. Economic advice in day-to-day politics is directed to all decision-makers, in particular to the public, the government, political parties and the public administration. In order to supply that information which appeals to the particular decision-makers, the economic advisers must actively participate in the politico-economic process. Only then will they find out the specific information requirements of the actors, and be able to advise them in a useful way. The advisers depend on their employers, and mostly they are integrated in an institution. They thus have an insider position.

16.2 INCENTIVES FOR ADVISING

A basic assumption throughout this book is that all decision-makers pursue their own selfish interests. This behavioural assumption naturally applies also to the economic advisers. It must therefore be assumed that they need certain incentives in order to offer advice. In some areas of economic advising spontaneous incentives arise because there is a market demand for such services. In other areas incentives for advising are insufficient or missing; there is 'market failure'. In this case, the incentives have to be created by appropriate rules set by social consensus.

Market Incentives for Advising

The services of economic advisers are demanded and payed for in the current politico-economic process by the government, the public administration and organized interest groups, which expect to reap direct benefits for themselves. Advice on social agreements, on the other hand, is rarely payed in the same manner; these services constitute a public good benefiting all individuals and groups. The supply of information on that level is rewarded when presented before a lay public, or published in books and articles in popular magazines.

Information may also be given because the economic advisers consider it an honour to become active for the government and/or certain interest groups. This motive may also play an important role when advising on social contracts. It is doubtful, however, whether such non-monetary incomes can create sufficient incentives to become active as intensively as when the advisory services are rendered to a well paying interest group.

Incentives Set by Social Consensus

Demand for advice will be insufficient or missing when the information leads to external effects or constitutes a public good (or, rather, service). As has already been discussed (in Chapter 12), individuals in general have few incentives to demand information about public policy issues because each one of them knows that he will have only a minute effect on the decisions made – especially through elections. Such a socially suboptimal demand may lead the population to agree to create incentives for advising other than those of the market. The social arrangements may above all refer to education, research on problems of economic policy, and public information.

Education. The work undertaken at universities and research centres can contribute to the formation of socially productive arrangements. Students are taught the fundamental social and technological relationships; this makes them better able to devise rules and institutions that are advantageous for all and on whose introduction a consensus may be reached. Research thus helps to find Pareto-superior arrangements.

In school, children and juveniles can be shown that keeping to the 'rules of the game' may be beneficial for all. This insight must be learnt by experience.

The educational sector can contribute to social agreements provided that it is not abused by the government. Social contracts can guarantee that education is not put into the service of the government of the day. This purpose serves, for example, the (partial) autonomy of the publicly run universities as instituted, for example, in Germany. Those employed in the university system are, to a certain extent, given a position independent of the government.

Research on Economic Policy. Under present conditions, economists have few incentives to do serious research on matters of practical economic policy. This is because the criterion for economic research is not the relevance for solving practical issues but rather the rigour of the analysis: a contribution is considered competent when the mathematics and statistics are handled well, when the scientific literature is known and quoted, and when the arguments are logically coherent and stringent. Another reason why there are relatively weak incentives is that research relevant for policy purposes is applied, and cannot often offer something new to academic colleagues. In order to become known and prominent, research must propose new results. This is rarely possible in practical work on policy problems.

Incentives to undertake research on practical economic policy can be strengthened by various means. Scholarships and research grants can be given to researchers dealing with immediate policy problems. In order to avoid undesired government interference, this task can be assigned to independent formations. This kind of support has the disadvantage that the input and not the output of the research is promoted. This would not be the case if scientific journals were founded that would pay good fees for articles of immediate policy relevance: the output, and not the input, of the research is then supported. Finally, prizes can be awarded to researchers in proportion to their contribution towards solving economic problems. The prizes should be the larger, the more serious is the problem attacked and solved.

Informing the Public. Economic advising on social agreements is useless if it is not communicated to the population. A social consensus may be reached that such advice has to be propagated by the mass media, in particular by radio and television. A public institution may be founded that buys time from radio and television stations and allocates it to policy advisers. Alternatively, private and public stations may be required to offer the time free of charge as a public service. In the 'constitution' of publicly regulated monopolies of radio and television (which applies in many countries) a general article may be included which gives them the task of informing the public about basic economic and social issues.

Avoiding a 'Dictatorship of Advisers'

As economic policy advisers, like everybody else, pursue their own utility, there is the danger that they impose their own preferences on the population. Such a 'benevolent dictatorship' can be made impossible by setting adequate rules through social consensus. An effective means is to secure competition among the advisers. This maintains the quality of the information provided while forcing the advisers to respect the preferences of the individuals. Competition among economic advisers can be secured by establishing a *market for advisers*, the entrance to which is kept open; the established advisers must then take potential competitors into account. Moreover, criticism of the established advisers can be supported. This can for example be institutionalized in the form of 'hearings' which can receive widespread publicity.

16.3 INSTITUTIONS OF ADVICE

Economic policy advising is possible in many different institutional forms.

Individuals

Economists can become active as individual persons. They can offer advice as *confidants* of politicians, write memoranda for politicians and public administrations, and influence the general public through the mass media. Finally, they can take up a political career themselves.

Examples

Some famous professional economists have attained high political ranks: Oscar Lange was vice-president of Poland, Ludwig Erhard was minister of finance and later chancellor and Karl Schiller was 'super-minister' of finance and of economic affairs in the Federal Republic of Germany; Raymond Barre was French, and Harold Wilson English, prime minister; Luigi Einaudi was Italian president; George Shultz was secretary of the Treasury and is now the Secretary of State, and Charles Schultze the director of the Bureau of the Budget in the United States; Antônio Delfim Netto and Mario Enrique Simonsen were for a long time ministers of economic affairs in Brazil.

Councils and Committees

Of special importance is the advice given by councils and committees. The collegiate form allows the use of more expert knowledge and of a broader spectrum of schools (for example monetarists and Keynesians), research fields (micro- and macroeconomics), qualifications (such as mathematically and institutionally oriented scholars) and political preferences. There are several types of such institutions.

Councils of Experts. These councils have scientists as members and are designed to work on a well defined task. Such institutions can be found in many countries and serving many different purposes. The best known and most important ones are the Council of Economic Advisors in the United States (founded in 1964) and the Sachverständigenrat zur Begutachtung der gesamtwirtschaftlichen Entwicklung ('Council of Experts for the Evaluation of Macro-economic Developments', founded in 1963) in the Federal Republic of Germany. They can be considered as two prototypes of councils of experts; they differ considerably from each other.

The Council of Economic Advisers consists of three members, usually leading economists, assisted by an excellent staff. The American president elects the members and decides the length of their tenure. They work full time in their advisory position. The results of their deliberations and findings are published in the yearly *Economic Report of the President*. The Council directly depends on the president. Its influence is determined mainly by the relationship of its members, especially of its chairman, to the president. The Council members accordingly consider themselves to be spokesmen of the administration's economic policy. The design and the activity of the Council make it an institution of government advising in the current economic process; this is documented by its complete dependence on the president and its intensive involvement in current economic policy debates. Advising the general public on matters to be decided on the level of the social consensus is of comparatively small importance. However, the Council makes an effort to educate the population in economics by writing its Report in a clear and simple language.

The German Sachverständigenrat has five members who must possess good scientific knowledge and experience in economic matters. A new member is chosen by the federal government, but the opinion of the remaining members of the Sachverständigenrat must first be heard. The members are appointed for a four-year period and may be re-elected. They work only part-time in their advisory position; most of them are professors who continue to teach. The law requires that the Council members be independent of interest groups, but by tradition one of them is considered to be the 'representative' of the trade unions, and another one the man of the employers and producers. The Council publishes a yearly report in the autumn, and there are also special reports. Minority opinions are admissible and are in fact regularly brought forward.

In the constituting law, the Council is given explicit economic goals to be achieved. The Council interprets each of the goals (price stability, full employment, balance of payments equilibrium, economic growth and 'just' income distribution) to be of equal importance. The law forbids the Council to make recommendations; it may only point out feasible alternatives. Actually, the Council does indirectly make recommendations by stressing the disadvantages of those alternatives that are considered not to be sensible. The reports are addressed to all decision-makers on economic policy, in particular to the government and parliament, but the public is also explicitly concerned as an addressee. The Council regularly criticizes the government by showing the opportunities missed by wrong policy. Some observers even speak of an 'extra-parliamentary' opposition. Owing to its construction, the Council is not equipped to advise the government because it is situated outside the current politico-economic process. Its tasks (to work out the long-run feasible alternatives and to make suggestions for productive social arrangements, as well as to have the general public as an addressee) show that it is at least partly designed as an advisory council for decisions on the level of the social consensus. In its reports, the Council often refers to 'social contracts, social agreements, or concerted actions'. It is, however, written in a form and language that appeals more to professional colleagues than to the lay public.

This discussion clearly shows that the Council of Economic Advisors and the Sachverständigenrat differ strongly in their institutional structure and activities.

Scientific Councils. This type of advisory institution by professional economists is appointed to particular ministries, departments or bureaus. The scientific councils are independent, and are not part of the public administration. Owing to their external position they have little influence on the current politico-economic process. The appointed scientists consider their membership as only one activity among many others; the sole motivation to participate is the honour of being a member. Often, few economists hold most of these jobs and council membership is by co-option. Scientific councils, for example, are appointed to the Ministry of Finance and the Ministry of Economic Affairs in the Federal Republic of Germany.

Mixed Councils. Economic advisers can take a seat in institutions that consist of professional economists, representatives of interest groups and members of the public administration. Because of their competence, academic economists often have much to say in mixed councils, especially when the rest of the members evenly consists of representatives of trade unions and employers' organizations. Mixed councils play a decisive role in the economic policy formation of a great many countries.

Examples

— the Socio-Economic Council in the Netherlands (founded in 1950);
— the Economic and Social Council in France (1958);
— the Advisory Council for Economic and Social Questions in Austria (1963);
— the Commission for Business Cycle Problems in Switzerland (1965).

Parliamentary Committees. Parliaments establish committees in order to study economic policy problems thoroughly. Of particular importance are those committees dealing with budgetary problems. In general, only few professional economists are members. An important exception to this rule is the Joint Economic Committee of the United States Congress, which consists of eight senators and eight representatives and is assisted by a highly qualified staff. It derives its influence partly from the hearings with leading economists which are heavily publicized by the media.

Official International Advisory Organizations.   The activity of many international organizations consists of economic policy advising. The value of the reports is reduced by the need to make the report acceptable to all member countries' interests.

Examples

The Organization for Economic Co-operation and Development (OECD) in Paris, with the Western European countries, the United States, Canada and Japan as members, regularly provides country studies in which the economic policy is evaluated and suggestions for the future policy are made. The OECD is also active in many other fields relevant for economic policy such as education, research and natural environment.

The Bank for International Settlements (BIS) in Basle, Switzerland, is another institution of this type; it concerns itself mainly with monetary and foreign trade problems.

Private Committees.   Economic advice may also be proffered by committees that do not have connections with governments or established interest groups. Often they consist of informal institutions of scientists forming an 'invisible college'.

Examples

A private committee of scientists that, in the beginning of the 1970s, had a considerable impact on economic thinking and policy was active within the framework of the 'Club of Rome'. This club was founded in 1968 and originally consisted of 30 persons concerned about the future. The Club had a major impact by sponsoring publications, the most famous being *The Limits to Growth*.

Specialized Institutes

In addition to the councils and committees just discussed, there are specialized advisory institutes. These have easy access to data, which they often collect and store themselves, and have scientific, technical and administrative personnel at their disposal. There are three main kinds of such institutes.

Government Institutes. In addition to the many university institutes, which mainly advise government, there are publicly run institutes outside the university system which make important contributions to economic policy-making. An example is the Wissenschaftszentrum (Science Centre) in Berlin, composed of institutes on management, natural environment and politics.

Independent Research Institutes. Many economic policy institutes of a non-profit-making kind are formally independent but rely indirectly on government support in the form of regular subsidies and long-term research contracts.

Example

In the United States, the Brookings Institution in Washington and the National Bureau of Economic Research in New York are world-famous. Similar institutes exist in other countries.

Profit-oriented Research Institutes. Private policy research institutes, which must make profit in order to survive, are subject to competitive pressure. This tends to raise the quality of the research reports, but may lead to time pressures, thus reducing the care taken with those parts of the reports that are difficult to check.

Examples

Among the best known private advisory institutes are

— the Rand Corporation in Santa Monica, California;
— Mathematica in Princeton;
— Battelle in Frankfort and Geneva;
— Prognos-European Center for Applied Economic Research in Basle.

CONCLUSION

Economic advisers are part of the politico-economic system in the same way as are all other actors. They can be expected to perform their task of bringing about and maintaining social consensus, and to inform the other actors about their possibilities in the daily politico-economic process, only if they have the incentive to do so. While some of the incentives arise automatically, others have to be consciously set by appropriate social rules and institutions, particularly with respect to advice on social contracts. There are many different forms in which economic advice may be institutionalized, each of which functions in a different way. The form chosen should depend on the particular purpose the advice is designed to serve.

FURTHER READING

Useful accounts of the problems of economic advising are given by two chairmen of the Council of Economic Advisers:

Walter W. Heller, *New Dimensions of Political Economy.* New York: Norton, 1967;

Arthur M. Okun, *The Political Economy of Prosperity.* New York: Norton, 1970.

Of similar interest is the book by

Charles L. Schultze, *The Politics and Economics of Public Spending.* Washington DC: Brookings Institution, 1968.

A comparison of the American and German councils of economic experts is undertaken by

Henry C. Wallich, The American Council of Economic Advisors and the German Sachverständigenrat. A Study in the Economics of Advice, *Quarterly Journal of Economics,* 82 (1968), 349–79.

The monetary benefits from teaching and publishing in professional journals and being therefore promoted in the academic hierarchy are calculated for the United States by

John J. Siegfried and Kenneth J. White, Financial Rewards to Research and Teaching: A Case Study of Academic Economists, *American Economic Review, Papers and Proceedings,* 63 (1973), 309–15.

The non-monetary rewards from publishing are discussed by

Lee S. Hansen and Burton Weisbrod, Towards a General Theory of Awards, or, Do Economists Need a Hall of Fame? *Journal of Political Economy,* 80 (1972), 422–31.

CHAPTER 17

From Economic Theory to Advice

INTRODUCTION

Economic advisers have to apply the results of economic theory to practical economic policy-making. They will succeed in doing this only if they all have, to some extent, compatible theories of economic relationships. Economists hold and proffer different opinions; there is, nevertheless, a large area of consensus. It consists of the type of analysis and the body of implicit normative views that leads to similar conclusions about economic policy. Disputes can arise when the complex theories are applied to practical economic policy-making, for this requires careful reasoning. Furthermore, advice on the formation of economic policy may be offered in various ways so as to make it more effective; this is what is referred to as the 'strategy of advising'.

17.1   THE ECONOMIC CONSENSUS

In Britain the story is told that three economists used to proffer four different opinions when they were asked for policy advice: two economists had one each; and John Maynard Keynes had two. Under such circumstances, it would not be surprising if the advisers had little influence in the current politico-economic process. Those in positions of power and authority would not know what to do when professional economists or even world-famous authorities gave conflicting advice. How could they decide which opinion was correct? They would either reject all suggestions (and renounce future 'advice'), or accept the opinion that best suited their own intuitive ideas, previously held.

Effective policy advising presupposes that the economists consulted agree on the major points and that they formulate a common suggestion. In economics – as in all sciences – there are many different views. This is due partly to the fact that each scholar likes to present his scientific achievements as novel and original. Uncontroversial questions are not a topic of scientific discussion. Moreover, divergent theories and quarrels are a good subject for the mass media. This applies, for example, to the disputes between monetarists and Keynesians, or between John Kenneth Galbraith and the orthodox economists.

In contrast to the general view, there is a large area of consensus in economics. While economists tend to take different positions in internal discussions, they often proclaim similar views towards outsiders. Non-economists, for example, are concerned almost exclusively with the distributional effects of price formation, while economists tend to stress the allocative consequences.

The consensus among economists refers to both the type of analysis and to their normative views. Modern economists share a common set of instruments of analysis and terminology – quite in contrast to other social sciences, in particular to sociology and political science. The great majority of Western economists is committed to an analysis based on the following assumptions:

— the acting unit is the individual, whose behaviour is systematically influenced by positive and negative incentives;
— the possibilities for marginal substitution are important and are evaluated at their opportunity cost;
— an effort is made strictly to separate positive and normative analysis.

Many economists hold the following normative views:

— the individuals' preferences are the measuring rod for economic policy behaviour;
— potential Pareto efficiency is a useful decision criterion;
— market solutions are preferable, especially in the micro-area, because of their high efficiency and low information requirements: accordingly, care should be taken not to interfere with the price system.

The range and content of the consensus among economists has been empirically studied in a survey. It turns out that there does indeed exist a consensus of the type indicated.

Empirical evidence

A random selection of over 2500 economists in five different countries (Belgium, France, West Germany, Switzerland, and the United States) (members of professional economics associations) were given 30 written statements about economic relationships on which to give their opinion. Two such statements were:

— 'Fiscal policy has a significant stimulative impact on a less than fully employed economy': 86 per cent of those answering 'agreed', and only 14 per cent 'disagreed'.
— 'A ceiling on rents reduces the quantity and quality of housing available': 82 per cent 'agreed', and 18 per cent 'disagreed'.

The degree of consensus among European and American economists proved to be considerable. Consensus is particularly high in those areas relating to the consequences of interfering with the price system: economists generally are of the opinion that the market is an effective way for allocating resources, particularly on the micro-economic level. Not surprisingly, there is more dissension on explicitly normative propositions, and on currently hotly debated issues such as monetarism.

On the other hand, the existence of a consensus does not mean that schools and trends with views differing from orthodox (neoclassical) economists do not exist. In addition to the Marxists (or radicals), one can call special attention to such unorthodox economists as Galbraith, Hirschman, Boulding, Myrdal or Perroux, or Veblen and Schumpeter of the previous generation. These economists can enrich traditional economics with new ideas and can help it to stay lively and to be able to deal with the urgent problems of our time. In particular, the unorthodox economists can make important contributions to economic policy-making; as has been stated before, innovative proposals are a prerequisite to effective economic advising.

17.2 FROM ECONOMIC THEORY TO ECONOMIC POLICY

Economic advisers can apply the results of economic theory only if they first transform their knowledge adequately. Complex theories cannot be used directly for economic policy-making, but must generally be simplified and reformulated for the specific problem. It is not enough to present theoretical knowledge to the politicians in the current politico-economic process; the advisers must reveal its *practical* consequences. Politicians are usually not ready or capable enough to undertake this transformation process themselves.

Economists distinguish two types of theories:

1 the *general* theory, which seeks to take all conceivable relationships into account and which rigorously derives its theorems from a background of a general equilibrium analysis;
2 the *pragmatic theory*, which is designed for immediate application.

The results of the two types of theories need not coincide; they sometimes even lead to opposing consequences. Such contrasting results may especially arise in three areas (all of which have been touched on in previous chapters).

1 *Theory of the second-best.* According to the pragmatic theory, a potential utility gain will be achieved when a policy succeeds in approaching the marginal conditions of Pareto efficiency.

Example

The pragmatic theory is applied in France and Great Britain with respect to the pricing policy of public enterprises. Following the marginal cost pricing rule, production is increased until the marginal costs have risen to the marginal product price. This corresponds to the marginal conditions of Pareto optimality: marginal utility equals price, and price equals marginal cost.

A theorem derived from the general theory of the second-best, which applies when prices lie above marginal cost in other areas of the economy, says however that, when deviations from optimal conditions exist, economic policy measures that remove *part* of these distortions only may lead to Pareto-inferior states. When the pragmatic marginality conditions are applied, the distance from Pareto optimality may thus increase. Economic advisers must decide how far they want to follow the pragmatic theory (which may lead to inefficient outcomes), or the general theory (which is difficult or impossible to apply in reality, and will therefore also lead to inefficiencies).

2 *Theory of external effects.* If externalities occur, the pragmatic theory suggests that, when there is a positive external effect, the

market activity is too small and should be increased. In the case of a negative external effect, the market activity is too large and should be diminished. According to the general theory, however, external effects may lead to a non-convex production possibility set, which results in the allocative function of the price system largely breaking down. Furthermore, it is even difficult to say in which direction a policy measure should be applied. It can be shown that the policy rules of the pragmatic theory are correct as long as there is only *one* activity that creates external benefits and cost. If a number of activities with externalities exists, the conditions of Pareto efficiency become very complex. It is thus no longer true that an activity that creates negative external effects should necessarily be reduced: it may well be Pareto-efficient to enlarge it. On the other hand, an activity with positive externalities need not necessarily be increased to approach a Pareto-efficient state.

3 *Stabilization policy*. Following pragmatic theory, government expenditures should be decreased and taxes increased in a state of over-employment and inflation. In case of a recession or depression, economic policy should be expansionary. According to the general theory of how to stabilize business cycles, an anti-cyclical policy of the type just described might well magnify business cycles. Whether the pragmatic policy rules are able to stabilize business cycles depends on the exact dynamic properties of the economic system and on the exact type and strength of intervention.

These three examples of how policy conclusions based on general and on pragmatic theory can conflict do not, luckily, describe the normal case of policy problems. The general theory encompasses a much larger set of assumptions necessary for a certain outcome; therefore the policy conclusions are by necessity much more careful. However, economic advisers will be listened to only when they can make clear-cut suggestions: economic policy decision-makers reject excessive non-binding and covered policy advice. Moreover, economic advisers must often act under pressure of time. They thus have no possibility to apply the general theory to the problems at hand, but must rely on the simpler pragmatic theory.

Applying the pragmatic theory is safe under two conditions:

1 *if the interdependence between the economic sectors is small:* the opposing results of the general theory reached in the cases of the theory of the second-best, of externalities and of stabilization are

due to its view of marked interdependence between the economic sectors. If it is possible to dissect the economy into sub-areas that are (relatively) independent of each other, the results of the general and of the pragmatic theory differ little;

2 *if the secondary effects are small:* when the initial impact of an economic policy action is all-important and any secondary effects are fairly insignificant, the general and the pragmatic theories will recommend similar policy measures.

Risk Minimization

Policy advice will be accepted only if the decision-makers can trust the recommendations made and are confident that they do not run a great risk if they follow the advice. The advisers must, therefore, make an effort to minimize the risk associated with the courses of proposed action. They can reduce this risk in several ways.

Limitation to Policies that Enjoy High Consensus among Economists. Economic advisers may hope that the large majority of economists do not err – which may be true or false. Such a view is, however, necessarily orthodox. The corresponding policy measures will be easy to predict; therefore they may cease to have much impact (see the theory of rational expectations, p. 202).

Selection of Theories on the Basis of Soft Modelling. Assume that an economic adviser believes that each one of two theoretical approaches is to some extent correct; he therefore does not reject either completely. He believes, however, that one of them is somewhat more likely to be true, although he is not able to state exactly what the corresponding probability could be. The 'limited probability information' (LPI) method allows us to derive an adequate evaluation of two or more theories by simply stating which theory is *more* likely (this is referred to as 'ordinal ranking').

Example

An economic adviser must decide whether he should recommend that the current macroeconomic policy be pursued further ('constant policy') or that stimulating measures be undertaken ('expansionary policy'). According to whether the 'true' nature of the economic system corresponds to theory I

(e.g. rational expectations) or to theory II (e.g. Keynesianism), quite different consequences will follow from the policy action. Assume that a 'constant' policy yields zero utility according to both theory I and theory II,
and that an 'expansionary' policy leads to a utility *loss* of 10 units according to the (rational expectations) theory I, and to a utility gain of 12 units
according to the (Keynesian) theory II. These outcomes are shown in Table
17.1. The utility units are chosen arbitrarily, the normalization to an outcome of zero utility for a 'constant' policy could be changed without affecting the decision procedure. If the economic adviser knew that theory I is
correct with 25 per cent probability, and theory II with 75 per cent probability, it would be rational for him to choose the 'expansionary' policy
because the mathematical expectation $(0.25 \cdot (-10) + 0.75 \cdot (12) = 6.5)$ is
higher than if 'constant' policy were chosen (expectation of zero).

It is very unlikely, however, that the economic adviser can assign exact
probabilities to the accuracy of the two models. In general, he will only
believe that theory II, for example, is more likely (or at least equally likely)
to be correct than theory I: $p_I \leq p_{II}$ (where p are the probabilities of the
theories, with $p_I + p_{II} = 100\%$). It follows that, in the extreme, both are
either equally likely ($p_I = 50\%$, $p_{II} = 50\%$) or that theory II is completely
correct and theory I completely wrong ($p_I = 0\%$, $p_{II} = 100\%$). The corresponding probability matrix is

$$\begin{bmatrix} 50\% & 0\% \\ 50\% & 100\% \end{bmatrix}.$$

The evaluation of the two policy measures can now be calculated by
multiplying the matrix of utilities contained in Table 17.1, with the above
probability matrix:

'Constant' policy:
'Expansionary' policy: $\begin{bmatrix} 0 & 0 \\ -10 & 12 \end{bmatrix} \cdot \begin{bmatrix} 50\% & 0\% \\ 50\% & 100\% \end{bmatrix} = \begin{bmatrix} 0 & 0 \\ 1 & 12 \end{bmatrix}$

A 'constant' policy yields an expected utility of zero in both extreme
cases – if the two theories are equally likely, or if only theory II is correct.

TABLE 17.1   *The Outcomes of a 'Constant' and an
'Expansionary' Policy According to Theory I and
Theory II*

	Theory I is correct	Theory II is correct
	(utility units)	
'Constant' policy	0	0
'Expansionary' policy	−10	12

An 'expansionary' policy yields a utility of 1 with the theories being equally likely, and a utility of 12 with theory II being correct. It is evident that the economic adviser should recommend an 'expansionary' policy because it dominates; that is, it is better under *all* circumstances than the 'constant' policy.

The 'soft modelling' approach allows economic advisers to make well-founded policy suggestions even if they are themselves not sure which theoretical approach is correct.

Suggestion of 'Robust' Measures.   Economic advisers can recommend policies whose effects depend only little on the exact size of the parameters of the economic system. Policy measures whose outcome completely changes (for example, has a contractive instead of an expansionary effect) when the size of a parameter slightly varies are not operational for the advisers and politicians. This will occur in particular when knowledge about the orders of magnitude in question is limited.

This discussion shows that the economic policy advisers have various approaches at their disposal to reduce the risk associated with their policy recommendations, and are thereby able to offer useful advice to the political decision-makers.

CONCLUSION

Though economists to a considerable extent hold similar views, it is nevertheless difficult to derive practical policy advice from general economic theories. It is argued that the pragmatic theory designed for immediate application may deviate from the general theory – particularly in the case of second-best problems, when significant external effects are present, and in the case of stabilization policy. The pragmatic theory may be safely applied, however, if the interdependence between the economic sectors is small and the secondary effects are also small. The advisers may also minimize the risk of giving bad advice by restricting themselves to policies having a greater consensus among economists, and by selecting theories on the basis of 'soft modelling'.

FURTHER READING

The study on the consensus among professional economists in various European countries and in the United States referred to was undertaken by

Bruno S. Frey, Victor Ginsburgh, Pierre Pestieau, Werner W. Pommerehne and Friedrich Schneider, Consensus, Dissension and Ideology among Economists in Various Countries. *European Economic Review*, forthcoming 1983.

Similar studies (with a smaller sample) have been undertaken for the United Kingdom and the United States by

Samuel Brittan, *Is There an Economic Consensus? An Attitude Survey*. London: Macmillan, 1973;
J. R. Kearl *et al.*, A Confusion of Economists? *American Economic Review, Papers and Proceedings,* 69 (1979), 28–37.

These studies find a considerable degree of consensus among economists of various party orientations.

Variants of economic theories are discussed in

The Crisis of Economic Theory. *Public Interest*, Special Issue 15 (1980).

The concepts of general and pragmatic theories are discussed in

William J. Baumol, Informed Judgment, Rigorous Theory and Public Policy, *Southern Economic Journal,* 32 (1965), 137–45.

The 'soft modelling' approach has been developed by

Eduard Kofler and Günter Menges, *Entscheidungen bei unvollständiger Information*. Lecture Notes in Economics and Mathematical Systems 136. Berlin: Springer, 1976.

The corresponding example given has been taken from

Heidi Schelbert, Marcel Chassot and Mark Granziol, Stabilisierungspolitik in kleinen offenen Volkswirtschaften am Beispiel der Schweiz empirisch illustriert, *Zeitschrift für Wirtschafts- und Sozialwissenschaften*. 101 (1981), 379–416.

CHAPTER 18

The Essence of
Democratic Economic Policy

The economy and the polity form an interdependent system of which the actors are endogenous parts. This applies in particular to the government and the public administration. These are no 'benevolent dictators', maximizing the welfare of society; rather, within the framework of the system, each actor pursues his own goals to the best of his ability. Only if the rules and institutions determining this framework are democratic can it be expected that economic policy will be designed according to the preferences of individuals. If, on the other hand, the basic framework is undemocratic, for example by severely restricting the political participation rights of certain sections of the population, or by leaving the government and the public administration a large discretionary power to pursue their own goals, the resulting economic policies will deviate significantly and systematically from the wishes of the population. For this reason it has been stressed that the theory of economic policy should be concerned first and foremost with the basic rules and institutions of society. This basic framework is not immutable; however, it can be introduced and changed only by social consensus.

A social consensus about rules and institutions is possible if the individuals and groups do not fully know their (future) positions in society, and therefore cannot defend their particular interests. Behind the veil of ignorance, agreements may be reached about limiting the government's power over individuals and about political and economic participation rights. A social consensus may also be reached about the roles to be played by the price system, by democratic or bureaucratic procedures or by bargaining. Each of these decision-making mechanisms has particular advantages and disadvantages, such that the individuals and groups behind the veil of ignorance will choose a (possibly varying) combination out of them. Shifting the point of view from decision-making systems to economic areas, social rules may be considered to guide the behaviour of the actors in the spheres of resources allocation, income distribution and the stabilization of the price level and of employment. Most of the rules established by social consensus serve either to induce the government and the public administration to undertake economic policies more closely in line with the population's preferences, or to overcome incentives for free-riding in the context of public goods supply.

Once the rules and institutions within which the decision-makers have to act are given, economic advisers can exert an influence on economic policy-making only by helping them better to reach their own goals. Individuals can be informed about how to make their wishes heard and followed in the political process, for instance by advising them about the most effective way to influence the government. The government can be advised about how to discover the preferences of the population, and to pursue economic policies approved by the voters. The advisers may also inform the government about the most effective economic policy-making instruments, in particular about the advantages and disadvantages of those based on changing incentives, as well as about the most suitable planning and forecasting techniques for decision-making.

As economic advisers themselves are a part of the politico-economic system, they will play the role accorded to them only if they can benefit by doing so, that is, if adequate incentives exist. While such incentives are provided partly by the market, in the form of monetary compensation, they can also be set by establishing appropriate institutions by social consensus, for example universities and independent research institutes.

The theory of democratic economic policy offers a quite different view from that of the traditional theory of economic policy. It requires a radical change in perspective. Confronted with a particular economic problem, the traditional approach would be to find out what action is optimal from the point of view of society, and to advise the political decision-makers of the corresponding policy to be undertaken. This approach neglects the political process, and as a result the policies suggested by the economic advisers will in general not be undertaken. The theory of democratic economic policy, on the other hand, takes the political process into account from the very beginning. The extent to which the existing politico-economic process is in line with the population's preferences is investigated, and also whether individuals' wishes are distorted or neglected. On the basis of such an analysis, the economic advisers then suggest rules and institutions that may serve to overcome such distortions, and will find a consensus among the individuals and groups making their decisions behind a veil of ignorance.

Economic advisers may also influence economic policy by advising those individuals and groups whose preferences are not adequately taken into account how to make their demands heard and followed by political parties and the public administration. Conversely, politicians can be informed that they could gain votes and win supporters if they would take up some wishes currently being disregarded. The theory of democratic economic policy thus works *through* the politico-economic process as it exists, and thereby serves to maximize the people's welfare.

Bibliography

Alchian, Armen A. and Demsetz, Harold, Production, Information Costs and Economic Organization, *American Economic Review*, 62 (1972), 777–95.

Arrow, Kenneth J., *The Limits of Organization*. New York: Norton, 1974.

Arrow, Kenneth J. and Hahn, Frank H., *General Competitive Analysis*. San Francisco: Holden-Day, 1971.

Ashenfelter, Orley and Smith, Robert S., Compliance with the Minimum Wage Law. *Journal of Political Economy*, 87 (1979) 333–50.

Bain, Joe S., *Industrial Organization*. New York: John Wiley, 1959.

Barkume, Anthony J., Tax-Prices and Voting Behavior: The Case of Local Educational Financing, *Economic Inquiry*, 15 (1977), Table 1.

Baumol, William J., Informed Judgment, Rigorous Theory and Public Policy, *Southern Economic Journal*, 32 (1965) 137–45.

Baumol, William J., *Welfare Economics and the Theory of the State* (2nd edn). London: Bell and Sons, 1975.

Baumol, William J. and Oates, Wallace E., *Economics, Environmental Policy, and the Quality of Life*. Englewood Cliffs, NJ: Prentice-Hall, 1979.

Baumol, William J. and Oates, Wallace E., *The Theory of Environmental Policy. Externalities, Public Outlays and the Quality of Life*. Englewood Cliffs, NJ: Prentice-Hall, 1975, part I.

Becker, Gary S., Irrational Behavior and Economic Theory. *Journal of Political Economy*, 70 (1962), 1–13. Reprinted in his collection of articles: *The Economic Approach to Human Behavior*. Chicago/London: Chicago University Press, 1976, 3–14.

Bernholz, Peter, Economic Policies in Democracy, *Kyklos*, 19 (1966), 48–80.

Bernholz, Peter, Dominant Interest Groups and Powerless Parties, *Kyklos*, 30 (1977), 411–20.

Bishop, John and Haveman, Robert, Selective Employment Subsidies. *American Economic Review, Papers and Proceedings*, 69 (1979), 124–30.

Black, Duncan, *The Theory of Committees and Elections*. Cambridge: University Press, 1958.

Blair, J. M., *Economic Concentration. Structure, Behavior and Public Policy*. New York: Harcourt, Brace, Jovanovich, 1972.

Blankart, Charles Beat, *Oekonomie der öffentlichen. Unternehmen.* Munich: Vahlen, 1980.

Borcherding, Thomas E., Pommerehne, Werner W. and Schneider, Friedrich, Comparing the Efficiency of Private and Public Production, *Zeitschrift fü Nationalökonomie,* 89 (1983), 127–56.

Bös, Dieter, *Economic Theory of Public Enterprise. Lecture Notes in Economics and Mathematical Systems.* Berlin/Heidelberg/New York: Springer, 1981.

Boulding, Kenneth E. and Pfaff, Martin, (eds), *Redistribution to the Rich and the Poor.* Belmont: Wadsworth, 1972.

Bradford, David F. and Rosen, Harvey S., The Optimal Taxation of Commodities and Income. *American Economic Review, Papers and Proceedings,* 66 (1976), 94–101.

Brams, Steven J., *Game Theory and Politics.* New York: Free Press, 1975, chapter 4.

Brams, Stephen J. and Fishburn, Peter C., Approval Voting, *American Political Science Review,* 72 (1978), 831–47.

Brennan, Geoffrey, Pareto-desirable Redistribution: the Non-Altruistic Dimension, *Public Choice,* 14 (1973), 43–67.

Brennan, Geoffrey and Buchanan, James M., *The Power to Tax. Analytical Foundation of a Fiscal Constitution.* Cambridge: University Press, 1980.

Breyer, S. G. and Macaroy, P. W. *Energy Regulation by the Federal Power Commission.* Washington, DC: Brookings Institution, 1974, table 5-1.

Brittan, Samuel, *Is There an Economic Consensus? An Attitude Survey.* London: Macmillan, 1973.

Brittan, Samuel with Lilley, Peter, *The Delusion of Incomes Policy.* London: Maurice Temple Smith, 1977.

Brunner, Karl and Meltzer, Allan H. (eds), *The Economics of Price and Wage Controls.* Amsterdam: North Holland, 1976.

Buchanan, James M., *The Limits of Liberty. Between Anarchy and Leviathan.* Chicago/London: University of Chicago Press, 1975.

Buchanan, James M., *Freedom in Constitutional Contract. Perspectives of a Political Economist.* College Station/London: Texas A & M University Press, 1977.

Buchanan, James M. and Bush, Winston, Political Constraints on Contractual Redistribution. *American Economic Review, Papers and Proceedings,* 64 (1974), 153–61.

Buchanan, James M. and Tullock, Gordon, *The Calculus of Consent. Logical Foundations of Constitutional Democracy.* Ann Arbor: University of Michigan Press, 1962.

Butler, David and Ranney, Austin, *Referendums. A Comparative Study of Practice and Theory.* Washington DC: American Enterprise Institute, 1978.

Cable, John R. and Fitzroy, Felix R., Productive Efficiency, Incentives and

Employee Participation: Some Preliminary Results for West Germany, *Kyklos*, 33 (1980), 100–21.

Chapman, Stephen, The Gas Line of '79, *Public Interest*, 60 (1980), 40–9.

Chenery, Hollis B. and Taylor, Lance, Development Patterns: Among Countries and Over Time, *Review of Economics and Statistics*, 50 (1968), 391–416.

Clandon, Michael P. and Cornwall, Richard R., (eds), *An Incomes Policy for the United States: New Approaches.* The Hague: Martinus Nijhoff, 1981.

Clawson, Marion and Knetsch, Jack L., *Economics of Outdoor Recreation.* Baltimore: John Hopkins Press, 1966.

Clayre, Alasdair (ed.), *The Political Economy of Co-operation and Participation.* Oxford: University Press, 1980.

Cohen, Davis K. and Farrar, Eleanor, Power to the Parents? The Story of Educational Vouchers, *Public Interest*, 48 (1977), 72–97.

Cowling, Keith and Mueller, Dennis, The Social Costs of Monopoly Power, *Economic Journal*, 88 (1978), 727–48.

Coxall, W. N., *Parties and Pressure Groups.* Harlow: Longman, 1980.

Culyer, Anthony J., *The Economics of Social Policy.* Oxford: Martin Robertson, 1973.

Curwen, P. J. and Fowler, A. H., *Economic Policy.* London: Macmillan, 1976.

Davidson, Paul, The Valuation of Public Goods. In Robert R. Dorfman and Nancy S. Dorfman (eds), *Economics of Environment* (2nd edn). New York: Norton, 1977, 345–55.

Davies, D. G., Property Rights and Economic Efficiency: The Australian Airlines Revisited. *Journal of Law and Economics*, 20 (1977), 223–6.

Downs, Anthony, *An Economic Theory of Democracy.* New York: Harper and Row, 1957.

Downs, Anthony, *Inside Bureaucracy.* Boston: Little, Brown, 1967.

Eckey, Hans-Friedrich, *Grundlagen der regionalen Strukturpolitik.* Cologne: Bund Verlag, 1978.

Econometric Models, *American Economic Review, Papers and Proceedings*, 63 (1973), 385–411.

Fair, Ray C., The Effect of Economic Events on Votes for President, *Review of Economics and Statistics*, 60 (1978), 159–73.

Faxén, Karl-Olof, Does Employee Participation in Decision-Making Contribute to Change and Growth? *American Economic Review, Papers and Proceedings*, 68 (1978), 131–4.

Finer, Samuel, *The Anonymous Empire. A Study of the Lobby in Great Britain* (2nd edn). London: Mall Press, 1966.

Flemming, John S., *Inflation.* Oxford: University Press, 1976.

Freeman, A. Myrick, Hedonic Prices, Property Values and Measuring Environmental Benefits: A Survey of the Issues, *Scandinavian Journal of Economics*, 81 (1979), 154–73.

Frey, Bruno S., Wahrscheinlichkeiten als gesellschaftliche Entscheidungsregel, *Wirtschaft und Recht*, 21 (1969), 14–26.

Frey, Bruno S., *Modern Political Economy*. Oxford: Martin Robertson, 1978.

Frey, Bruno S., Politico-economic Models and Cycles. *Journal of Public Economics*, 9 (1978), 203–20.

Frey, Bruno S.; Ginsburgh, Victor; Pestieau, Pierre; Pommerehne, Werner W. and Schneider, Friedrich, Consensus, Dissension and Ideology among Economists in Various Countries, *European Economic Review*, forthcoming 1983.

Frey, Bruno S. and Pommerehne, Werner W., Measuring the Hidden Economy: Though this be Madness, yet there is Method in it? In Vito Tanzi (ed.), *The Underground Economy in the United States and Abroad*. Lexington, Mass.: Heath, 1982.

Frey, Bruno S. and Schneider, Friedrich, A Politico-economic Model of the UK: New Estimates and Predictions. *Economic Journal*, 91 (1981), 737–40.

Friedman, Milton, *The Optimum Quantity of Money and other Essays*. Chicago: Aldine, 1969.

Frisch, Helmut, Inflation Theory 1963–1975: A 'Second Generation' Survey, *Journal of Economic Literature* 15 (1977), 1289–1317.

Fromm, Gary and Klein, Lawrence R., A Comparison of Eleven Econometric Models of the United States, *American Economic Review, Papers and Proceedings*, 63 (1973), 385–93.

Fuchs, Victor R., The Economics of Health in a Post-industrial Society, *Public Interest*, 56 (1979), 3–20.

Furubotn, Eirik G. and Pejovich, Svetozar, Property Rights and Economic Theory: A Survey of Recent Literature, *Journal of Economic Literature*, 10 (1972), 1137–62.

Galbraith, John K., *The Affluent Society*. Boston: Houghton Mifflin, 1952.

Galbraith, John K., *The New Industrial State*. Boston: Houghton Mifflin, 1967.

Gordon, Robert J., Recent Developments in the Theory of Inflation and Unemployment, *Journal of Monetary Economics*, 2 (1976), 185–219.

Gordon, Robert J., *Macroeconomics* (2nd edn). Boston: Little, Brown, 1981.

Gordon, Robert J., The Effect of Aggregate Demand on Prices, *Brookings Papers on Economic Activity*, 6 (1975), 613–62.

Gordon, Scott, The New Contractarians, *Journal of Political Economy*, 84 (1976), 573–90.

Gramlich, Edward M., *Benefit–Cost Analysis of Government Programs*. Englewood Cliffs, N.J.: Prentice-Hall, 1981.

Hamermesh, Daniel S., *Economic Aspects of Manpower Training Programs*. Lexington, Mass.: Heath, 1971.

Hansen, Lee S. and Weisbrod, Burton, Towards a General Theory of

Awards, or: Do Economists Need a Hall of Fame? *Journal of Political Economy*, 80 (1972), 422–31.

Harberger, Arnold C., Monopoly and Resource Allocation, *American Economic Review, Papers and Proceedings*, 44 (1954), 77–92.

Hayek, Friedrich A., *Legislation and Liberty. A New Statement of the Liberal Principles of Justice and Political Economy*. London: Routledge & Kegan Paul, 1973–79.

Hayek, Friedrich A., *Denationalisation of Money* (2nd edn). London: Institute of Economic Affairs, 1978.

Heller, Walter W., *New Dimensions of Political Economy*. New York: Norton, 1967.

Hirshleifer, Jack, Where Are We in the Theory of Information? *American Economic Review, Papers and Proceedings*, 63 (1973), 31–9.

Hirshleifer, Jack, *Price Theory and Applications*. London: Prentice-Hall, 1976.

Hirshleifer, Jack and Riley, John G., The Analytics of Uncertainty and Information – An Expository Survey. *Journal of Economic Literature*, 17 (1979), 1375–1421.

Intriligator, Michael D., A Probabilistic Model of Social Choice, *Review of Economic Studies*, 41 (1973), 553–60.

Jencks, Christopher, *Inequality*. New York: Basic Books, 1972.

Johansen, Leif, The Report of the Committee on Policy Optimisation – UK. *Journal of Economic Dynamics and Control* (1979), 101–9.

Johnson, Edwin L., A Study of the Economics of Water Quality Management, *Water Resources Research*, 3 (1967), 297.

Johnson, Dudley, *Poverty*. London: Macmillan, 1972.

Kahn, Alfred E., Applications of Economics to an Imperfect World, *American Economic Review, Papers and Proceedings,* 69 (1979), 1–13.

Kaldor, Nicholas, Alternative Theories of Distribution, *Review of Economic Studies*, 23 (1956), 83–100.

Kamerschen, David, Estimation of the Welfare Loss from Monopoly in American Economy, *Western Economic Journal*, 4 (1966), 221–36.

Kamien, Morton I. and Schwartz, Nancy L., Market Structure and Innovation: A Survey, *Journal of Economic Literature*, 13 (1975), 1–37.

Kearl, J. R. *et al.*, A Confusion of Economists? *American Economic Review, Papers and Proceedings*, 69 (1979), 28–37.

Kennedy, Charles and Thirlwall, A.P., Surveys in Applied Economics: Technical Progress, *Economic Journal*, 82 (1972), 11–72.

Kesselmann, Jonathan R., A Comprehensive Approach to Income Maintenance: SWIFFT, *Journal of Public Economics*, 2 (1973), 59–88.

Kesselman, Jonathan R. *et al.*, Tax Credits for Employment rather than Investment, *American Economic Review*, 67 (1977), 339–49.

Kirschen, Etienne S. et al., *Economic Policy in Our Time*. Vol. I: *General Theory*. Amsterdam: North Holland, 1964.

Kirschen, Etienne-Sadi (ed.), *Economic Policies Compared; West and East.*
Vol. I: *General Theory.* Amsterdam: North Holland, 1974.

Klapper, Joseph T., Effects of Mass Communication. In David L. Sills (ed.),
International Encyclopaedia of the Social Sciences. New York: Macmillan 1968, Vol. 3, 81–9.

Kofler, Eduard and Menges, Günter, *Entscheidungen bei unvollständiger Information. Lecture Notes in Economics and Mathematical Systems 136.* Berlin: Springer, 1976.

Kydland, Finn E., and Prescott, Edward C., Rules rather than Discretion: the Inconsistency of Optimal Plans, *Journal of Political Economy,* 85 (1977), 473–91.

Ladd, Helen F. and Tideman, T. Nicholas (eds), *Tax and Expenditure Limitations. Papers on Public Economics,* 5. Washington, DC: Urban Institute Press, 1981.

Laffer, Arthur B. and Seymour, Jan P., *The Economics of the Tax Revolt: A Reader.* New York: Harcourt, Brace, Jovanovich, 1979.

Lamberton, Donald M. (ed.), *Economics of Information and Knowledge.* Harmondsworth: Penguin, 1971.

Layard, Richard, Education versus Cash Redistribution: The Lifetime Context. *Journal of Public Economics,* 12 (1979), 377–86.

Leibenstein, Harvey, *Beyond Economic Man: A New Foundation for Microeconomics.* Cambridge, Mass.: Harvard University Press, 1976.

Lerner, Abba and Collander, David, Anti-Inflation Incentives, *Kyklos,* 35 (1982), 39–52.

Littmann, Konrad, Oeffentliche Ausgaben II, *Handwoerterbuch* der *Wirtschaftswissenschaften, Band I.* Stuttgart, Tuebingen and Goettingen: Fischer, Mohr, and Vandenhoeck and Ruprecht, 1977, 349–63.

Luce, Duncan and Raiffa, Howard, *Games and Decisions.* New York: John Wiley, 1967.

McGraw, Kenneth O., The Detrimental Effects of Reward on Performance: A Literature Review and Prediction Model. In Mark R. Lepper and David Greene (eds), *The Hidden Cost of Reward: New Perspectives on the Psychology of Human Motivation.* New York: Erlbaum, 1978.

McKean, Roland, Products Liability: Implications of Some Changing Property Rights, *Quarterly Journal of Economics,* 84 (1970), 611–26.

Malinvaud, Edmond, *The Theory of Unemployment Reconsidered.* Oxford: Basil Blackwell, 1977.

Martin, John P., *Public Sector Employment Trends in Western Industrialized Economics,* mimeo. Paris: OECD, 1980, table 1.

Meade, James M., *Efficiency, Equality and the Ownership of Property.* London: Allen & Unwin, 1964.

Milbrath, Lester W. and Goel, M. L., *Political Participation. How and Why Do People get Involved in Politics?* (2nd edn). Chicago: Rand McNally, 1977.

Mincer, Jacob, Unemployment Effects of Minimum Wages, *Journal of Political Economy*, 84 (1976), 87–104.

Moore, Thomas G., The Effect of Minimum Wages on Teenager Unemployment Rates, *Journal of Political Economy*, 79 (1971), 897–902.

Mueller, Dennis C., Constitutional Democracy and Social Welfare, *Quarterly Journal of Economics*, 87 (1973), 60–80.

Mueller, Dennis C., Voting by Veto, *Journal of Public Economics*, 10 (1978), 57–75.

Mueller, Dennis, *Public Choice*. Cambridge: University Press, 1979.

Niskanen, William A., *Bureaucracy and Representative Government*. Chicago: Aldine, Atherton, 1971.

Noam, Eli M., The Valuation of Legal Rights, *Quarterly Journal of Economics*, 96 (1981), 465–76.

Nutter, G. Warren, *Growth of Government in the West*. Washington DC: American Enterprise Institute, 1978.

Oates, William E., *Fiscal Federalism*. New York: Harcourt, Brace, Jovanovich, 1972.

Oates, Wallace E. (ed.), *The Political Economy of Fiscal Federalism*. Lexington, Mass.: Lexington Books, 1977.

OECD, *Consumer Policy in the Member Countries*. Paris: Organization for Economic Co-operation and Development, 1972.

OECD, *National Account Statistics of OECD Countries*. Paris, various years.

Okun, Arthur M., *The Political Economy of Prosperity*. New York: Norton, 1970.

Olson, Mancur, *The Logic of Collective Action: Public Goods and the Theory of Groups*. Cambridge, Mass.: Harvard University Press, 1965.

Orzechowski, William, Economic Models of Bureaucracy: Survey, Extensions, and Evidence. In Thomas E. Borcherding (ed.), *Budgets and Bureaucrats. The Sources of Government Growth*. Durham, North Carolina: Duke University Press, 1977, 229–59.

Peacock, Alan, *Structural Economic Policies in West Germany and the United Kingdom*. London: Anglo-German Foundation, 1980.

Pechman, Joseph A. and Timpane P. Michael (eds), *Work Incentives and Income Guarantees*. Washington DC: Brookings Institution, 1975.

Phelps, Edmund S. (ed.) *Economic Justice. Selected Readings*. Harmondsworth: Penguin, 1973.

Pommerehne, Werner W., Institutional Approaches to Public Expenditure: Empirical Evidence from Swiss Municipalities, *Journal of Public Economics*, 9 (1978), 255–80.

Pommerehne, Werner W. and Frey, Bruno S., Public versus Private Production Efficiency in Switzerland: A Theoretical and Empirical Comparison. In Vincent Ostrom and Frances P. Bish (eds), *Comparing Urban Service Delivery Systems. Urban Affairs Annual Reviews*, vol. 12. Beverly Hills: Sage, 1977, 221–41.

Pommerehne, Werner W. and Frey, Bruno S., Bureaucratic Behaviour in Democracy: A Case Study, *Public Finance*, 33 (1978), 98–112.

Posner, Richard A., Theories of Economic Regulation. *Bell Journal of Economics*, 5 (1974), 335–58.

Posner, Richard A., The Social Cost of Monopoly and Regulation, *Journal of Political Economy*, 83 (1975), 807–27.

Pratten, C., *Economies of Scale in Manufacturing Industries*. Cambridge: University Press, 1971.

Preston, M. H., *Theory of Macroeconomic Policy*. London: Philip Allan, 1974.

Rawls, John, *A Theory of Justice*. Cambridge, Mass.: Harvard University Press, 1971.

Rowley, Charles, *Anti-trust and Economic Efficiency*. London: Macmillan, 1973.

Schattschneider, E. E., *The Semi-sovereign People*. New York: Holt, Rinehart & Winston, 1960.

Schelbert, Heidi, Chassot, Marcel and Granziol, Mark, Stabilisierungspolitik in kleinen offenen Volkswirtschaften am Beispiel der Schweiz empirisch illustriert, *Zeitschrift für Wirtschafts- und Sozialwissenschaften*, 101 (1981), 379–416.

Scherer, Frederic M., *Industrial Market Structure and Economic Performance*. Chicago: Rand McNally, 1970.

Schon, Donald A., The Blindness System, *Public Interest*, 18 (1970), 39–51.

Schotter, Andrew, *The Economic Theory of Social Institutions*. Cambridge: University Press, 1981.

Schultze, Charles L., *The Politics and Economics of Public Spending*. Washington DC: Brookings Institution, 1968.

Schwartzman, David, The Burden of Monopoly, *Journal of Political Economy*, 68 (1960), 627–30.

Sen, Amartya, *Collective Choice and Social Welfare*. Edinburgh: Oliver and Boyd, 1970.

Sen, Amartya, *On Economic Inequality*. London: Clarendon, 1973.

Siegfried, John J. and White, Kenneth J., Financial Rewards to Research and Teaching: A Case Study of Academic Economists, *American Economic Review, Papers and Proceedings*, 63 (1973), 309–15.

Silberston, Aubrey, Economies of Scale in Theory and Practice, *Economic Journal*, 82 (1972) (Supplement), 369–91.

Simon, Herbert A., Rationality as Process and Product of Thought, *American Economic Review, Papers and Proceedings*, 68 (1978), 1–16.

Sinden, John A. and Worrell, Albert C., *Unpriced Values. Decisions without Market Prices*. New York: John Wiley, 1979.

Smith, Peter and Swann, Dennis, *Protecting the Consumer: An Economic and Legal Analysis*. Oxford: Martin Robertson, 1979.

Stigler, George J., The Economics of the Minimum Wage Legislation, *American Economic Review*, 6 (1946), 358–65.

Stigler, George J., The Economics of Information, *Journal of Political Economy*, 69 (1961), 213–25.

Strauss, Robert P. and Hughes, G. David, A new approach to the demand for public goods, *Journal of Public Economics*, 6 (1976), 191–204.

Stroebe, Wolfgang and Frey, Bruno S., In Defense of Economic Man: Towards an Integration of Economics and Psychology. *Schweizerische Zeitschrift für Volkswirtschaft und Statistik*, 116 (1980), 119–48.

Stuart, Charles E., Swedish Tax Rates, Labor Supply and Tax Revenues, *Journal of Political Economy*, 89 (1981), 1028–38.

Tanzi, Vito (ed.), *The Underground Economy in the United States and Abroad*. Lexington, Mass.: Heath, 1982.

The Crisis of Economic Theory, *Public Interest*, Special Issue 15 (1980).

Theil, Henry, *Optimal Decision Rules for Government and Industry*. Amsterdam: North Holland, 1968.

Thimm, Alfred L., How Far Should German Co-determination Go? *Challenge*, 24 (1981), 13–22.

Tideman, Nicholas and Tullock, Gordon, A New and Superior Process for Making Social Choices, *Journal of Political Economy*, 84 (1976), 1145–59.

Tinbergen, Jan, *Economic Policy: Principles and Design*. Amsterdam: North Holland, 1956.

Tuerck, David G. (ed.), *Political Economy of Advertising*. Washington DC: American Enterprise Institute, 1978.

Tufte, Edward T., *Political Control of the Economy*. Princeton: University Press, 1978.

Tullock, Gordon, *The Politics of Bureaucracy*. Washington, DC: Public Affairs Press, 1965.

Turnovsky, Stephen J., *Macroeconomic Analysis and Stabilization Policies*, Part III. Cambridge: University Press, 1977.

Union Bank of Switzerland, *Social Security in Ten Industrial Nations*. Zurich, April 1977.

Twenty-Five Years Kaldorian Theory of Distribution, *Kyklos*, 34 (1981), fasc. 4 (in particular the article by Gottfried Bombach).

van den Doel, Hans, *Democracy and Welfare Economics*. Cambridge: University Press, 1979.

Vanek, Jaroslav, *The Participatory Economy. An Evolutionary Hypothesis and a Strategy for Development*. Ithaca, NY: Cornell University Press, 1971.

Wallich, Henry C., The American Council of Economic Advisors and the German Sachverständigenrat: A Study in the Economics of Advice, *Quarterly Journal of Economics*, 82 (1968), 349–79.

Wallich, Henry C. and Weintraub, Sidney, A Tax-based Incomes Policy, *Journal of Economic Issues*, 5 (1971), 1–19.

Weidenbaum, Murray L., The High Cost of Government Regulation, *Challenge*, 22 (1979), 37, table 4 (excerpt).

Weingast, Barry R., Shepsle, Kenneth A. and Johnsen, Christopher, The Political Economy of Benefits and Costs: A Neoclassical Approach to Distribution Politics, *Journal of Political Economy*, 89 (1981), 642–64.

Williamson, Oliver E., *The Economics of Discretionary Behavior. Managerial Objectives in a Theory of the Firm.* Englewood Cliffs, NJ: Prentice-Hall, 1964.

Wilson, James Q., *Political Organizations.* New York: Basic Books, 1973.

Author Index

Subject Index

DATE DUE

BRODART, INC.   Cat. No. 23-221